COUNTRY INNS
OF THE OLD SOUTH

COUNTRY INNS OF THE OLD SOUTH

By
ROBERT W. TOLF

Illustrations by
ANDRA RUDOLPH

101 PRODUCTIONS
San Francisco

COVER ILLUSTRATION: River Forest Manor, Belhaven, North Carolina. Drawing by Andra Rudolph. Color rendering by Patricia Glover.

The illustrations in this book are by Andra Rudolph, except for the following, which were furnished by the inns and are reproduced with their permission. The name of the artist, when known, follows the name of the inn. Anchuca; Bailey House; Bay Street Inn, George Bauman; Dairy Hollow House, Jacqui Froelich; De Loffre House, William Scheele; Kenwood Inn; Myrtles Plantation; Oglethorpe Inn; St. Louis Hotel; 17 Hundred 90 Inn; The 1735 House, David Clar; Williamsburg Inn, Richard J. Stinely.

Maps designed and executed by Patricia Glover

Copyright © 1978, 1983 Robert W. Tolf
Drawings copyright © 1978, 1983 Andra Rudolph

Printed in the United States of America

Published by 101 Productions
834 Mission Street, San Francisco, California 94103
Distributed to the book trade by
Charles Scribner's Sons, New York

Library of Congress Catalog Card Number 82-24659
ISBN 0-89286-208-4

CONTENTS

INTRODUCTION

Country Inns are very much In.

When I first traveled the highways and byways of the South searching for special innings, I came up with a grand total of sixty-eight. This time around I came to a halt with more than 160.

I walked the real estate, interviewing dozens and dozens of innkeepers from one end of Dixie to the other—and back again. I studied and surveyed others, under the cloak of anonymity, and in a very few cases I used trusted, experienced sources to add their reconaissance to my judgments. But in no instance did I accept any favors or freebies or otherwise allow my decisions to be influenced by external pressures.

No fees are requested or required from the inns included in this book; there is no association or organization to join, no requirement to buy or sell books. That kind of copout is, for this writer, as dishonest, as great a disservice to the reader, the traveler, the inn-goer, as those guides which routinely list inns that have not been personally inspected. It's much more expensive—a far greater investment of time and treasure—to drive, fly, train, and walk the dozen states making on-scene inspections, but for me it's the only way.

And four years after the first edition I still come to the same conclusion about the ways and means of defining an inn. Webster calls it "a public house for the lodging and entertainment of travelers or wayfarers for a compensation"; but for me the modern-day inn of the Old South is almost a state of mind, a place of refuge in town or country, an escape, whether high on a wooded hill or deep in the heart of some concrete canyon—a place where one can find safe haven from mass-produced lodgings that don't tell a traveler whether he's spending the night in Dallas, Denver, or Detroit.

My kind of inn, be it a rustic lodge in the highlands, a refreshingly rural farmhouse, a century-old village tavern, a seaside shack, even a railroad car bolted securely into its sense of place—my kind of inn is an experience apart, an escape from the monotony and mediocrity of Samesville, USA.

Give me floors that squeak, windows that open, closets I can walk into, and innkeepers who are expatriates rather than corporate clones; innkeepers doing their own thing, serving food that is not the prepackaged, preportioned, pre-who-cares variety; innkeepers who have the time and talent to talk with their guests, who want to know them, to advise, perhaps even console.

Give me an experience removed from the routine of shag carpeting, computerized staffs, and chain reactions. Give me something that's one-of-a-kind, a remembrance of things past, a hope for vibrant alternatives in the future. Give me transport from the realities, relief from the world of plastic.

Give me the kind of innkeeper who has the spirit to mount on his wall a faded photograph of an old-fashioned room key plaque, a portrait of someone's ancestor, an old-timey please-ring-for-clerk bell, and these words:

> Such hotels will soon be gone forever, in favor of Holiday Inns everywhere, and then somebody very rich will build a whole antique hotel with everything in it the way things were a hundred years ago, and only very rich people will be able to go there.

RULES OF THE INN

Reservations, Deposits and Rates

Reservations are required for every inn in this book and should be made as far in advance as possible, especially during peak travel times. Many inns require a deposit of at least one night's lodging, others require a minimum stay during certain periods. Call or write to determine current requirements and current rates. For obvious reasons, we do not quote specific rates. When we use the word inexpensive, we mean just that: less than an average motel in the area. Expensive is equivalent to the tariff at a first-class, maybe a super-luxe, hotel. Moderate is somewhere in between.

Bar Service

In most of the inns it is nonexistent, but in some setups are provided and brown-bagging permitted; in others, especially in the Carolinas, local regulations are rather restrictive and no drinking is permitted outside one's own room. Ask the innkeeper before doing something that might embarrass all concerned.

Housekeeping

In the smaller inns with shared baths this is an important responsibility of the guest: cleaning sink and tub, taking your towels. Rooms, often cleaned by the innkeeper who doubles as chambermaid, should be kept in good order.

Tipping

In the smaller inns this should be discussed with the innkeeper; many would be embarrassed or insulted by the offer of a gratuity, but would welcome a thank-you note and would accept the kind of bread and butter gift you'd send if staying at someone's home.

KENTUCKY

WEST VIRGINIA

VIRGINIA

NORTH CAROLINA

TENNESSEE

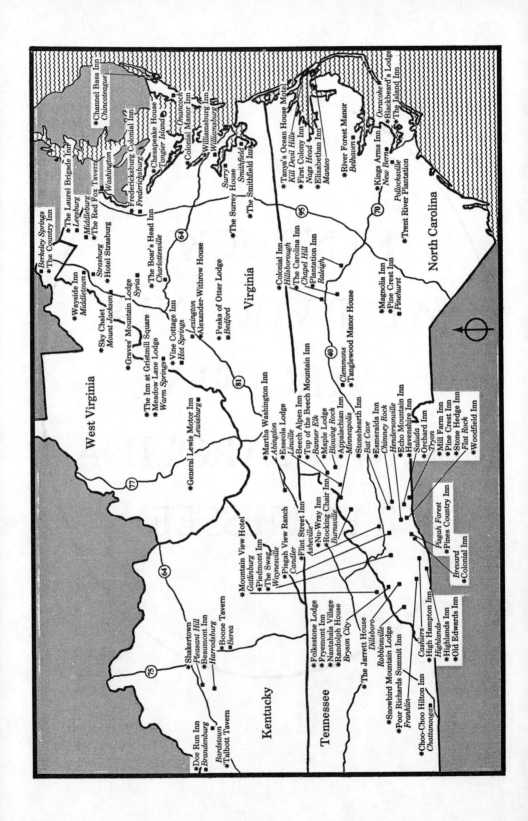

KENTUCKY

DOE RUN INN
Brandenburg, Kentucky

The site of Doe Run Inn was first discovered by Daniel Boone's brother, Squire, a famed Indian fighter and scout who was also a Baptist minister. Reverend Boone preached the first sermon in Louisville and performed the first white marriage in Kentucky. Two years after the Declaration of Independence, he came across this idyllic spot alongside one of the fast-flowing feeder streams of the Ohio River.

Named for the multitude of deer Boone found in the area, Doe Run has a counterpart across the river a few miles into Indiana: Buck Creek, where Squire Boone and his sons Moses, Isaiah, Jonathan, and Enoch (the first white male child born in Kentucky) built a gristmill. The remains can be seen near the entrance to Squire Boone Caverns, opened in 1973 without the excess of hokum that usually plagues such places. Surrounded by reconstructed pioneer log cabins and trails for exploring the countryside, the caverns are well worth the eighteen-mile drive from Doe Run.

Also worth visiting is the Fort Knox Military Reservation with its George S. Patton Museum of Cavalry and Armor. Now the state's most popular tourist attraction, the museum is an indoor-outdoor crash course in the development of armor. Fort Knox is near the route taken by Confederate General Morgan and his twenty-two hundred mounted troopers to cross the Ohio River for daring raids on northern cities.

Morgan's troops also crossed near the Doe Run Inn. Started in 1816, the five-story original section of hand-hewn timbers and native limestone was completed in 1821, and a smaller, two-story section was built a decade later. Abraham Lincoln's father worked on the building as a stonemason; his uncle, Josiah, settled across the river not far from the Boones. Josiah Lincoln's descendants are still living in that area.

3

The building was used initially as a mill, first for wool, then for grain. It has been owned by the same family for five generations and has been an inn since 1927. The ancestors of the present innkeepers, H. Curtis and Lucille Brown, were among the early flour millers.

A pair of oversize millstones form part of the front walk, leading to a door a Kentucky howitzer couldn't penetrate, through thick-as-a-fortress walls that could have withstood any Indian attack. Inside, the Browns have preserved a sense of history, furnishing their inn with an ancient spinning wheel and butter churns, a 150-year-old standing desk of oak used by the millers, a high-standing secretary owned by Henry Watterson, cherry chests brought by packet boat down the Ohio before the War Between the States. In the Honeymoon Room there is a handsomely carved walnut bed that belonged to Mrs. Brown's great-grandfather. Next to it is a marble-topped dresser and washstand with a gigantic mirror framed in ornate carving—part of Mrs. Brown's dowry.

The third-floor single rooms are far more rugged, with spartan furnishings but comfortable beds; looking out the small-paned windows you almost expect to see Indians scurrying off into the woods. At breakfast on the porch overlooking Doe Run, with a basket of warm homemade biscuits before me, while spooning a little red-eye gravy on my fried Kentucky country ham, I thought I saw Daniel and Squire running along the creek. And in the dining room, sitting under the sixty-five-foot yellow poplar beam that's been holding up the floors for more than 160 years, I saw the ghosts of those old "Kaintucks" who ground their grain behind these walls when Monroe was in the White House and Louisville was just another river port town.

Lunch and dinner are as good as the breakfast, and on Fridays and Sundays there's a belt-buster of a buffet with close to eighty dishes spread across the room. To walk off those calories, there are the surrounding woods—one thousand acres owned by the inn—nearby Otter Creek Park, and part of the old Enoch Boone farm. Tennis and swimming at the Doe Valley and Hillcrest country clubs can be part of the exercise by prior arrangement with the innkeepers.

DOE RUN INN, Route 2, Brandenburg, Kentucky 40108. Telephone: (502) 422-9982. Accommodations: 17 single and double rooms, five with a private bath. No telephones; television in lobby only. Rates: inexpensive. Meal service: breakfast, lunch, and dinner. Beer only. Children and pets welcome. Cards: MC. Open all year except December 24 and 25.
Getting There: The inn is four miles from Brandenburg via State Highway 448; from Elizabethtown, the inn is 28 miles northwest via

Doe Run Inn, Brandenburg, Kentucky

Routes 31-W north to 1638 and then 448. From Louisville it is 38 miles southwest via U.S. 31-W to Mudraugh and 1638, which only runs from Muldraugh to 448. Turn south on 448 a half mile to entrance.

TALBOTT TAVERN
Bardstown, Kentucky

Bardstown is Stephen Foster's town. America's troubadour is memorialized by a state park containing a grand old mansion on Federal Hill officially declared to be "My Old Kentucky Home," the inspiration for the song that serves as the state anthem. Hoopskirted guides point out the very desk in the very room where Foster wrote the song, although biographers question the fact that Foster ever saw more of the South than he could observe in New Orleans or from the deck of a paddle-wheeler along the Mississippi. But why bicker when the story is so romantic, the home so handsome, and the belles so beautiful? And when there's an outdoor drama performed from mid-June to Labor Day under the stars—Paul Green's *Stephen Foster Story*, a lively, knee-slapping, sentimental whoop-de-doo.

Talbott Tavern, situated in the center of town, honors Foster's memory with a room named in his honor and a letter in the lobby attesting to his presence in Bardstown. Many other figures from the pages of American history have passed through this solidly built stone inn since it first opened its doors in 1779. During the American Revolution, George Rogers Clark used the tavern as a base, storing provisions and ammunition in the cellar. Lewis and Clark, Andy Jackson, Henry Clay, William Henry Harrison, Zachary Taylor, Audubon, Lincoln, even Queen Marie of Rumania passed through this one-time western stagecoach stop. Washington Irving used the inn as setting for his story *Ralph Ringwood*—the stolen kiss in that tale took place in the inn in 1802, and the scene is duplicated with mannequins in one corner of the lobby. It's a unique display, but then the rest of Talbott's Tavern's lobby is also unique—sloping floors, an undersize reception desk, and a collection of Greenough's lithographs of Indian chiefs, done in 1836.

Upstairs there's another remarkable artistic achievement: wall murals apparently painted by one or several members of the court of Prince Louis Philippe while the prince stayed at the inn in 1797 during his exile in this country. He later sent a collection of paintings to the church of St. Joseph, in gratitude for the hospitality shown him by the

Talbott Tavern, Bardstown, Kentucky

people of Bardstown. St. Joseph's, which was built in 1812, was the first cathedral west of the Alleghenies.

The cathedral is well worth a visit, as is My Old Kentucky Home and the Barton Museum of Whiskey History. Bardstown is also bourbon country—ironically, considering the fact that Foster's last years were spent in a less-than-sober state: he wrote music in the morning and sold it in the afternoon for just enough to buy a bottle.

The tavern hasn't stopped serving the public since it first opened that heavy door in 1779. Meals are taken in the oldest section of the building, which once housed the original inn. Heavy timbers and thick stone walls were built to withstand attacks from Indians and the British. Through deep wooden window casings, the inn's stagecoaches could be seen arriving along the post road. All the cooking was done in the two fireplaces; overhead was the loft with a pair of sleeping rooms lined with small cots; one room was for men and one for women. This is a historic setting for a meal of pan-fried chicken served with cream gravy and hot-baked bread, followed by a slab of chess pie.

At night you can sleep in a hand-carved four-poster, bathe in claw-footed tubs large enough to accommodate a Lincoln, walk along floors pushed out of plumb by the settlement of centuries, every creak and crack stirring up memories of generals and kings, presidents and artists.

TALBOTT TAVERN, Bardstown, Kentucky 40004. Telephone: (502) 348-3494. Accommodations: Six rooms, each with a private bath, one with television, none with a telephone. Rates: inexpensive. Meal service: lunch and dinner. Full bar service. Children welcome; pets not allowed. Cards: AE, MC. Open every day but Christmas.
Getting There: Bardstown is 39 miles from Louisville and 65 from Lexington via the Blue Grass Parkway, at the intersection of U.S. 150, 31E, and 62. The tavern is in the center of town across from the old courthouse and welcome center.

BEAUMONT INN
Harrodsburg, Kentucky

The year was 1917. Woodrow Wilson was in the White House, American forces were in Europe, and, in far-off Kentucky, the Glave Goddard family purchased a historic old building to convert to an inn. In the past sixty years, an incredible, often incomprehensible series of events has occurred in Washington and Europe. But in Kentucky, the Glave Goddard family is still in charge of that same inn. The stability,

8

the sense of place, the appreciation of tradition are all apparent today as Charles Dedman, of the fourth generation of the family, goes about the business of running this very special place.

The origins of the inn go back to 1845 when the site was one of the town's famous spas, Greenville Springs. For a short period it was transformed to the Greenville Female Academy and then in 1885 renamed Daughters' College. In 1894 Colonel Thomas Smith, a Confederate veteran, bought the institution and named it Beaumont College, granting "mistress of science" degrees. It was a school whose motto declared it to exist for the promotion of "exalted character graced by elegant culture and refined manners." Mrs. Goddard was dean of the college—she had graduated from Daughters' College in 1880.

Faded photographs, graduation certificates, prints and portraits on the walls of the inn provide visual records of the past. The spacious hallways and the pair of high-ceilinged Victorian sitting rooms are filled with family heirlooms and museum pieces. On the second floor, some of the bedroom windowpanes have students' names scratched onto the glass.

This quiet, refined setting gives the visitor a feeling of the richness of the Goddard family history. In addition to the seventeen rooms in the inn there are accommodations in two other buildings on the well-tended thirty-two acres. Goddard Hall, a two-story frame structure built in 1935, has porches, pineapple four-posters, and connecting rooms ideal for families using the pool or tennis courts.

Then there's Greystone, a stone structure built in 1931 as a private residence for the present manager's parents, the Dedmans. They still live on the ground floor, surrounded by antique treasures. The four large bedrooms on the second floor are rented to guests and are superbly furnished and immaculately maintained, as are all rooms in this inn. In 1977 the inn and the two buildings underwent a major refurbishing.

The Beaumont air of quiet dignity, established comfort, taste, and restraint strikes you immediately as you enter the large entryway and register in the reception area, which is also the library. The aura is repeated in the dining rooms appointed with white napery, shining hotel flatware, brass candelabra, and paddle fans—a Southern colonial setting with pleasant service and excellent food. Luncheon offerings include chicken pot pie, fruit salad, little biscuits served hot and chock-full of chopped country ham; dinners feature rainbow trout, steaks, memorable corn pudding, and special desserts: prune cake, butterscotch pie, strawberry meringue glace, and an orange-lemon cake named in honor of Robert E. Lee.

The senior Dedman is a dedicated admirer of General Lee, and

Beaumont Inn, Harrodsburg, Kentucky

evidenced by a wall in the inn's entry hall displaying Lee portraits and a copy of his farewell speech to the army of northern Virginia. There could be no better backdrop for a Lee memorial (even though Kentucky, with split loyalties, remained in the Union) than this splendidly appointed inn gracing a town whose origins date back to 1774.

Harrodsburg is the oldest permanent English settlement west of the Alleghenies. In town there's Old Fort Harrod, where General George Rogers Clark planned his Revolutionary War strategy. Next to it is the outdoor amphitheater where *The Legend of Daniel Boone* is performed from mid-June to the end of August. And for harness and thoroughbred racing fans there are the spring and fall seasons at nearby Keeneland and Red Mile. There's also a private golf course in town open to guests of Beaumont Inn.

BEAUMONT INN, 638 Beaumont Drive, Harrodsburg, Kentucky 40330. Telephone: (606) 734-3381. Accommodations: 27 rooms, suites; single, double, and king-size beds; all rooms with a private bath, television, and telephone. Rates: moderate, including Continental breakfast. Meal service: breakfast, lunch, and dinner. No bar service (a dry county but setups provided). Children welcome; pets not allowed but kennel space may be arranged. Cards: AE, MC. V. Open March 1 to November 30.
Getting There: Harrodsburg is 32 miles from Lexington via the Blue Grass Parkway and U.S. 127. The inn is three-fourths of a mile from 127 in the southern end of the town, clearly marked by signs.

SHAKERTOWN
Pleasant Hill, Kentucky

The last Kentucky Shaker died fifty years ago, but the sect's works survive with a magnificent vibrancy in the perfectly restored buildings of Pleasant Hill. Ten of these offer accommodations for those who want to immerse themselves totally in the spirit of the Shakers, whose settlement was the model farm of Kentucky. Five thousand acres were cultivated by these early-day conservationists, who developed the most modern agricultural techniques, introducing crop rotation and Chinese sugarcane and perfecting new strains of sheep, hogs, and cattle. Some Leicester sheep and Durham cows are still in Pleasant Hill pens, but no mules or dogs are to be found; mules were not one of God's natural creatures, and dogs were neither useful nor edible.

Settled in the early 1800s by a trio of believers dispatched from the mother church, Pleasant Hill had by 1820 a population of five hundred industrious souls obedient to the teachings of the movement's founder, Mother Ann Lee. She advised her flock to "put your hands to work and your hearts to God," and to work "as though you had a thousand years to live, and as if you were to die tomorrow."

With unceasing devotion, discipline and labor the Shakers created an orderly ("There is no dirt in Heaven," Mother Lee advised), immensely fruitful and prosperous community with important cottage industries inspired by the demands of self-sufficiency. Part of this strict discipline included celibacy; there were separate quarters for men and women with separate doors in all the buildings except the Trustees' House, which is where those from the outside world came to barter and buy Shaker produce. Shakers were the nation's first commercial seed producers and the first to put seeds in packets; they invented or improved upon the circular harrow, the buzz saw, the self-acting cheese press, the cream separator, the wooden clothespin, the washing machine, the flat broom, the metal writing pen, and a device to core and peel apples. The Pleasant Hill waterworks was the first west of the Alleghenies, and the cypress tank still stands.

The Shakers' ingenuity led to the practice of storing ice cut from nearby ponds, the development of double-chamber heating stoves, and the cultivation of mulberry trees for silkworm culture. The sisters spun the silk thread, hooked rugs, wove willow baskets, put up preserves, and dried herbs for medicine and food. And always the surplus was sold throughout the South and Midwest; a Shaker name on a label was a hallmark of excellence.

The Pleasant hill label on food is also a hallmark today. In the dining room (located in the Trustees' House), gingham-gowned waitresses serve back-to-the-farm breakfasts of fruits, melons, juices, grits, eggs, bacon, sausage, cereal, homemade jellies, hot biscuits, bran and pumpkin muffins. For lunch there are cornsticks and fresh salads, vegetables fresh picked from the garden, rhubarb and strawberry cobblers as impossible to resist as the lemon and chess pies, the latter an old Kentucky "receipt" made with custard and brown sugar. Dinner is at two sittings, 6:00 and 7:15 (make your choice when making your room reservation), and offers stomach-stretching servings of more home-baked bounty, an overflowing relish bowl, entrees of roast beef, chicken, steak, and ham. No tipping is allowed here or anywhere in Pleasant Hill.

After one of these meals you'll want to walk around the mortarless stone walls that now border the pastures and fields and once extended some forty miles. The two dozen buildings are a study in soaring strength and unspoiled simplicity. The Shakers built some with mitred

12

Shakertown, Pleasant Hill, Kentucky

clapboards, others with limestone they quarried or bricks they fired in their own kilns. There's also a leisurely stroll past pasture and farmland, past the ravine to the river, on a road it took the brethren two years to cut; you'll pass a profusion of wild flowers, and herbs such as liverwort, snakeroot, and buckberry, which the sisters once picked for use in their medicines.

On the Kentucky River, starting from Shaker Landing, there are hour-long excursions on an authentic paddle-wheeler from the end of May to the end of October. The river was the Shakers' highway: they floated flatboats along the Kentucky, Ohio, and Mississippi rivers to the markets of New Orleans, St. Louis, Louisville. Later in the nineteenth century, steamboats regularly stopped at Shaker Landing to pick up the fruits of Shaker industriousness and ingenuity.

The whole Shaker record of achievement and innovation is explained on the self-guided tours through the ten exhibition buildings, open daily and run by a nonprofit corporation that turns all admission charges into further development and restoration.

After a day of feeling the spirit and sense of mission of the Shakers, what could be more fitting than to sleep in a Shaker room? Ten of the original twenty-seven village buildings have been converted into individual lodgings furnished with reproductions of Shaker tables and chairs, writing tables, handwoven rugs and curtains, and high-standing beds (many with trundle beds underneath) covered with heavy hand-loomed quilts. On the chests of drawers there are no brass pulls or knobs, no veneer or inlay work to hide the natural wood. There are three-slat chairs and perhaps the best known of all Shaker creations, the starkly elegant four-slat brethren's rocker—a bit more massive than the New England prototype and usually made from native Kentucky wild cherry or black walnut. It's the kind of chair whose "peculiar grace" Thomas Merton once explained came from the fact that "it was made by someone capable of believing that an angel might come and sit in it."

SHAKERTOWN, Route 4, Pleasant Hill, Harrodsburg, Kentucky 40330. Telephone: (606) 734-5411. Accommodations: 65 rooms, single and double, each with a private bath, television, and telephone. Rates: inexpensive. Meal service: breakfast, lunch, and dinner. No bar service. Children and pets welcome, but pets not allowed in dining area or exhibition buildings. No credit cards. Open all year.
Getting There: Pleasant Hill is eight miles northeast of Harrodsburg, 22 miles southeast of Lexington, just off U.S. 68, where there's a sign.

BOONE TAVERN
Berea, Kentucky

The Boone Tavern, opened in 1909, is the wholly owned showplace of that remarkable work-study institution known as Berea College. Founded in 1855 and named for the Biblical town (Acts 17:10) where Paul was received by noble, open-minded people, the college currently has an enrollment of some fifteen hundred students. Eighty percent of these come from Appalachian counties in eight Southern states, to receive a liberal arts education within the context of the Christian faith. A Bachelor of Arts degree is offered in twenty-three major fields of study and a Bachelor of Science in agriculture, business, home economics, industrial arts, and nursing. Each student works a minimum of ten hours a week.

Over 90 percent of the staff in the Boone Tavern are students—and they accept no tips. The students' pride of participation and their belief in the dignity of labor are everywhere apparent. This is a crisply and pleasantly maintained inn. The furniture in the rooms, much of it handsome reproductions of early American pieces, is made by Woodcraft, part of the Berea College Student Industries. If you want to learn more about the school and its programs, sign up for the student-conducted tours—they run hourly from a nearby information center during summer months and twice daily from Boone Tavern during the school year.

Also save enough time for a visit to the Appalachian Museum with its evocative series of photographs and displays depicting the lifestyle and daily routine of the fiercely independent mountaineers. Close at hand is the Log House with its collection of early American furniture and its sales room (there's also a sales outlet in the tavern) with displays of the products of the College Student Industries—beautifully finished wooden artifacts, brooms, needlecraft, weaving, ceramics, and stonework.

From late June until Labor Day there are performances of Paul Green's *Wilderness Road,* an outdoor drama depicting in song, dance, and pageant the crises the Civil War brought to Kentucky. Performances are in the Indian Fort Theater, situated in the College Forest, six thousand acres of land used by students for study and research and just plain picnicking and hiking. The theater is also the site of the Kentucky Guild of Artists and Craftsmen May Fair.

Also on the must list in this town of some seven thousand souls is the headquarters of the highly regarded Churchill Weavers, and the Appalachian Village, a collection of stores and displays turning profits over to self-help projects for the people of Appalachia.

Touring and walking are absolutely essential for anyone who takes his meals at the Boone Tavern. The food is served in generous portions by smiling students in a dining room with fresh white napery, student-made chairs and tables, and a general atmosphere of Southern gentility. And the food is excellent. The spoon bread is spooned onto your plate, and the cornsticks are as good as I've ever tasted. There are some special flavors imaginatively assembled out back: baked Swiss steak in dill sauce, roast leg of lamb with caper gravy, chicken flakes on a mound of Southern dressing with sweet-pepper jam; side dishes of Spanish eggplant, nutmeg-spiced sweet potato, fresh Brussels sprouts with Roquefort; desserts of blackberry cobbler, pies of lemon and toasted Brazil nut meringue. Solid, honest flavors. There's as much chance of finding additives in Boone Tavern fare as there is of finding a student-waitress with false eyelashes and bleached-blond hair.

BOONE TAVERN, Berea College Hotel, Berea, Kentucky 40404. Telephone: (606) 986-9341. Accommodations: 59 rooms; single, double and twin beds; all rooms with a private bath, television, and telephone. Rates: inexpensive. Meal service: breakfast, lunch, and dinner (reserve for lunch and dinner; no one over 12 allowed in shorts; jackets required at dinner and on Sunday). No bar service. Children and pets welcome. No credit cards. Open all year.
Getting There: Berea is 40 miles from Lexington, 120 from Louisville, and a mile from I-75 on U.S. 25. The hotel is in the center of town, across from the campus.

WEST VIRGINIA

GENERAL LEWIS MOTOR INN
Lewisburg, West Virginia

In the heart of the Allegheny Mountains, some twenty-three hundred feet above sea level and a short drive from the elegant Greenbrier, there's a little sleeper of an inn tucked into a tree-shaded street in a little sleeper of a town. Lewisburg is dotted with century-old houses, an 1837 courthouse, and a 1796 stone Presbyterian church used as a hospital during the Civil War. Its center of commerce hasn't been troubled much by modernity.

The main building of the inn dates from the turn of the century—not our century, but the previous one. John Adams and Thomas Jefferson were then running the country, long before the western counties of Virginia broke away from the mother state and formed their own. The inn was constructed a few years after the town was incorporated in 1782, the year after the death of General Andrew Lewis, an Irish-American for whom the town was named. Lewis built Fort Savannah in the area as a defense outpost against the Indians. In 1774 he mustered a thousand militia to battle the Indians at nearby Point Pleasant.

Some of the weapons they might have used, along with a great variety of kitchen and farm utensils, are on display along a back hall of the inn—it's called the Hall of Memories. But the entire inn is an Inn of Memories. In the raftered lobby with its fireplace, ancient rockers, and clocks, just past a few spinning wheels, are cabinets of old and rare china. In the bedrooms is a variety of furniture collected over the years—carved, high-standing beds, Victorian dressers, Oriental carpets, and converted kerosene lamps, all under the crisp control of innkeeper Col. Charles May.

17

The veranda stretching along the front of the inn provides the shade and setting for rocking away your cares and concerns, while the garden out back is a perfect place for a quiet stroll after indulging in some of the solid fare that flows from the kitchen. At the General Lewis you can start your day with country ham and end your day with country ham. And I'm automatically prejudiced in favor of a place that serves apple butter for breakfast.

A meal like this puts me in the right mood for touring the Greenbrier Valley, for swimming and playing golf at the Greenbrier Country Club, or for making a pilgrimage to "the Stulting Place," the birthplace of Pearl Buck, thirty miles away. It's now a fully restored home on a sixteen-acre farm, furnished in late nineteenth-century style so that an admirer of one of our most prolific writers can see the homestead as it was when Miss Buck was a young girl.

A little farther north in Marlington there's also a small historical museum. And close to Lewisburg, at Locust, Milligan, and Second creeks, are three of West Virginia's covered bridges.

GENERAL LEWIS MOTOR INN, 301 East Washington Street, Lewisburg, West Virginia 24901. Telephone: (304) 645-2600. Accommodations: 29 rooms; single, double, and twin beds; all rooms with a private bath, television, and telephone. Rates: inexpensive (moderate during the annual August State Fair when the inn is on a modified American plan). Meal service: breakfast and supper, Sunday dinner. No bar service. Children welcome; daily pet charge. Cards: AE, MC, V. Open all year.
Getting There: From Interstate 64 take exit 169 and Route 219 to Lewisburg 1-1/2 miles south. Lewisburg is 105 miles east of Charleston and nine west of White Sulphur Springs; the inn is at the crossroads of Routes 219 and 60.

THE COUNTRY INN
Berkeley Springs, West Virginia

George Washington bathed here! He also might have slept here. Not in the Country Inn—that wasn't built until 1932—but in a shelter next to the mineral springs that have been warming bodies in water of a constant seventy-four degrees since 1748. Berkeley Springs is the nation's oldest spa, developed on land donated by Lord Fairfax and now part of Berkeley Springs State Park, a lushly landscaped area the size of a village green. The park is surrounded by freshly painted white buildings with green trim. Inside are the Turkish and Roman baths that

The Country Inn, Berkeley Springs, West Virginia

generations of spa-goers have used to treat rheumatism, infantile paralysis, and other maladies.

The inn is a few meters away from the springs, which must have been its initial reason for being. But now, with or without immersion in the curative waters, there are enough attractions in the Berkeley Springs area to make a stay at the inn well worthwhile. And the inn is so proficiently run, so immaculately maintained, that it's a pleasant stopover point for one or many days. In fact, the whole town seems immaculately maintained—its twenty-five hundred people keep it neat as that proverbial pin.

Inn breakfasts are hearty, the country ham and chicken authentic, the serving staff back-country friendly. Soups are a specialty at the inn, homemade daily and guaranteed to break the hohums caused by canned brews—cucumber-chicken, salmon, and corn chowder are three of the favorites—the perfect way to start an old-fashioned meal. Follow up those honest flavors with baked ham, pot roast, or stuffed pork chops. Then have a slice of pie or baked-out-back cake before retiring to the spacious lobby with its collection of comfortable couches and overstuffed chairs, its racks of travel brochures, its lounge and gift shop.

It's all as carefully maintained as the thirty-four rooms with their solid colonial furnishings and multipaned windows looking out over the park and mountains, rooms that are perfect retreats for relaxing after touring some of the most spectacular scenery in the nation.

"Wild and Wonderful" is the way state tourism sloganeers describe West Virginia, and a trip to Prospect Peak looking over the Great Cacapon and Potomac valleys should convince even the most doubting Thomas of the truth of their claim. The Cacapon State Park, ten miles from the inn, has hiking and horse trails, golf, tennis, boating, and swimming, while just a few minutes away is a magnificently situated championship golf course designed by Robert Trent Jones.

An hour of easy, scenic driving through the eastern panhandle of the state brings the tourist to the National Park of Harpers Ferry, completely restored to the way it was when John Brown staged his raid on the arsenal. Living-history programs, antique and craft shops now ring the area, and the view is still sensational from the nearby rock named for Thomas Jefferson after he declared: "This view is well worth a trip across the Atlantic."

Charles Town is also just an hour away. In addition to the racetrack here (the thoroughbreds also run at Shenandoah Downs), there's the Old Opera House with a repertoire ranging from *Goodbye Charlie* to *Wild Wonderful West Virginia*. In neighboring Martinsburg there's the Adam Stephen house to see—home of the town's founder and built in 1789 of local limestone. In Berkeley Springs there's another stone structure, this one built to look centuries older, but actually completed in the last century. It's a hillside-dominating crenelated castle, with a medieval round tower that looks real enough for Rapunzel.

THE COUNTRY INN, Berkeley Springs, West Virginia 25411. Telephone: (304) 258-2210. Accommodations: 34 rooms; single, double, and twin beds; some rooms with a basin only, others with a private bath; all with televisions and telephones; also suites and master rooms with two double beds and a bath. Rates: inexpensive to moderate. Meal service: breakfast, lunch, and dinner. Full bar service. Children and pets welcome, but deposit required for a pet against possible damage. Cards: AE, MC, V. Open all year.
Getting There: From Interstate 70 the inn is six miles south via State Route 522. It is just over 100 miles from Washington, D.C.

VIRGINIA

MARTHA WASHINGTON INN
Abingdon, Virginia

If ever you imagine that Virginia is not George Washington Country, travel its length and breadth and start counting the memorials and namesakes—from Mount Vernon and Alexandria's towering Masonic monument in the north, to the central regions with the Houdon statue in Richmond's Capitol, across apple-rich Shenandoah (where landowner Washington required that each of his tenants plant at least four acres of apples), to Winchester with its headquarters used by Washington as a surveyor and as a military commander. In the southwest tip of the state is Washington County, chartered in 1776 and the first county in the country to honor the General's name. Two years later the county seat was named Abingdon for the ancestral home of Martha Washington. Seventy-five years later a women's college was established in the town and named after the wife who, in the words of a local Washington worshipper, "shared his anxieties and hope in our struggle for liberty, and whose virtues made her a perfect model of womanly excellency."

Martha Washington College was housed in a converted private home that had been built in 1830 by Gen. Francis Preston. For three-quarters of a century the Methodist Church operated the college, until the financial pressures of the Great Depression forced it to shutter the school, which merged with the nearby Emory and Henry College.

In 1937 the historic building, with new wings added over the years by the college, was converted into an inn. It was named the Martha Washington, of course, and designed to provide housing for the increasing numbers of out-of-towners discovering this little town put on the map by a group of actors across the street from the inn. The Barter

22

Martha Washington Inn, Abingdon, Virginia

Theatre had been established four years earlier and so named because the performers bartered some of their tickets for food. It's now the State Theatre of Virginia, the longest-running professional resident theater in the country and the stage where such actors as Gregory Peck, Patricia Neal, Hume Cronyn, Claude Akins, and Fritz Weaver received their early training and exposure. The season now runs from April through October with a dozen plays in a wide-ranging repertory—Agatha Christie to Shakespeare.

Abingdon is also in the center of some of the most spectacular scenery in the state. Twelve miles south are the Bristol Caverns, and through twenty miles of pine forest to the east there's White Top Mountain (fifty-five hundred feet) and Mount Rogers, tallest in the state at fifty-seven hundred feet. To the north there's a five-mile-long, sixteen-hundred-feet-deep gorge at Breaks Interstate Park on the Kentucky border. And at Big Stone Gap there's the South West Virginia Museum and the summertime outdoor musical *Trail of the Lonesome Pine,* depicting in song and dance life in the Highlands.

Closer to town are 220 miles of shoreline ringing South Holston Lake, one of the largest earth-filled dams in the world. Right in town is the Cumbow China Company, whose hand-decorated Ruskin line is probably the best known of the several local industries. In August there is an annual two-week Virginia Highlands Arts and Crafts Festival with music and art programs, lectures, house tours, and displays of local handicrafts.

There is much more to do and see in and around this town of some six thousand Virginians. On most weekends in May and June this historic shrine is filled with wedding receptions; the bride's descent down the sweepingly elegant colonial staircase into the wide, wide hall is one of the local traditions. The inn's bridal suite, room No. 202, has a grand old four-poster complete with canopy! But of all the handsome colonial rooms in this inn, I prefer No. 214 with its fireplace and its matched set of four-poster, acanthus-leaf beds covered with heavy white quilts.

All those rooms are in the original section, as are the lobbies and sitting rooms with chandeliers hanging down from the high ceilings, ancient grandfather clocks, and a fine portrait of Thomas Jefferson. In the dining room, past a small gift shop and a series of meeting rooms, white napery and an atmosphere of dignity and grace encourage guests to avoid the big-city gulp-and-run approach to a meal. Instead you can relax, visit with neighbors, discuss the town and its history, ponder the life and lessons of Washington, and enjoy a little more spoon bread and another hot biscuit while you finish that piece of country ham.

24

MARTHA WASHINGTON INN, 150 West Main Street, Abingdon, Virginia 24210. Telephone: (703) 628-3161. Accommodations: 65 rooms; single, double, twin beds; all rooms with a private bath; telephones; half of the rooms have television. Rates: inexpensive to moderate. Meal service: breakfast, lunch, and dinner. Full bar service. Children and pets welcome. Cards: AE, DC, MC, V. Open all year. *Getting There:* Take exit 8 from Interstate 81 and follow signs to Barter Theatre a mile into Main Street; the inn is across the street from the theatre.

PEAKS OF OTTER LODGE
Bedford, Virginia

The Peaks of Otter Lodge is located midway in the Virginia section of the overwhelmingly beautiful Blue Ridge Parkway—470 miles ribboning along the mountain crests of the southern Appalachians, linking the Great Smoky Mountains National Park with the Shenandoah National Park. The lodge ambles along a little lake in the shadow of the Peaks of Otter, whose pyramid shapes tower nearly four thousand feet into the Virginia sky. The inn is a model of handsome and harmonious architecture, a quiet blend of functional utility totally at home in the mountains—there's no shouting at the wilds of the Blue Ridge. The site is also convenient, just a few minutes off the Parkway.

The room terraces, the balconies, and the lodge lounge—with its copper-topped stone fireplace—command views of grassy meadows, and blue Otter Lake reflecting the greens of the forest climbing the peaks. The rooms blend peacefully with the panoramic views— wooden-raftered ceilings; soft brown and beige drapes, bedspreads, and upholstery; tables and dressers topped with thick slate; an oversize rocking chair from which you can enjoy the scene.

In the main lodge there is similar attention given to preserving the presence of the woods while providing modern conveniences in a nonplastic manner. The ground-level cocktail lounge is old-Virginia tavern, but the dining room with its windows looking out to lake and mountains is more elaborate than one would expect to find in the semi-isolated reaches of the Blue Ridge: fresh napery and baskets of flowers adorn the tables nightly and during the bounteous buffets on Sundays and Fridays, when seafood is the specialty. The presentation is reminiscent of a Caribbean grand hotel with a Swiss chef running things, while the food is reminiscent of many historic inns closer to the state's main population centers, inns that no longer take lodgers but still serve the honest Southern country fare that has kept them on the culinary map for decade after decade.

A small coffee shop tucked into one corner of the lodge provides a snacking outlet as well as box lunches for guests wishing to explore the hiking and nature trails close to the lodge or the numerous nearby fishing possibilities. The Park Service Visitor Center—only a few hundred yards from the lodge—has all the information and trail maps. Be sure to pick up a copy of the Blue Ridge Parkway brochure containing a complete map of the region, special places to stop, and areas and seasons for the best viewing of the flame azalea, mountain laurel, and rhododendron.

PEAKS OF OTTER LODGE, P.O. Box 489, Virginia 24523. Telephone: (703) 586-1081. Accommodations: 58 rooms, each with two double beds, a private bath, a balcony; no televisions or telephones. Rates: moderate. Meal service: breadfast, lunch, and dinner. Full bar service. Children and pets welcome. Cards: MC, V. Open all year. *Getting There:* The lodge is 34 miles from Lynchburg and 29 from Roanoke, a half mile from Mile Marker 86 Visitor Center of the Blue Ridge Parkway. From Bedford take Route 43 eleven miles north to Parkway, the Visitor Center, and the lodge.

ALEXANDER-WITHROW HOUSE
Lexington, Virginia

This magnificently restored building is one of the best-kept secrets in the South, and after a dozen uncrowded hours in two-hundred-year-old Lexington, I came to the same conclusion about the town. Of course Civil War buffs know the place—both Robert E. Lee and Stonewall Jackson are buried here. Lee was president of Washington College after the war, and his final resting place (along with that of his father, Revolutionary War hero Light Horse Harry) is in the Lee Chapel on the campus of what is now Washington and Lee University. It's a splendid complex of early nineteenth-century architecture—red brick and white-pillared neo-Classical buildings.

Jackson is buried in the town cemetery along with hundreds of other Confederate veterans. His house in town is now the Jackson museum, restored by the Historic Lexington Foundation, established to help preserve Lexington's distinctive architecture. The foundation purchases, restores, and eventually sells the buildings with easements that safeguard forever the facades; sales proceeds are then applied to other purchases and the process is repeated. It's a practical approach to the problem of retaining if not nurturing the architectural roots in our historic cities. The foundation also sees that utility lines are buried, street lighting is installed, and brick sidewalks are laid.

It takes only a few minutes of strolling through town to discover how well this group has succeeded in achieving its goals in a relatively short time. The first project was completed as recently as 1970—the Alexander-Withrow House on the main crossroads of the town. Solidly built of brick and stone about the time that George Washington was becoming our first president, the house was one of the few that survived Lexington's city-leveling fire of 1796. In the following century this sturdy structure served as the town's first school, its first post office, and its first bank, as well as home to a string of shopkeepers.

There is no building like it in Lexington, perhaps anywhere else in Virginia or the South. Glazed brick headers form elaborate diamond patterns that zigzag along the top two stories; above the first story is a wrought-iron balcony, and overhead is an Italianate roof crowned with a quartet of corner chimneys pointing severely at the sky.

The Historic Lexington Foundation sold the building, now on the National Historic Register, to Harriet and Carlson Thomas, who run an antique store on the ground floor and are innkeepers for the five suites on the two floors above. They furnished these rooms with antiques from their collections and with superbly executed reproductions, creating an opportunity for total immersion in the spirit of this charming little town.

Room No. 5, the attic suite, is the most functional; i.e., the least charming—clean but colorless—so when making reservations and sending in deposits specify that rooms on the lower levels are desired.

Lexington took its name from the town in Massachusetts where the minutemen stood up to the redcoats. The town's history is intertwined with American military history, much of which is associated with the Lees and the Jacksons. Stonewall was an instructor in artillery tactics at the other college campus in town—the Virginia Military Institute, the nation's oldest state-supported military college, founded in 1839 and now a National Historic District. There's a Jackson Memorial Museum on campus with displays depicting the history of VMI, and at the far end of the parade field, there's a newer museum, bringing up to date the town's two-century-old military record books. It's the George C. Marshall Museum and Library, which presents a graphic review of the active life and many contributions of this distinguished VMI graduate, class of 1901. He's the only military figure ever to win the Nobel Peace Prize—that too is on display.

For information on the museums and for walking-tour brochures of this town that seems made just for walking, visit the Welcome Center, a few hundred bricks from the Alexander-Withrow House on

27

Washington Street. The center is also in a restored historic structure, a merchant's home built in 1845.

ALEXANDER-WITHROW HOUSE, 3 West Washington Street, Lexington, Virginia 24450. Telephone: (703) 463-2044. Accommodations: five suites, all with a bedroom, bath, kitchenette, living room, fireplace, and television but no telephone. Rates: inexpensive to moderate. No meal service, but there is instant coffee/tea in kitchenette and a bakery next door that delivers fresh rolls Monday through Saturday. No bar service. Children welcome if supervised; pets not allowed. No credit cards. Open all year.
Getting There: Take exit Route 60 West from Interstate 81 and go three miles, following the signs to the Welcome Center; the house is two blocks past the center.

VINE COTTAGE INN
Hot Springs, Virginia

Visitors to Virginia's fabled Hot Springs area who don't have the wherewithall to stay at the grand and glorious Homestead can check into this eighty-year-old Victorian rambler that used to house the domestics of those who vacationed at the Homestead five hundred yards away. It's owned and operated by Doug and Jacquie O'Brien, the dynamic duo that also runs the Sam Snead Tavern in town. The tavern is an architectural abomination that looks as though it was air-lifted from the wild, wild West, but the Vine Cottage Inn has in recent years been carefully restored and revitalized.

The inn has also been refurnished, filled with period pieces that lend an air of authenticity as distinctive as that found in the Homestead. The bathtubs have claw feet, the wraparound porch has lots of rockers for easy-going contemplation of the passing parade, and the turn-of-the-century living room is filled with books and comfortable chairs for guests to relax in in front of the cheerful fire—welcome after a run on the Homestead's ski slopes or a brisk winter walk.

The inn's restaurant features fresh trout (or you can catch your own in the nearby streams), chili, ribs, chicken, and beef tenderloin dolloped with bearnaise and labeled O'Brien. The salad dressing is from the same recipe that earned Jacquie a blue ribbon at a state fair a few years back.

VINE COTTAGE INN, Highway 220, P.O. Box 205, Hot Springs, Virginia 24445. Telephone: (703) 839-2422. Accommodations: 17

rooms, ten with a private bath, three with beds for families or groups up to six, one with a pair of double bedrooms, kitchen, sitting room, private entrance. Rates: inexpensive to moderate; includes complimentary breakfast. Meal service: breakfast and dinner year round, lunch from April through November. Inquire about pets. No cards. Open year round.

Getting There: The inn is on State Road 220, five miles south of Warm Springs, next door to the Homestead.

THE INN AT
GRISTMILL SQUARE
Warm Springs, Virginia

Two centuries after the first mill was built on the site, local landowners with an overdose of imagination and determination brought it back to life, opening a formally rustic restaurant in the old mill with its ancient overshot wheel; establishing an art gallery (using old chestnut siding from one of their own barns to decorate the interior), a general store, and a few other boutiques; and restoring several other old buildings to serve as overnight accommodations.

All that was the work of Catherine and Phillip Hirsh. Their successors on the scene, Janice and Jack McWilliams, who took over during the summer of 1982, immediately demonstrated their own dedication to the trying trade of innkeeper, their own multitalented approach to the fine art of pleasing the public.

Rooms were refurbished, and additional buildings taken over for accommodations, including the miller's house dating from the 1820s, now with a pair of suites and two rooms named Barley and Wheat. The tower apartment has its own wraparound porch and a full kitchenette, a washer and dryer, and a wood-burning fireplace—it's perfect for two couples traveling together.

There is also a fireplace and a washer and dryer in the so-called Main Street Apartment with its own balcony, and more wood-burning hearths in five of the other six single rooms, named Silo, Quilt (with double quilts on the bed), Board and Croft, Dinwiddie, and Singapore. The last-named has an Oriental motif and an ingeniously hidden bathtub tucked into a closet.

The complimentary breakfasts are delivered to the rooms, and the Waterwheel Restaurant on campus, in the old mill, provides some of the best eating in the Allegheny Valley for lunch (during the summer months) and dinner. Ever since the rebirth of Gristmill Square the restaurant has been reliable, initially run by a German chef with previous tours at the Waldorf-Astoria, and now by a Frenchman.

Chef Louis is in charge of a menu bristling with a spicy, cognac-kissed terrine of chicken livers, sausage, and pork; stuffed mushroom caps en croûte; shrimp provençale; fresh mountain trout stuffed with backfin crab meat and baked, or sautéed in butter and given an almondine shower, or broiled with herb butter.

For those who want to make their own meals, in the rooms or on the road, the Gristmill Hodge Podge Store run by a sprightly Pomeranian, Sabine von Arnswaldt, has a wide variety of foodstuffs. There's also a neighboring art gallery with the works of local artists, and across the road is the Bath and Tennis Club, with a swimming pool, a sauna, and a trio of tennis courts. The Cascades and Lower Cascades golf courses are only minutes away; there are numerous hiking and horseback-riding trails; and, in wintertime, the ski slopes at the Homestead beckon—those at Snowshoe, a bit more challenging, are an hour's drive.

At any time of the year, the return to Gristmill Square after a day of activity is a happy, satisfying experience, a perfect combination of old and new. Where else do they chill their wine with the cooling millstream waters that keep the heat out of the cellar? What other inn has its own pub named for one of the great frontiersmen, Simon Kenton? He passed through Warm Springs the year the first mill was built, in 1771, and stayed with the miller until he earned enough to buy a rifle and provisions to cross the frontier into Ohio country.

Pub and restaurant, shops and galleries, accommodations—all are easy to recommend with great enthusiasm. The highly personal and professional supervision of the innkeepers will keep it that way, but then the McWilliamses are hardly newcomers to the business: they had an inn in Vermont for seventeen years.

THE INN AT GRISTMILL SQUARE, P.O. Box 359, Warm Springs, Virginia 24484. Telephone: (703) 839-2231. Accommodations: twelve units; some suites with a washer-dryer, most with a fireplace; fully equipped kitchen in two apartment units; all with a color television, no telephone. Rates: moderate to expensive; includes complimentary Continental breakfast. Inquire about pets. Cards: AE, MC, V. Open year round.
Getting There: From Hot Springs drive five miles north on U.S. Highway 220 to Warm Springs at the intersection with State Route 39, and look for the signs pointing the way to the square.

MEADOW LANE LODGE
Warm Springs, Virginia

When that imaginative couple, Catherine and Phillip Hirsh, pulled out of the unique Gristmill Square project they had spun from the past in the early seventies, they held on to a very special structure in that complex, the Francisco Cottage. Hand-hewn out of local logs by Charles Lewis Francisco in the 1820s, it's one of the most appealing accommodations in the South. Furnished with the kind of taste exhibited by the Hirshes in their other projects, the cabin has been thoroughly modernized in a manner that protects its authenticity.

To book that time capsule into the long ago, the visitor contacts Hella Armstrong, the super-efficient manager for the Hirsh holdings at Meadow Lane Lodge and Meadow Lane Farm, the spectacularly laid-back family farm four miles west of Gristmill Square and the Francisco Cottage.

Those holdings include some sixteen hundred acres of working farm and two miles of the Jackson River, stocked by Hirsh as well as the state and brimful of rock and smallmouth bass, rainbow trout, eastern chain pickerel, sunfish, and chub—the last-named are game fighters but inedible; when caught they're tossed up on the riverbank.

Also on the estate is an ancient Indian burial mound, a Dynaturf tennis court, a mini-zoo of animals—sheep and goats, horses, ducks, geese, guinea fowl, bluetick hounds—and the site of Fort Dinwiddie, the frontier outpost where Virginia Militia Commander George Washington defended his colony against the Indians.

In other corners of the farm are the accommodations: suites and bedrooms in the lodge, and Craig's Cottage with its own kitchen, a splendid bay window, a deep walk-in closet, a corner fireplace, and a delightful little dressing table. One of the two suites in the lodge has a fireplace, and the lodge is also the location of the cheery breakfast room where the complimentary full breakfast is served, and the comfortable common room with its double fireplaces, television, and still more proof of the high level of taste of the people in charge.

The dozen guests luxuriating in the lodge facilities are offered a sometimes-stunning array of antiques—in their rooms, in the common room, or in the breakfast waker-upper with its oak sideboard dating from 1710. And everywhere there is the view, and endless possibilities for hiking, bird-watching, and wild-flower identification, or what the Hirshes call, in their inimitable way, "creative loafing."

31

Meadow Lane Lodge, Warm Springs, Virginia

MEADOW LANE LODGE, Star Route A, Box 110, Warm Springs, Virginia 24484. Telephone: (703) 839-5959. Accommodations: Francisco Cottage in Gristmill Square, with a fireplace, kitchen, twin-bedded room, sitting room with sofabed, private bath, washer-dryer, porch, television, and telephone. Seven units in Meadow Lane; four with three baths in lodge, two with screened-in porches; Craig's Cottage with a telephone, television, kitchen. Rates: moderate to expensive; includes full breakfast. Pets allowed only in Craig's Cottage, but inquire. Cards: AE, MC, V. Open from March 15 to January 2.
Getting there: Follow Andrew Lewis and Charles Lewis Memorial Highway, State Route 39, from Warm Springs west four miles, and turn into the Meadow Lane farm at the hard-to-miss sign.

THE BOAR'S HEAD INN
Charlottesville, Virginia

When Thomas Jefferson was a student at William and Mary, an inn known as Terrill's Ordinary occupied the site of the present Boar's Head Inn. Later, when Jefferson was building his beloved Monticello, he on occasion purchased his venison from the innkeeper. But there's certainly no similarity between an "ordinary" and the Boar's Head Inn that graces the countryside today. The inn is a total reconstruction, a restoration similar to the kind that brought colonial Williamsburg back to life. Boar's Head is now more modern resort than wayside tavern, but there are some important distinctions that hold it apart from the typical convention center.

In the older section with its grand collection of antiques, there are rooms with hand-hewn pine beams and high-pitched ceilings, solid frame beds tucked into alcoves, and fireplaces and Windsor chairs providing a pleasant combination of solid historical tradition and modern comfort. The candlelighted dining room with its roaring fireplace and its 150-year-old gristmill is a most appealing and appropriate setting for this section of the commonwealth. The serving personnel, garbed in colonial dress, are as pleasant and polite as the bygone era this setting evokes.

Then the boar's head was considered a symbol of hospitality. Out in a garden fountain there's a boar's head modeled on the famous bronze boar in the flower market, Mercato Nuovo, in Florence—itself a copy of the ancient marble boar in the Uffizi Gallery. The inn's boar also has flowers for neighbors. Carefully tended beds of blossoms, changed with the season, guide the stroller past stone arches and boxwood, around the millstones that once ground wheat and corn, to a peaceful little pond with ducks to feed.

Beyond this gentle sylvan scene is a pair of all-weather Grasstex tennis courts and a nine-hole golf course. The inn also offers fishing, swimming, badminton, and a sports club with a daily membership fee for outdoor and indoor tennis, squash, paddle tennis, and health salons.

Those who want to pay proper tribute to America's Renaissance man can take easy driving trips to Monticello, there to be humbled if not overwhelmed by trying to comprehend all that Jefferson achieved. And when that is partially digested, there's the trip to the serene campus of the University of Virginia with its rotunda designed by Jefferson and perfectly restored as a Bicentennial project.

THE BOAR'S HEAD INN, P.O. Box 5185, Ednam Forest, Charlottesville, Virginia 22903. Telephone: (804) 296-2181. Accommodations: single, double, and twin-bedded rooms, all with private baths, televisions, telephones, and coffee service; honeymoon suite with complimentary champagne and fruit. Rates: moderate. Meal service: breakfast, lunch, and dinner. Full bar service. Children welcome; charge for pets. Cards: AE, DC, MC, V. Open all year.
Getting there: Take U.S. 250 Bypass around Charlottesville and exit at Route 250; proceed a mile west to the entrance to the inn.

GRAVES' MOUNTAIN LODGE
Syria, Virginia

Here is the perfect mountain hideaway, tucked between two Blue Ridge peaks—on one side Old Rag Mountain at thirty-three hundred feet and on the other Hazeltop at thirty-eight hundred feet. The lush farmlands rolling up to the hillsides are as carefully tended as they have been for the past 250 years, when the first settlers streamed in from Tidewater Virginia and as far away as Germany. The German Lutheran church in the Hebron Valley, a few miles south of Syria, is the oldest church built, owned, and still in use by American Lutherans; the original section dates from 1740.

The Graves family had farmed the area for many years and in the mid-1960s decided to become innkeepers. Anyone who wants to go back in time a few dozen decades should pay a visit to Graves' Mountain Lodge. Bring the family and reserve a cabin—one of them is 3-1/2 miles from the lodge. The cabins are rugged log structures with porches, stone fireplaces, and wooden benches. Or take a turn in the old

34

Graves Mountain Lodge, Syria, Virginia

farmhouse with its seven rooms of rustic furnishing. There are a couple of cottages, as secluded as the log cabins, with kitchenettes and porches.

Behind the main lodge building are newer units that are called motels, but that's only because a car can be driven to the door. Considering the handsome colonial furnishings of these rooms and the balconies looking out over the Blue Ridge Mountains, the term motel seems chained to something far less individual and appealing.

After eating a family-style meal, served at precise times (except on weekends) in the lodge dining room, you will welcome the three-mile hike to one of the cabins or cottages, to walk off those back-to-the-farm portions of mountain trout, chicken, or country ham. There is enough food to stoke a farmhand for a full day in the fields or a tourist planning a horseback ride on the many trails. Breakfast is served at the tables; lunch and dinner are buffet style; all meals are informal and most of the produce comes from Jim Graves's six-thousand-acre farm.

Supervised trail riding is available, as is stabling, at an extra charge, for those who travel with a horse. There is also a junior Olympic-size pool, eight paved tennis courts including two under lights, streams and stocked ponds for the anglers, the Greene Hills Country Club for the golfers, games galore in the lodge's recreation room, and hiking paths of all degrees of difficulty around the lodge. A short drive away is the Rapidian Wildlife Area and the Shenandoah National Park.

The nearby Skyline Drive, the northern extension of the Blue Ridge Parkway, provides over a hundred miles of winding road and dazzling beauty with dozens of scenic overlooks. Nine miles from the drive are the most popular caves in the eastern United States, the Luray Caverns, which have been attracting tourists for more than a century. In that same direction is the 160-acre park commemorating the Civil War battle at New Market, where the young cadets of the Virginia Military Institute stood up to the invading Yankees. Two years before that heroic action, Stonewall Jackson came through this country, camping with his troops near Graves' Lodge, rushing to join Lee at Fredericksburg. This is a historic area, a quiet area, and a great place to escape.

GRAVES' MOUNTAIN LODGE, Syria, Virginia 22743. Telephone: (703) 923-4231. Accommodations: single, double, twin, and bunk beds in houses, cabins, cottages, motels; all with a private bath, some with television, none with telephone. Rates: inexpensive to moderate; special reduced weekly rates. No bar service. Children welcome; pets allowed only in certain units. Cards: MC, V. Open April through November.

Getting there: From Culpepper take U.S. 29 fifteen miles south to Madison, turn right, and go north on 231. Proceed seven miles and turn left on Route 670; drive 3.8 miles to lodge on the left.

SKY CHALET
Mount Jackson, Virginia

This mountaintop country inn is a four-season retreat, with a swimming pool and shuffleboard court on campus and all kinds of athletic activities at neighboring Bryce Resort: boating and fishing, golf, horseback riding, and skiing—including grass skiing in summer months. The slopes and chair lift are just a short walk through the woods from the Sky Chalet.

It's an appropriate name. The eleven-acre complex of main lodge and cottages straddles the Supin Lick Ridge at seventeen hundred feet; there's a breathtaking view of the Allegheny and Massanuttin mountains in the distance; and the fresh mountain air stimulates the appetite.

The Sky Chalet kitchen takes care of that, with back-to-the-farm breakfasts and dinner entrées of fried chicken, country ham, one-pound porterhouse steaks; excellent salads; freshly baked bread served in its own flowerpot; scrumptious coconut cake; dumplings, pies, and cakes made with apples plucked on the premises. The back room tries hard to live up to its proud claim that it has the best apple pie, served hot, and the best apple cake, sprinkled with raisins, not only in Shenandoah County but in the whole country.

The rooms, each bearing the name of a tree (but none called Ash or Hemlock, which the owners deemed inappropriate or too easily misinterpreted), are comfortable in a homey, rustic way suitable to the surroundings, and they are well maintained. Bud and Mary Felsburg, who took over Sky Chalet in August 1980, are careful custodians. They are also highly personable innkeepers who mean it when they write their guests after their departure that it was a pleasure to have them at the Chalet: "It is our goal to make life-long friends of our guests, and we want you to think of Sky Chalet as your home away from home."

It's a good base camp for exploring the Shenandoah Valley, that rolling stretch of peaceful, fertile fields that once lay burnt and barren. Sheridan, when he was finished with the Confederate forces in the valley, boasted that a crow flying over it would have to bring its own rations.

To the north of the Sky Chalet are the Luray Caverns, well worth the trip. Other underground adventures in the area, places to learn once again the difference between stalagmites and stalactites, are not as well known as Luray but are still interesting—the caverns of Shenandoah, Endless, Massanutten, Skyline, Grand, and Dixie.

The Skyline Drive is only a half hour away, and Interstate 81 takes the tourist north to the Apple Capital of Winchester, which has an annual Apple Blossom Festival each April, and two historic buildings that operate as museums: the 1756 log cabin that George Washington used as headquarters during the Indian wars, and the headquarters used a century later by another famous general, Stonewall Jackson.

The military genius of Jackson's sweeping 1862 Shenandoah Valley strategy is explained in an excellent sixteen-minute film at the New Market Battlefield, a 160-acre site off Interstate 81 at exit 67, a few miles from the Chalet. Another film tells the story of the cadets from Lexington's Virginia Military Institute who marched ninety miles in three days to do battle with the Yankees. Of 247 of them—average age eighteen—10 were killed and 47 wounded, and their bravery is commemorated today in the battlefield's Hall of Valor. The vivid displays are brought to life in a very real way each May when the Battle of New Market is reenacted on the second Sunday of the month.

SKY CHALET, Star Route, Box 28, Mount Jackson, Virginia 22842. Telephone: (703) 856-2147. Accommodations: 17 rooms, all with a private bath, some with a sitting area, some with a shared common room; no telephones or televisions. Rates: moderate; includes complimentary Continental breakfast and special dinners. Meal service: breakfast, lunch, and dinner. Full bar service. No credit cards, but personal checks are welcome. Open year round.
Getting there: The Chalet is ten miles west of Mount Jackson on Route 263, reached by taking exit No. 69 off Interstate 81. Shuttle service is provided from the Mount Jackson bus terminal and from the Sky Bryce Airport.

HOTEL STRASBURG
Strasburg, Virginia

Thirty-two miles north of the town of New Market, with its memorials to the Confederate cadets who fought in the 1864 Battle of New Market, is the somnolent little settlement of Strasburg. It's a town with its own Civil War memories: the battles of Cedar Creek and Fishers Hill were fought there. In the mini-museum on King Street there are rusted relics from those struggles, along with Indian artifacts and fossils found in the area, and exhibits explaining the various crafts produced by the farming community. The Strasburg Museum is in the former Southern Railway Depot, originally built as a steam pottery. The first potter arrived as early as 1765, and at one time, a century later, there were no fewer than five pottery shops, including the Bell Company, which shipped its wares all over the East.

The other museum in town is the Strasburg Hotel, a beautifully restored four-story vestige of the Victorian era. Erected originally as a hospital and recently revitalized as a high-ceilinged hostelry filled with Victorian furnishings, the hotel also boasts a reliable restaurant served by a smiling staff.

After a drink in the Depot Lounge with its stained-glass windows, its highly polished bar, and a collection of model trains, the Strasburg diner is ushered into the dining areas, three rooms with old art— portraits and landscapes—on the walls, ladder-back and bentwood chairs, and turned-wood pedestal tables. It's an atmosphere more Colonial or Federal than Victorian, but most of the food is strictly Shenandoah Valley, with excellent fresh-baked breads and desserts. Shenandoah Blanc from nearby Edinburg heads the wine list, along with a Chancellor Noir, a very dry red.

The wine is a product of the Shenandoah Vineyards, located on Route 686 off the Edinburg exit of Interstate 81. The view of the Blue Ridge Mountains is sensational from the miniscule winery, which offers informal tours and tastings.

HOTEL STRASBURG, 201 Holliday Street, Strasburg, Virginia 22657. Telephone: (703) 465-9191. Accommodations: 17 rooms, six with a private bath; no televisions or telephones. Rates: inexpensive to low moderate. Meal service: breakfast, lunch, and dinner; full bar service. Inquire about pets. Cards: AE, MC, V. Open year round.
Getting there: Take exit No. 75 off Interstate 81 and drive on Route 11 about 1.5 miles to the first light; turn right and then left at the next light. The hotel is on the corner of Holliday and Queen streets, a block from Main Street.

WAYSIDE INN
Middletown, Virginia

The first travelers to this inn in the northwest boonies of Virginia started coming in 1797, pausing for bed and board as they journeyed across the Shenandoah. The Wayside was then known as Wilkinson's Tavern. When rugged highways were hacked out of the wilderness twenty years later and the Valley Pike (now Route 11) came through Middletown, the tavern became a stagecoach stop, a relay station where fresh teams of horses were ready and where bounce-weary passengers could rest and refresh themselves.

The inn escaped the ravages of the War Between the States, though Stonewall Jackson's famous Valley Campaign swept past a few miles away. In May of 1862, Jackson attacked the Yankees retreating from Strasburg and forced them to divide their army, but Sheridan, headquartered in Winchester fourteen miles north of Middletown, eventually held sway, leading the boys in blue to victory in the beautiful Shenandoah.

Jacob Larrick bought the inn after the war, changing the name to Larrick's Hotel. In the early part of this century, when it was again sold, the new owner added a third floor, wings on each side, and a new name, the Wayside Inn. In the next few years, as pot-holed pikes were transformed to paved roads, the automobiles touring the valley caused the inn to lay claim to being "America's First Motor Inn."

In the 1960s Leo Bernstein, a Washington financier and antiques collector with a restless energy for new projects and a fascination with Americana, took over. He restored and refurbished with a happy abandon, bringing in dozens of antiques, decorating the rooms individually. The colonial motif prevails, but there are Chinese, Empire, and Victorian rooms as well. The discriminating guest with a strong aversion to a particular period might want to specify that when making a reservation.

On the ground floor, the rooms are loyal to their origins, although a radio station and a gift shop bring a bit of plastic to the fore. The Coachyard cocktail lounge helps compensate—it's a wine cellar in the spirit of an English pub. The Slave Quarters dining room, especially on a cold winter night with the fire crackling, is my favorite among the several eating areas, all decorated with high-backed chairs and bare wooden tables that look as though they've been there since Stonewall rode through town. Peanut soup, hot breads, country ham, and pan-fried chicken, along with tempting pastries for tea time, are among the

Wayside Inn, Middletown, Virginia

inn specialties. And all of the food is delivered by a young staff garbed in period gowns and bonnets.

A few yards away from the inn is the Wayside Theatre, a 260-seat enterprise staffed by professional actors who perform from June through September. In the fall there are drama workshops and in the summer film festivals.

WAYSIDE INN, 7783 Main Street, Middletown, Virginia 22645. Telephone: (703) 869-1797. Accommodations: 21 rooms; single, twin, double beds; all rooms with a private bath, none with television or telephone. Rates: moderate. Meal service: breakfast, lunch, dinner, and afternoon tea. Full bar service. Children welcome; pets not allowed. Cards: AE, MC, V. Open all year.
Getting there: Take exit 77 from Interstate 81 and proceed on Route 11 a half mile directly to the inn.

THE RED FOX TAVERN
Middleburg, Virginia

Some eight hundred horse-lovers and probably ten times as many horses live in and around Middleburg, where five of Virginia's twenty recognized hunt meets take place. The Red Fox Tavern, a 250-year-old hostelry that started out in life as Chinn's Ordinary a half century before the American Revolution, is the perfect inn for the heart of Virginia's horse country. Its thirty-inch-thick stone walls have hosted many an early-morning hunt breakfast and many a late-evening celebration after point-to-point races, the National Beagle Trials, and the Upperville Horse Show, oldest in the country.

Ghosts of the past stride the tavern's historic halls—a teenage George Washington surveying the area, British redcoats, back-country planters plotting against the King. During the Civil War, Confederate Gen. Jeb Stuart came galloping through town. He slept in the tavern and met there with Col. John Singleton Mosby, his one-time scout. Mosby's Partisan Rangers spread terror and destruction behind Union lines, at one point capturing a general, at another Sheridan's entire supply train. After the war Mosby was credited with originating the phrase "the solid South."

When Stuart was meeting with Mosby, the inn was known as the Beveridge House and already had been expanded to its present three-story size. After the war, in the mid-1880s, the name was changed to the Middleburg Inn, and in 1937 came the final rechristening as the Red Fox Tavern.

The Red Fox Tavern, Middleburg, Virginia

The fox and hunt theme inspires much of the decor of today's tavern. There is a Nobel J. Beveridge room—where the bar and intimate little lounge are located, of course. There is also a Mosby Room and a Jeb Stuart room, where the inn's only television set is wheeled out for world-shaking events—the Derby or the Preakness.

Everywhere there are fireplaces, bouncing the glow of their flames off warm woods and well-worn floors; off paints, fabrics, and wallpapers selected from the authenticated eighteenth-century Williamsburg collection. That's all part of the careful and all-encompassing restoration and renovation undertaken in early 1976, resulting in a welcome springburst colonial freshness, with hooked rugs, quilts, and canopied four-poster beds. The furnishings reflect the history of the inn and the beauty and tradition of its setting, while offering all the modern comforts.

There's a similar blending of early American tradition in the dining room with its wooden-pegged, wide-plank floors, its rafters and hand-hewn sturdy pillars hung with brass and pewter, its stone walls and fireplaces. Windsor chairs surround handsomely appointed tables laid with the bounty from a kitchen with a veteran staff. From seven in the morning until eleven at night, there are huge country breakfasts, lunches of crab cakes and fat sandwiches, and dinners of backfin crab imperial, ham steak, prime rib, and Southern fried chicken, followed by pecan pie or carrot cake.

THE RED FOX TAVERN, Washington and Madison Street; P.O. Box 385, Middleburg, Virginia 22117. Telephone: (703) 687-6301. Accommodations: six rooms, each with a twin, double, or king-size canopied bed, fireplace, private bath; telephones but no televisions. Rates: moderate. Meal service: breakfast, lunch, and dinner. Full bar service. Children and pets welcome. Cards: AE, V. Open all year.
Getting there: Middleburg is 40 miles from Washington, D.C., via Route 50 and six miles from the intersection of Route 50 with Route 15; the tavern is on the main street, Route 50.

THE LAUREL BRIGADE INN
Leesburg, Virginia

The dining room of this inn is a popular pilgrimage for residents of the surrounding area as well as for eating enthusiasts from as far afield as the nation's capital. Especially on Sundays the hungry diners congregate, eager to partake of what the inn calls "Colonial Cookery for Gentle Palates." In Laurel Brigade vernacular that translates to noteworthy prime rib and crab Newburg, to meals that start with fruit shrub and end with memorable lemon cheesecake. Meals are served by an experienced staff in a setting reminiscent of many inns in the Virginia countryside, although here one is spared the ubiquitous Washington/Lee memorabilia and decorative pieces that explain the origin of the inn's name.

Built on a lot platted in the original 1758 town plan, the inn, then known as an ordinary, took in its first guests in the 1760s. In 1817 the Peers family purchased it, renaming the property the Peers Hotel. When the Marquis de Lafayette came through town on his triumphal 1825 tour, the banquet meal in his honor—attended by President Adams, James Monroe, and other distinguished guests—was prepared in the Peers Hotel kitchen and possibly served in a special ballroom (now the long ell at the back of the inn) built for the occasion.

In 1837 the hotel was converted to a private home, and it was not until 1946, when the Roy Flippos bought the property, that it once again opened its heavy wooden doors to the public. The Flippos' son and daughter, Roy and Ellen, are now in charge of the two stories of local stone painstakingly hammered and chipped to fit one on top of the other. This craft is not lost in today's Leesburg, where old and new buildings are being restored and constructed in the same manner.

The distinctive name the Flippos selected for their inn honors the memory of a Civil War brigade made up of local Leesburg and Loudon County men. Noted for heroic exploits along the border, they made the last cavalry charge of the war, part of the corps of riders in gray who swept across the plain west of Appomattox Court House.

The Flippos keep a spotless inn—there's no sparing of fresh paint or elbow grease when cleaning the five upstairs rooms. These have spacious baths, four-posters with quilted spreads, solid colonial furniture, and windows looking out on other historic buildings or to a small garden out back, a Georgetown-style enclosure ideal for a quiet stroll or chat.

The town of Leesburg has brick sidewalks, interesting buildings, and antique stores. Start with a visit to the Information Center a block from the inn. Located next to a log cabin built about the same time as

The Laurel Brigade Inn, Leesburg, Virginia

the inn, the center has walking-tour brochures for Leesburg's sixty-acre historic district and nearby sites of interest. One of these is Morvan Park, a two-hundred-year-old, two-hundred-acre estate entered by a mile-long avenue of trees leading to outstanding boxwood gardens. The Greek Revival mansion has a Renaissance hall, a Jacobean dining room, Flemish tapestries, art nouveau pieces, and displays on the life and times of Virginia's reform governor, Westmoreland Davis.

Oatlands is another estate not to be missed, an 1803 Classical Revival home on 260 acres of green and gently undulating farmland that is a center of county equestrian happenings: point-to-point races, a horse show and a foxhound show in the spring, and hunter trials in the fall.

THE LAUREL BRIGADE INN, 20 West Market Street, Leesburg, Virginia 22075. Telephone: (703) 777-1010. Accommodations: five rooms; double and twin beds, private baths; no televisions or telephones. Rates: inexpensive. Meal service: lunch and dinner (closed Mondays). Full bar service. Children and pets welcome. No credit cards. Open all year. *Getting there:* Leesburg is 25 miles from Washington, D.C., via U.S. 7, and the inn is on Route 7, Market Street, in the center of town.

FREDERICKSBURG COLONIAL INN
Fredericksburg, Virginia

Midway between Richmond, Virginia, and the nation's capital is a town the natives like to refer to as the "Most Historic City in America": Fredericksburg, site of the famous Civil War battle of the same name, fought in December 1862. The vastly superior Union forces, led by General Burnside, crossed the Rappahannock to attack the Confederate Army of Northern Virginia commanded by Robert E. Lee. Five days later, after close to thirteen thousand Union casualties, more than twice the Confederate losses, Burnside retreated. It was one of the bloodiest engagements in the war; Burnside later was relieved of his command, and one of his key generals resigned.

There were other titanic Civil War battles in this burned-over region—Chancellorsville, the Wilderness, and Bloody Angle—and the Colonial Inn has established a mini-museum with war memorabilia just off the lobby; the gun collection of the owner, Alton Echols, is on display in the conference room.

But there's more history in Fredericksburg. John Smith visited the area as early as 1608, but the first settlers did not arrive until 1671 when they laid out the town. A half century later it was named for the father of George III, Frederick, Prince of Wales. George Washington went to one of the local schools—his mother lived in Fredericksburg for several years and her home is now a museum and her grave marked with a monument. His sister's home also survives, as does the Masonic Temple of which Washington was a member. The law office of James Monroe now serves as another museum, as does the old and honorable Rising Sun Tavern with all its venerable associations—Lafayette was entertained there.

Alton Echols and his innkeeper, James Herst, will be happy to fill in the details, to defend that boast that they live in the country's "Most Historic City." They will also be glad to see to the needs of their guests, providing modern conveniences in the only "country inn" in the immediate area.

FREDERICKSBURG COLONIAL INN, Wakefield Square, 1707 Princess Anne Street. Telephone: (703) 371-5666. Accommodations: 26 units, each with a color television, sink, refrigerator, alarm clock; no telephones; some rooms with a private bath; some suites with a queen-size sofa bed in the sitting room. Rates: inexpensive; includes Continental breakfast. Pets accepted. Cards: MC, V. Open year round.
Getting there: Fredericksburg is off the U.S. 17 exit of Interstate 95; the inn is two blocks from the historic district, past Herndon Street. Princess Anne Street runs parallel to the Rappahannock River, two blocks distant.

CHESAPEAKE HOUSE
Tangier Island, Virginia

Of all the inns I stayed in during my research and reconaissance forays into the far reaches of the Old Confederacy, none was more unusual than the Chesapeake House, in the middle of the bay James Michener has described in such exhausting detail. Reached only by boat and populated by direct-line descendants of seventeenth- and eighteenth-century pioneers—they still speak with a bit of an Elizabethan accent and rhythm, and their ancestors are buried here—Tangier Island is a place removed from what most of us consider the realities of today.

There are only a couple of cars, one for the one-man police force, one to collect garbage on the narrow paths just wide enough to accommodate a single vehicle. The islanders walk, or they cycle. Thus the yard at the Chesapeake House is filled with two-wheeled transportation used by the local women. They stream into the large kitchen to prepare belt-busting meals served family style to overnight guests and visitors from the cruise ships that depart all summer from Redville,

48

Virginia, and, on the other side of the bay, Crisfield, Maryland. Crab cakes, clam fritters, incredibly good coleslaw and potato salad, Virginia ham, and a soufflé of a corn pudding that is nothing short of sensational— and the only limit on portions is on the crab cakes: two is tops. But when we spent a long weekend on the island we bought a school of soft-shell crabs from a local fisherman and had the back room sauté them lightly—it was an epicurean pigout.

Unless one fishes, going out with one of the locals or chartering a boat, there is little to do on the 3-mile-long-by-1-1/2-mile-wide island—our major occupation, after we realized there were too many giant jellyfish for swimming and too many stinging flies to try the rocky beach, was watching the crabs moult! And reading about the Beautiful Swimmers and their importance to the bay.

The rooms are summer-camp simple, and air conditioning is nonexistent, but there are fans, and on most nights the breeze blows across the bay as one contemplates the insularity of this special slice of contemporary life.

CHESAPEAKE HOUSE, Tangier Island, Virginia 23440. Telephone: (804) 891-2331. Accommodations: ten rooms, all with shared baths; no telephones; television only in the common parlor. Rates: inexpensive; includes full breakfast and family-style dinner. No pets. No cards, but checks are welcome. Open April 1–November 1.
Getting there: From Redville, Virginia, there are regular summer cruises to Tangier (contact the boat at 804-333-4656), and a daily mail boat along with summer cruises departing from Crisfield, Maryland (contact the dock at 804-891-2240).

CHANNEL BASS INN
Chincoteague, Virginia

The most unlikely people turn up in the most unlikely places. Would you expect to meet a classical and flamenco guitarist, who is also a master chef, on a small island off Virginia's Eastern Shore? Or a teacher with a master's degree in special education waiting tables and cleaning rooms in a fishing village where the illiteracy rate is said to run as high as 30 percent?

It was back in the spring of 1972 when Jim and Kathleen Hanretta made their decision to plunge headlong into new careers. They were vacationing in Chincoteague (pronounce that Shin-ko-teeg if you want to pass for a "teeger") and came across a huge old house for sale, the last one of its pedigree on the market. The main section was built in the

49

Channel Bass Inn, Chincoteague, Virginia

1870s, with additions hammered on in the 1920s when it served as a boardinghouse. When the Hanrettas first saw the three-story, twenty-eight-room structure, it was still taking in lodgers.

Their decision to purchase the building and convert it to a first-class inn was an instant one, though neither had any prior experience in any phase of innkeeping. Kathy had been teaching in Alexandria's Montessori school, and Jim was practicing his guitar eight hours a day in preparation for a tour on the recital circuit. In the next three years of the finger-numbing, fingernail-smashing, muscle-weary labor that left them deep in debt, they questioned their decision, but not their stubborn determination.

Kathy did the scrubbing, polishing, sewing, and decorating. Jim took on-the-job crash courses in electricity, plumbing, carpentry, and painting. He also spent countless hours organizing his kitchen and perfecting his recipes, developing a menu that is as Spanish inspired as a painting by Goya, a poem of Cervantes, or an olé-producing veronica by Manolete—as Spanish as the music Jim plays.

It took him four years to settle on the menu, to carefully coax into being the best dining room on Virginia's Eastern Shore. He constantly experimented to find the proper blend of spices and herbs to enhance the succulence of the clams and oysters found in such abundance off Chincoteague shores, and to salute rather than defeat the flavor of the flaky fillets of flounder. He grows many of the herbs and much of the produce, and has bake-it-yourself sourdough flown in from San Francisco. Spanish saffron and olive oil are basic ingredients, but in the best manner of a Spanish chef who understands French cooking, he also favors tarragon in many of his dishes, and uses a brown wine sauce for sautéed veal. Other dinner specialties are his oysters Basque, which translates to a hearty tomato sauce spiked with Parmesan and chorizo. He sautés shrimp, scallops, and lobster in a white wine-butter-garlic sauce and serves broiled shrimp on saffron rice with green peppers, onions, and tomatoes. Breakfast favorites include pecan pancakes; omelets made with oysters, backfin crab, or mushrooms and truffles; and eggs Benedict.

Why all the Spanish emphasis? Jim is a true *afficionado*, converted when serving with the Marines in Spain. Later he went back to learn more about the music, the culture, and the cooking. He has never really left the country in spirit, though his inn does not reflect the heaviness of Spanish decor and there's not a bullfight poster in sight in the dining room, the front sitting room and porch, or the bedrooms that he and Kathy have been renovating.

They began with basic cleaning, then rewiring and repair, then major refurbishing, starting with the third floor. The four rooms there are now completed with new carpeting and handsome furnishings, surely the most luxurious accommodations on the island.

The island is ideal for watching the traffic on the fish docks and checking the clam-shuckers; for sitting on a bench watching the sunset; or for wandering along the miles of National Wildlife Refuge and National Seashore with its unlimited opportunities for isolated hiking, bird-watching, and seeking sandy stretches of solitude conducive to thinking deep thoughts and searching for new truths.

And if you want to talk about new truths back at the inn, James Hanretta is only too willing—his definition of innkeeper encompasses not only the roles of general manager, bookkeeper, handyman, entertainer, gardener, and super-chef, but also father confessor and cultural guide.

CHANNEL BASS INN, 100 Church Street, Chincoteague, Virginia 23336. Telephone: (804) 336-6148. Accommodations: 11 rooms; double, twin, queen- and king-size beds; eight rooms with a private bath; no televisions or telephones. Rates: inexpensive to moderate. Meal service: breakfast and dinner. Bar service: beer and wine. No children under ten and no pets. Cards: AE, MC, V. Open all year except month of December.
Getting there: Take Route 175 eleven miles from U.S. 13, which runs from Salisbury, Maryland, to the Chesapeake Bay Bridge-Tunnel; turn left at the traffic light in Chincoteague, proceed three blocks to Church Street, and turn right; the inn is the second building on the right-hand side of the street.

COLONIAL MANOR INN
Onancock, Virginia

On the water-surrounded finger of Virginia that flanks the eastern shore of Chesapeake Bay, ranging from New Church and Chincoteague in the north, through Temperanceville, Accomac, Wachapreague, Nassawadox, and Birdsnest all the way down to Cape Charles at the tip, there's one sleepy little town after another. One of my favorites is Onancock, because it's quintessential mainstream-America.

The name is Indian for "foggy place," but I saw little fog when I was in town on the occasion of their centennial celebration, complete with a parade and placards lauding such landmarks as the twenty-third-oldest drugstore in the country. They also have the Kerr House, a brick mansion built in the nineteenth century for a Scotch merchant-shipper who was a prosperous entrepreneur when Onancock was a key coastal port. It's now a museum open to the public.

The Colonial Manor Inn is not nearly as historic, but the three-story, twenty-room converted home is one of the most immaculately maintained, fussily kept hostelries I've ever had the pleasure of seeing. Run by Norman F. Horsey, a retired employee of the Department of Agriculture who took over after the death of his wife in 1979, the inn has a cozy, at-home kind of friendly atmosphere. No meals are served (his wife used to serve breakfast), but there's enough good eating in the immediate area that the guests will never go hungry. Phil Martin's honest little eatery in town opens at five in the morning—for the early-rising fishermen—and in Wachapreague there's the Island House with reliable, fresh seafood.

On the back of innkeeper Horsey's card there's the kind of sentiment I like to find when touring the backroads of America:

> We're glad to have you as our guest,
> And hope you have a good night's rest.
> Tomorrow, you again may roam,
> But while you're here, just feel at home.
>
> And when your journey starts anew,
> Please take this little card with you—
> To wish you Godspeed on your way.
> And bring you back again some day.

COLONIAL MANOR INN, 84 Market Street, P.O. Box 94, Onancock, Virginia 23417. Telephone: (804) 787-3521. Accommodations: 15 rooms, five with a private bath, all with black/white television; no telephones. Color television in common sitting room. Rates: inexpensive. No pets. No cards. Open year round.
Getting there: Onancock is one mile west of U.S. 13 via State Road 316; Market Street is the town's main street, and there's a prominent sign in front of the inn.

WILLIAMSBURG INN
Williamsburg, Virginia

Over the past quarter-century I've been to Williamsburg at least a dozen times. I've stayed at that aristocratic pamperer of a place known as the Williamsburg Inn, overnighted in one of those colonial houses strategically scattered in the historic area, and also in a room tucked into a historic-area tavern—all maintained in a style, outside and in, loyal to eighteenth-century Williamsburg. I even remember a weekend in the Williamsburg Inn when it was much more rustic, with a bare wood floor and a mountain inn feeling rather than its present-day spring-colored, flowery modernism.

No matter what time of year I was there, I always loved it: in the winter with soft candlelight bouncing off Christmas wreaths, in spring with the Virginia countryside coming back to life, in summer with tourists from around the world visiting the city that served as the capital of Virginia from 1699 until 1780, in the fall when the trees are dropping their multihued colors on brick walkways. I never tire of strolling the thoroughfare President Roosevelt called "the most historic avenue in all America": Duke of Gloucester Street with the Capitol at one end, the College of William and Mary (second only to Harvard as the nation's oldest institution of higher learning) at the other end, and the home of the royal governor, "the Palace," halfway between.

I never tire of hearing the story of the reconstruction and restoration of Williamsburg, financed by the Rockefellers who poured $45 million into the project. They were convinced of the unique importance of the town by Episcopal minister William Archer Rutherfoord Goodwin, rector of the local Bruton Parish Church and a visionary Virginian. Goodwin outlined the initial plans, engaged architects, and bought up properties along Duke of Gloucester Street.

Complete authenticity and no compromise became the bywords during the years of restoration and reconstruction. Buildings were moved or demolished, gardens planted in strict accord with the plants and practices of the eighteenth century, and furnishings of the period purchased after worldwide searches. Thousands and thousands of bricks were hand-molded from red clay and fired with oak in the manner employed two centuries earlier, to create the same gray-green glazed ends that provide a distinctive accent when laid in Flemish bond.

The first restoration was the building named for Christopher Wren on the campus of William and Mary. In 1926 it was the scene of the 150th-anniversary celebrations of Phi Beta Kappa, founded at the college. Restoration could not be completed until the discovery of a contemporary copper engraving in Oxford's Bodleian Library—in which the Wren building was clearly outlined, as was the Governor's Palace. Other aids for the total rebuilding of the Palace and Capitol were provided by drawings made by a Swiss visitor in 1702, a map drawn by a Revolutionary War French soldier, and floor plans executed by Thomas Jefferson when he was governor.

In the mornings after a quiet stroll I always look forward to settling into a colonial breakfast in the Williamsburg Inn and, at the end of a long day of absorbing colonial America, to a formal dinner in the inn, grateful for the requirement that puts coats and ties on male tourists who spend their days in a variety of undress.

At this time, when so many other cities and towns and villages have done what was pioneered here, a visit to Williamsburg is really a pilgrimage to pay tribute to those who had the wisdom, courage, and tenacity to complete the task and provide such a superlative model for others to follow.

I'm already making plans for another excursion, looking forward to another trip back in time, starting and ending my day in one of the inn's expensively appointed rooms, reading my morning paper under a shining brass chandelier in the lounge, greeting other guests under glistening crystal in the lobby, looking out of my bedroom window at the living bit of British colonial America spread out before me. This inn of inns offers a unique opportunity to live in grace and style while studying a setting so important to the development of our nation.

WILLIAMSBURG INN, Post Office Drawer B, Williamsburg, Virginia 23185. Telephone: (804) 229-1000. Accommodations: bed-sitting rooms, suites in main inn, and 26 colonial houses; twin and double beds; private baths, televisions, telephones. Rates: moderate to expensive. Meal service: breakfast, lunch, and dinner. Full bar service. Children welcome; pets not allowed. No credit cards. Open all year.
Getting there: Williamsburg is 50 miles southeast of Richmond and 30 west of Norfolk via Interstate 64 to U.S. 60. The inn is at the fringe of the historic area, reached by South England or Francis Street.

THE SURREY HOUSE
Surry, Virginia

When I first came across this unheralded place not far from the James River, I found two men in the office getting advice on some of the local attractions. They were dressed rather formally for American travelers (even in the sometimes more formal Tidewater Virginia) in light gray, conservatively cut suits and black shoes that couldn't have come from this country, with prim little worn briefcases under their arms. They had to be British, and indeed they were.

These two ruddy-faced men had come from the mother city in the mother county in the mother country—all the way from Surrey. They were heading for Jamestown, driving to the car ferry four miles away and taking the twenty-five-minute ride from Scotland Wharf to the birthplace of America. There they would see the wattle-and-daub reconstructed James Fort, modeled on the one built in 1607 by those first settlers who crossed the mighty Atlantic in a trio of ships. These ships, which are also reconstructed and lying at anchor near the fort, look more like toys than vessels capable of carrying over one hundred very cramped colonists to the New World.

By staying in Surry and using the ferryboat, history buffs can avoid the crowds at the compacted motels and eateries on the other side of the James River. Surry affords the tourist a sleepy little town with a few off-the-beaten-path sights of its own. There's the Rolfe-Warren House built in 1652 on land that once belonged to the son of Pocahontas and John Rolfe, land where Captain John Smith had built a fort. There's the architecturally interesting Bacon's Castle, built in 1660 and called the oldest brick house in English North America. The castle's name resulted from its occupation by rebellious colonists, led by Nathaniel Bacon, resisting the tyranny of their British sovereign—one hundred years before the Declaration of Independence.

A short distance away is the Chippokes State Park, a working plantation for more than three centuries, with the same boundaries it had when patented in 1619; it is now planted with handsome gardens circling the antebellum mansion with many outbuildings.

The innkeeper of Surrey House, Mrs. Will M. Gwaltney, will provide detailed instructions and information on all there is to see in her town, just as she did for those two Englishmen—in between baking a wedding cake for one of her nieces. Her kitchen is just behind her tiny, homey office with a large easy chair planted in front of the television. It's an informal and pleasant place to chat with her about the area.

At the Surrey House don't expect a historic inn filled with antiques—it's really more like a tiny two-story motel. But it's meticulously maintained, lovingly cared for, and has one of the best restaurants in Surry and a good many other cities and counties in the commonwealth.

Mrs. Gwaltney's sister-in-law runs the splendid kitchen. There are memorable crab cakes, crab imperial spiked with fresh pineapple, ham that's cured six months served in a variety of shapes and sizes, warm yeast rolls and apple fritters. Then there's peanut-raisin pie and soup made from peanuts, popular in these parts long before the Carters started promoting them: in Surry County eighty-five hundred acres of peanuts are harvested each fall.

Printed on the menu is a touch of homey poetry that says a lot about the reason Surrey House is in this book:

> I like to live in a little town,
> Where the trees meet across the street
> Where you wave your hand and say hell-o
> To everyone you meet.

THE SURREY HOUSE, Surry, Virginia 23883. Telephone: (804) 294-3191. Accommodations: 11 rooms, pairs of double beds, private baths, televisions, no telephones. Rates: inexpensive. Meal service: breakfast, lunch, and dinner. No bar service. Children welcome; pets not allowed. Cards: MC, V. Open all year.

Getting there: Surrey is halfway between Richmond and Norfolk on Route 10; turn at the intersection with Route 31; the house is a block from that center crossroads.

THE SMITHFIELD INN
Smithfield, Virginia

The name should be familiar to any lover of Virginia ham, and slices of the salty Smithfields, cured in this sleepy little city, are, of course, among the headliners of the inn dining room. But innkeepers Twyla and Doug Gregory are Southern enough to also have fried chicken, black-eyed peas, hand-beaten biscuits, corn bread, and collards on their menu.

And they've been loyal enough to the long history of their proud possession to work a careful, gradual restoration of a building that's been catering to the public as a tavern, a public house, and a stagecoach inn since the early years of the nineteenth century. Built in 1752 as a simple two-story cottage and expanded to its present size in 1870, the inn was operated by the Skyes family for four decades—it was then known as the Sykes Inn.

We're grateful to the Gregorys for their choice of name and for their dedication to the proposition that the inn is worth saving—as a historic site in the heart of some of the country's most historic real estate. Williamsburg is only twenty-five miles away, Norfolk and Newport News even closer. The Smithfield Inn makes a good headquarters for day-tripping into the past.

THE SMITHFIELD INN, 112 Main Street, Smithfield, Virginia 23430. Telephone: (804) 357-4358. Accommodations: six rooms, two with a private bath; no televisions or telephones. Rates: inexpensive. No pets. Cards: AE, MC, V. Open year round.
Getting there: Smithfield is 18 miles southeast of Surry and ten miles northwest of Newport News via State Road 10.

NORTH CAROLINA

TANYA'S OCEAN HOUSE MOTEL
Kill Devil Hills, North Carolina

Tanya Young, the owner-operator of this unique complex spread along the sands of the Outer Banks in Kill Devil Hills, doubles as a teacher-historian of the development, culture, and rich past of North Carolina. The designer-decorated rooms in this hostelry each represent some special facet of North Carolina's history or geography, and the details are discussed in the eminently readable *Tanya's Tarheel Times*.

Among my favorite rooms is the Library, honoring the state's first public library and built into an eighteenth-century accommodation in blue and beige, with one wall filled with bookcases divided by a fireplace, which is flanked by comfortable chairs for reading. Next to the canopy bed are antique oak tables, matched by an antique oak dresser and a delicately constructed lady's writing desk.

The Currituck Barn Loft room is named for the neighboring county and is barnlike in feeling, with shuttered windows, an antique corn shucker converted to a table, a variety of old and honorable farm implements dangling from ceiling and wall, and a canopy-covered bed that looks like an old tobacco wagon.

There's another reminder of tobacco, an industry so important to North Carolina, in Tanya's Tobacco Belt room done in brown and gold tones and reminiscent of a curing barn with old implements of the industry affixed to the walls.

Jonathan Livingston Seagull's Nest defines itself, and Tanya declares that Jonathan had to be an Outer Banker. The Wright Brothers Camp is modeled after the one in the nearby Wright Brothers

Museum, and Tanya is certain "we have the Wright stuff in the Wright Brothers Camp for your comfort!"

What fun! I'd like to spend six weeks in Tanya's Tarheel Collection, moving from room to room, from historic happening to historic happening, enjoying the pool, the ocean, the courtyard, and learning about the Tarheel State.

TANYA'S OCEAN HOUSE MOTEL, Milepost 10, P.O. Box 747, Kill Devil Hills, North Carolina 27948. Telephone: (919) 441-7328. Accommodations: 42 rooms, each with a private bath, television, refrigerator; no telephones. Rates: moderate. No pets. Cards: MC, V. Open year round.
Getting there: Tanya's inn is located at Milepost 10 on State Route 12, halfway between Kitty Hawk and Nags Head.

FIRST COLONY INN
Nags Head, North Carolina

The First Colony Inn is the oldest continuously operating inn on the Outer Banks, and, as the locals tell it, the landmark has been there as long as they can remember. But it doesn't go back to the Wright brothers, whose monument is just a few miles up the beach at Kitty Hawk—it dates only from 1932. That's when the three-story classic was constructed in vintage Nags Head style: cedar-shake siding, a dormered roof with protruding gables, and wide breeze-catching verandas.

Built directly on the beach, where innkeeper Betty Clarke now hosts watermelon parties, and supplied with an ample number of rockers for watching the surf and thinking great thoughts, the First Colony was named for Roanoke, the English settlement established twenty years before Jamestown and thirty-five before Plymouth. Roanoke is the subject of America's longest-running outdoor drama, *The Lost Colony,* performed nightly from the first week in June to the last week in August at nearby Roanoke Island; 1983 is its forty-third season.

First Colony Inn rooms are simple but not severe—precisely what one wants when searching for an oceanfront holiday without motel trappings.

The inn is across from Jockey's Ridge, the largest sand dune on the East Coast and a staging area for hang gliders. They move through the air as effortlessly as the ghosts that reportedly haunt the inn. Maybe one of them looks like Sir Walter Raleigh—or even Andy Griffith: he played Sir Walter in *The Lost Colony* early in his career.

FIRST COLONY INN, State Route 158 Business, P.O. Box 726, Nags Head, North Carolina 27959. Telephone: (914) 441-7365. Accommodations: 18 rooms; singles, doubles, suites, and cottages, all with private baths; no televisions or telephones. Rates: inexpensive to low moderate. Meal service: none. No pets. Cards: MC, V. Open May 1 through mid-October.

Getting there: The inn is on 158 Business, the main artery running north and south from Whalebone to Kitty Hawk, across the road from Jockey's Ridge State Park.

ELIZABETHAN INN
Manteo, North Carolina

In style and spirit the Elizabethan is more like a motel than an inn, but its builders did make an effort to construct their buildings with a facade of Olde English Tudor; and with a name honoring the great queen how could I exclude it from a book on country inns of the South? Not when it was Elizabeth who sent Sir Walter Raleigh to colonize the New World. Not when the Elizabethan Gardens are nearby for horticulturists and anglophiles to appreciate. And not when Paul Green's outdoor drama, the longest-running in the nation, is performed each summer to enthusiastic audiences eager to learn the history of the colonists who came to Roanoke Island in 1585 and "walked away through the dark forest into history."

The Lost Colony is performed minutes away from the Elizabethan Inn, on the shores of Roanoke Sound. The two thousand-seat Waterside Theatre is next to the Elizabethan Gardens and reconstructed Fort Raleigh. From the first week in June to the last week of August the story is unfolded, from Raleigh pleading with his queen to be allowed to accompany the expedition he was sponsoring, to the birth of Virginia Dare (who is memorialized in the Gardens by a nineteenth-century sculpture). The presentation includes the harvest dance of the Hatteras Indians and a brilliant display of fireworks.

In 1984 local shipwrights will have completed their replica of Raleigh's lead ship, the sixty-eight-foot *Elizabeth.* Using tools of the 1500s—adzes and broadaxes—the shipbuilders will have the pine and juniper vessel, *Elizabeth II,* ready for the kickoff of the quadricentennial of the first English settlement in this country.

During the three-year celebration the Elizabethan Inn will be bustling with guests enjoying the swimming pool, the quiet of the courtyards separating the trio of buildings, and the Elizabethan dining

61

room where the specialties include excellent clam chowder, a harvest from nearby waters, hush puppies, and choice steaks.

On Tuesdays and Fridays they serve a boiled dinner with ham and cabbage, potatoes, and cornmeal dumplings. On any day—starting at six in the morning for the fishermen and other early risers—they present pancakes sprinkled with bits of bacon, and a special "Coastal Breakfast": herring roe and eggs.

ELIZABETHAN INN, U.S. 64 and 264, P.O. Box 549, Manteo, North Carolina 27954. Telephone: (919) 473-2101. Accommodations: 50 rooms, all with private baths, telephones, cable color televisions; some rooms with refrigerators. Rates: moderate. Meal service: breakfast, lunch, and dinner; no bar. No pets. Cards: AE, MC, V. Open year round. *Getting there:* Highway 64 and 264 is the main street of Manteo, and the inn is between the Lost Colony complex and the Christmas Shop, with clearly marked signs.

BLACKBEARD'S LODGE
Ocracoke, North Carolina

For a rustic introduction to this island in the Atlantic, an integral part of the Cape Hatteras National Seashore, check into this lodge. Each and every room is named after a famous port, each riser on the stairs bears the name of some notorious pirate, and the decor is straight from the sea. As management states in its flyer, "Blackbeard's Lodge is a link with a colorful period of Ocracoke's history... not the 'plushiest' Lodge you have ever visited but it is by far the friendliest! Ya' all come, ya' hear?"

While there are signs of modernity popping up from the sand here and there on the barrier island, Blackbeard's holds on to the past, as does the Ocracoke Lighthouse, built in 1823, the oldest lighthouse still in use on the East Coast, and the hidden, sandy lanes of Ocracoke, which take the walker ever so gently into yesterday.

The lodge is convenient to sixteen miles of virgin beach, as well as to the National Park Service Visitor Center where there's information on the Summer National Seashore Programs (from the first week in June to the first week in September). The programs include narrations about the pirates, the early history of the island, and the landings of Verrazzano, Raleigh, and Sir Francis Drake; seashore and woods walks; and snorkeling and evening campfires.

Doward H. Brugh, the owner-manager of Blackbeard's Lodge, can provide his own insights into the lore and legends of the little (pop. 500) village, can advise on chartering boats for trips to Bird, Pelican, and Portsmouth islands, and will recommend local restaurants—such as one of the newest, the Pelican, with its excellent sautéed lump crab meat, clam chowder, fresh vegetables, and combination seafood platters.

BLACKBEARD'S LODGE, P.O. Box 37, Ocracoke, North Carolina 27960. Telephone: (919) 928-3421 and 928-9591. Accommodations: 44 rooms, including two bedroom efficiencies, all with private baths; no telephones or televisions. Rates: low moderate, with lower rates in winter months. No pets. No cards. Open year round.
Getting there: The lodge is just off the main road spearing into Ocracoke, Route 12, a few hundred yards from the Island Inn.

THE ISLAND INN
Ocracoke, North Carolina

Larry Williams, one of the twosome now running this relaxed, informal rambler on the Outer Banks, is a living, working, and happy contradiction of that old maxim that you can't go home again. He was born on Ocracoke, raised on Ocracoke, and remembers well the fire of ships burning on the horizon and the thudding explosion of depth charges during World War II. German submarines preyed on shipping all along this coast; four of their victims, British seamen on a torpedoed antisubmarine trawler, are buried on the island in a British cemetery, a small square plot of four white stone crosses behind a white picket fence.

Williams left the island shortly after the war, moving farther north to Virginia Beach, where he worked as a schoolteacher until 1977 when he started a new career as innkeeper. He remembers the days when the only contact with the mainland was the old mail boat and the arrival twice a week of the supply ship sailing out of the Pamlico River and across the sound from Washington. He recalls fondly the balmy summer evenings when a song started by someone sitting outside his cracker-box house would soon be picked up by others until the whole island was singing in chorus.

Larry Williams is a Howard on his mother's side, and you don't have to be in Ocracoke very long to understand how deep those roots go. Walk down the sandy path between the Methodist church and the post office—that's Howard Street, a narrow lane shaded by water oaks and yaupon, which preserves the spirit of the isolated island the way it used to be. The lane goes past the Howard Cemetery, one of several little family plots that dot the flat landscape. There was even a Howard who sailed with Edward Teach—otherwise known as Blackbeard.

63

The Island Inn, Ocracoke, North Carolina

Blackbeard's favorite harbor was Ocracoke. Its treacherous inlet provided a natural barrier against heavier British warships, and it was in the Ocracoke channel that Blackbeard met his end. In the fall of 1718 a lieutenant of the British Royal Navy beheaded the pirate after a violent hand-to-hand struggle and threw him overboard. According to legend, the headless Blackbeard swam around the ship seven times before finally sinking into a place forever after known as Teach's Hole.

Another Blackbeard story concerns the name of the island—said to have come from the pirate's prayers as he waited for dawn on that fateful autumn day, still hoping to escape the navy: "O Crow Cock, O Crow Cock!"

It's all part of the lore and legend of this strip of sand that was the first landfall of the colonists sent out by Sir Walter Raleigh in 1585. Their settlement at Roanoke Island to the north is commemorated at the restored Fort Raleigh, a 144-acre National Historic Site with a Waterside Theatre where Paul Green's symphonic drama, *The Lost Colony,* is performed during the summer. Farther north along another finger of Outer Bank is Kitty Hawk, site of the Wright Brothers National Memorial with its reconstruction of the hangar and house, and replicas of the launching gear used in Orville and Wilbur's first powered flight in 1903.

Between that memorial and Ocracoke is the splendid solitude of sand and stunted forest, coves, and dunes, whose stillness is broken only by the steady roar of the surf, the screeching of the gulls, and the less harsh tones of many other birds—Ocracoke is on the eastern flyway. In the forty-five square miles from Whalebone to Ocracoke, there are sixteen miles of virgin beach, of National Seashore—a seemingly limitless expanse to get away from it all, to beach walk, surf fish, and swim, to sail and bird-watch, to paint and photograph, even to write travel books.

But you will always want to return to the village and inn that Larry Williams never really left in spirit. He runs his Island Inn with the capable aid of partner Foy Shaw who, like Larry, was a teacher in Virginia Beach. The inn's original building was constructed in 1901 as an Odd Fellows' Lodge, and the first floor served as Ocracoke's first public school. In the 1930s the building was moved across the road to its present location and became a private home. Ocracokan R. S. Wahab bought the building in 1941 and converted it to an inn he called the Crow's Nest; his nephew, Larry Williams, helped him run it. Then during World War II the navy established a base on the island with some five hundred men. The old inn became the local Officers' Club. The navy also brought the first public telephones and paved roads.

Subsequent owners of the inn added wings with rooms to accommodate more travelers, and when Larry and Foy took over they started a refurbishing program that is still under way. There's now a splendid little lobby and a variety of comfortable, though not elaborately furnished rooms—seashore rustic is the prevailing style. A new unit with nineteen rooms was opened in the first months of 1982. The dining room is fish-house straightforward, with anything from the deep the specialty—excellent clam chowder, mountains of sautéed crab meat, a generous combination seafood platter—all at moderate prices.

After a meal at the inn, walk around the village. In one direction are rows of well-maintained cracker-box houses leading to the oldest operative lighthouse on the East Coast, built of five-foot-thick walls in 1823; during hurricanes and high waters, the lighthouse has provided shelter for natives fleeing flooded homes. In the other direction is old Howard Street, the church, and the family burial plots. Around the enclosed harbor called Silver Lake there are ferry docks, marinas, and a National Park Service Visitor Center housed in a building put up by the navy.

THE ISLAND INN, Box 7, Ocracoke Island, North Carolina 27960. Telephone: (919) 928-4351. Accommodations: 39 rooms; single and twin beds; four rooms with shared baths, 35 with private baths; some rooms with television, none with a telephone. Rates: low moderate, with lower rates off season. Meal service: breakfast, lunch, and dinner. Wine and beer. Children welcome; pets not allowed. Cards: MC, V. Open all year.
Getting there: From the north take Route 158 to Whalebone Junction and from the west Route 64–264 to Whalebone; there proceed on Route 12, taking the free car ferry across Hatteras Inlet, a 45-minute trip departing every 25 minutes from 5 am to 11 pm. From the south and Morehead City take U.S. 70 to Cedar Island and the two-hour car ferry that runs from 7 am to 1, 4, or 5 pm, depending on the season. There's also a 2-1/2-hour ferry that connects at Swan Island at Route 264 west of Belhaven, with four trips a day: 7 and 10 am, 1 and 4 pm. Make reservations at ferry terminals or by phone: Swan Island 926-1111 and Cedar Island 225-3551.

TRENT RIVER PLANTATION
Pollocksville, North Carolina

William Parker is the innkeeper's innkeeper. A veteran of this most rewarding profession in Cape Cod, he discovered the Carolinas long ago, but only in the past few years did he determine to create a special inn here, in the flatlands on the edge of the Croatan National Forest, halfway between the towns of Belgrade and New Bern.

This time around he was not content merely to create an inn in a stately old manor house; he had to have a petting farm, a barnyard with a couple hundred animals, and a river where he could show guests the best fishing spots. Here visitors on board the *Carolina Blue* can glide under the cypress trees thick with ghostly whirls of Spanish moss. When the moon is full, there are special nighttime excursions—certain routes to romance. This inn also has a swimming pool, handsomely landscaped, of course; and a small antique store, positioned perfectly in the old smoke house.

There are more antiques displayed throughout the mansion—all of them for sale, and that means a steadily changing array of furnishings. When I made my first foray into Bill Parker's little kingdom, my corner room with its three windows was home to a mint-condition mahogany tester bed with dust ruffles, dating from the early 1800s; a handsome two-drawer cherry night table; an eighteenth-century Southern-made walnut beaded-drawer bow chest; an early American chest of walnut with richly elaborate inlay; a Chippendale-style mirror with more inlay; a Martha Washington armchair; and a walnut drop-leaf table, made about 1790 in the South, probably Virginia.

There are other treasures in the splendid living room, and everywhere the thickest of carpeting, along with walk-in closets, windows that open, and champagne and fresh flowers upon arrival. In the mornings there's silver-tray breakfast delivery to the rooms: orange juice with a sprig of freshly plucked mint, coffee or tea, and such goodies as cinnamon swirls presented with a rose and spiked with a few splashes of pistachio liqueur.

Pollocksville is not much more than a crossroads, but New Bern with its magnificent Tryon Palace is close at hand; the ocean and the port of Morehead City (with its superlative seafood restaurant on the waterfront, the Sanitary Fish Market) is less than an hour's drive.

TRENT RIVER PLANTATION, Highway 17 at the Trent River, P.O. Box 154, Pollocksville, North Carolina 28573. Telephone: (919) 224-3811. Accommodations: four rooms, none with a private bath; televisions but no telephones. Rates: moderate; includes Continental breakfast. No pets. No cards. Open year round.

Getting there: The plantation is 12 miles south of New Bern on U.S. 17 at the Trent River.

KINGS ARMS INN
New Bern, North Carolina

In the heart of the historic district of the second oldest town in the state, settled by German and Swiss émigrés in 1710 (led by Baron von Graffenried, who named the city for his native town), three couples have restored a fine old frame structure, converting it to a modern inn. Built in the 1840s with various Victorian additions a half century later, the inn was named for the royal coat of arms that glowers mightily from the pediment on the north facade of Tryon Palace; and it's furnished in a manner generally loyal to the Colonial and Federal periods.

The Federal style had a tenacious hold on the port city at the confluence of the Neuse and Trent rivers, lasting almost until the Civil War and coinciding with the growing prosperity of the town in the post-Revolutionary period. The Eli Smallwood House at 524 Front Street, now a private residence, is a superb example of the style, a quintessential expression built by a successful planter-merchant in the years 1810–16. The scale is perfect, the hand-carved ornamentation solidly exquisite. A similar elegance is found in the New Bern Academy and its New Street Building dating from 1806; the Masonic Temple and Theatre completed in 1809; the 1821 First Presbyterian Church with its magnificent pedimented Ionic portico and a total sense of symmetry outside as well as in; and the Harvey Mansion at 221 Tryon Palace Drive, a three-story structure built in 1797 by a shipowner-merchant and containing the finest Adamesque Federal woodwork in the city if not the state.

The Harvey Mansion, beautifully restored and revitalized, now serves as a restaurant that is clearly the class act of New Bern. The wine list is adequate, the beef and veal reliable, and the oysters outstanding. The house specialty of scampi Italiano, blessed with sherry and tarragon with a touch of tomato and garlic, is worth writing Venice about.

And the nearby Tryon Palace is worth writing Williamsburg about. It's a painstakingly perfect reconstruction of the residence of royal governor William Tryon. During the American Revolution it became the capitol of the newly independent state. In 1798, thirty years after it was completed, the palace burned, but in the 1950s, aided by the original plans of architect John Hawks, various artifacts uncovered during excavations, and the inventory of the royal governor, the Tryon Palace Commission worked the miracle of reconstruction. To furnish the palace, antiques and works of art were imported from England— only items contemporary to Tryon's time—including paintings by George Romney, Claude Lorrain, and Gainsborough. The palace boasts the oldest Gainsborough in the country.

George Washington never slept at the palace, but he did spend two nights in the neighboring John Wright Stanly House, built by a prominent New Bern shipowner, merchant, and Revolutionary War patriot, and restored a decade ago. It too has been carefully furnished with period antiques, primarily American, but also a few Irish and English pieces from the 1750–80 period.

On the palace grounds are magnificent eighteenth-century English gardens, always bright with blooms of the season, and the Stevenson House, built in 1805. The influence of the port and the presence of shipwrights and boat builders are gracefully apparent in the roping of the original wood cornices, and the widow's walk.

Tryon Palace and the two houses are open to the public, which is advised to watch a short informative film before being escorted through the buildings by one of the lovely guides, resplendent in a farthingale.

Tryon Palace is only four blocks from the Kings Arms Inn, and the trio of innkeepers—Bettye and Walter Paramore, Evelyn and John Peterson, Uzie and John Thomas—can provide information on the complex and the many other architectural attractions of New Bern. On two days early in April there's a home and garden tour with more than twenty-five residences, gardens, and landmarks on display.

Kings Arms guests are sent off for their day of touring with a complimentary breakfast delivered to the rooms and consisting of juice, coffee or tea, and toast, blueberry or English muffins, pastries or ham biscuits.

KINGS ARMS INN, 212 Pollock Street, New Bern, North Carolina 28560. Telephone: (919) 638-4409. Accommodations: eight rooms, each with a private bath and a television; no telephones. Rates: moderate; includes Continental breakfast. No pets. Cards: AE, MC, V. Open year round.
Getting there: Pollock Street runs parallel to and between Tryon Palace Drive and Broad Street (U.S. 17); the inn is around the corner from East Front Street and next door to the Henderson House, a late eighteenth-century mansion that is now a restaurant—start your meal with peanut soup and finish it with buttermilk pie!

RIVER FOREST MANOR
Belhaven, North Carolina

Since the first edition of *Country Inns of the Old South*, innkeeper Axson Smith has gone on to that great inn in the sky; but his spirit survives, in fact, it thrives, in the historic mansion he converted to a hostelry in 1947. His wife Mabel and son Axson Smith, Jr., see to that. The grounds are well kept—and were filled with townspeople celebrating Independence Day in real down-home, Music Man style, when I last surveyed the scene, on July 4, 1982. And the dining rooms never looked better to me, crisp with fresh napery and with a high level of fussy maintenance everywhere apparent.

The man who liked to boast that he could devour a whole ham in one sitting, that he once consumed eight two-pound chickens, can rest assured that his beloved Belhaven inn is in very competent hands. The Goliath of a buffet with its seventy-five-item groaning table of good eating is still bringing in the trenchermen and the gourmands, to feast on everything from country-style souse to sweet potato fluff, Pamlico fried oysters, and clam fritters, to the Manor's famous pickled country sausage, Down East country ham with raisin sauce, homemade biscuits, hush puppies, lemon pie, and Mattie's caramel cake. No wonder they proclaim on the menu for the smorgasbord (served daily from 6 to 9 and Sundays from 12 to 9) that their guests should "Eat, Drink and be Merry for Tomorrow You May Diet."

There's enough good food here to keep sailors alive for weeks at sea. Or to send manor guests walking the eighteen miles to historic Bath, North Carolina's oldest incorporated town (1705), with guided tours of the dwellings and a summer outdoor drama entitled *Blackbeard, Knight of the Black Flag*. Bath's St. Thomas Episcopal Church is the oldest one in continuous use in the state—the bell of the church was presented by Queen Anne in 1732, and the candelabra is Georgian Sheffield.

Sixteen miles from Bath is the charming waterfront settlement of Washington, named for our first president and incorporated in 1776. A map outlining a self-guided walking tour of the historic district is available at the town's visitor center on Market Street.

The little coastal town of Belhaven is also worth some touring time: in the center of the city is the Belhaven Memorial Museum, and two of the largest crab processing plants in the Carolinas are not far away. There's swimming in the river, and fishing and hunting in the countryside.

River Forest Manor, Belhaven, North Carolina

The River Forest Manor, tucked into a grove of long-needle pines, is the ideal base camp for exploring the area. Restored in great part by the tireless Smith, whose father used to run Belhaven's old Carolina Hotel, the manor was built in the grand Victorian style at the turn of the century by a local lumber and railroad magnate, John Aaron Wilkinson. He spared no cost in building this elaborate home, the largest in town. Italian artisans were imported to carve the ceiling moldings and the ornate oak mantels for the eleven fireplaces. Crystal chandeliers were installed, cut glass leaded into transoms, polished mahogany fitted into place on the dining room walls, two-story Ionic columns added to the main entrance.

Today Wilkinson's labor of love, so carefully restored by Axson Smith (who added a marina, a tennis court, and a hot tub to the property) and lovingly tended by his wife and son, transports the tourist back in time as soon as the building is first sighted from the drive. Decades drop with each step up the elaborate staircase that leads up to the game hall and the bedrooms. Memorable among the rooms is No. 2, with its marble-topped tables, high-standing bed, oversize old chests, and wagon-wheel lamp; the extra-large No. 7, with a row of windows and twin Victorian beds that could accommodate giants; and No. 3, with a mahogany four-poster and a ballroom of a bathroom with a tub for two and its own balcony. This grand old manor offers a carefully preserved feeling of Victorian times.

RIVER FOREST MANOR, 600 East Main Street, Belhaven, North Carolina 27810. Telephone: (919) 943-2151. Accommodations: 12 rooms, all with private baths, televisions, and telephones, but some are in an adjacent motel unit, so be sure to specify if the new or old rooms are preferred. Rates: inexpensive to low moderate. Meal service: breakfast and buffet dinners; bar service: beer, wine, and "brown-bag social club." No pets. Cards: MC, V. Open all year.
Getting there: Belhaven is 52 miles from Greenville via Route 264, on the Pungo River emptying into Pamlico Sound. At the intersection of 264 with 92, continue on 264, Main Street, to the waterfront and the manor. With a full-facility marina, the manor monitors VHF Channel 16 and CB Channel 9; it has an entrance channel 8 feet MIW and 700 feet of dockage.

MAGNOLIA INN
Pinehurst, North Carolina

Just as the Pine Crest Inn (following) does not have the pizzazz of the prestigious Pinehurst Country Club, so the Magnolia does not measure up to the Pine Crest. It's more of an old-timey Southern guest house, one with a crackling living room fire to warm guests in the wintertime, and a small pool out back to cool them in the summer. Porches on both floors allow ample space for rocking and relaxing, and the shops and galleries of the town center are seconds away.

Tennis and golf are minutes away—the inn will make starting-time arrangements at the country club as well as at other courses; there's also a health spa at the club, and a local riding club as well as a gun and archery club.

The Magnolia Inn goes back to the origins of Pinehurst. It was built as an inn in 1896, the year after its owner, James Walker Tufts, paid a dollar an acre for some five thousand acres in an area then known as the Pine Barrens. It is now called the Sandhills of North Carolina, and it's one of the most meticulously manicured tracts of land in the country—for golfers and all other visitors.

MAGNOLIA INN, P.O. Box 266, Pinehurst, North Carolina 28374. Telephone: (919) 295-6900. Accommodations: 13 rooms, including three large enough to accommodate threesomes, all with private baths; no televisions or telephones. Rates: inexpensive; includes full breakfast. No pets. No credit cards. Open year round.
Getting there: The inn is on the corner of Magnolia and Chinquapin roads, one block from the post office and the village green.

PINE CREST INN
Pinehurst, North Carolina

Donald Ross was the owner of the Pine Crest Inn for more than twenty years, and if you don't recognize his name, you're no golfer. Ross designed some six hundred golf courses all over the country. His portrait hangs behind the reception desk of this grand old inn, which first opened its doors to guests in 1913.

Innkeeper Bob Barrett has been in command since 1961, and he's now turning over active management to son Pete, a graduate of the excellent Hotel, Food and Travel School of Florida International University in Miami. They should put up a portrait of Bob Barrett. One of chef Carl Jackson graces a wall in the dining room—over the fireplace. But then Jackson has been behind the Pine Crest burners for close to fifty years. He used to spend his summers cheffing at the Roaring Gap Inn and the White Elephant Inn in Nantucket, but when Barrett decided to keep the Pine Crest open during the summer—starting in 1981—Jackson stayed in place. At his side is nephew Peter Jackson—he's been there for close to thirty years. Together they produce a menu that has earned the inn an enviable reputation for fine food: home-baked breads, homemade soups, fresh fish, superb crab and scallop casseroles, fantastic pork chops, solid steaks, and such reliable all-American fare as ham steak with the obligatory slice of pineapple, and calves' liver with onions and bacon. No wonder his portrait hangs so proudly in the dining room!

The Barretts are happy to award such recognition, and Bob is particularly proud of his Waterford chandelier hanging in a dining room usually used for private parties. His Irish shows as he explains how the chandelier was a gift from a guest, one of the many repeaters who come back year after year. When Bob sees them coming he also sees their room number etched on their forehead, and he often has to do a bit of juggling to satisfy personal requests for a particular room. My favorite is No. 212, a corner room with three walls of windows and pictures of hunt scenes on the wall.

The atmosphere at the Pine Crest is vintage New England inn, with all the modern conveniences and such extras as Mr. B's Old South Lounge with a tinkling piano and with Dixieland on the weekends. There's a lovely little lattice-lined bar in another cozy corner, a suitable staging area for discussing a day on the links.

Pinehurst is a golfer's Mecca. The nearby country club has six courses, and the World Golf Hall of Fame is behind the fourth green of the famous No. 2 course. The inn has a set daily allotment of starting times, and they reserve those times on Pinehurst courses five days in advance. For other area courses reservations can be made thirty days in advance.

For non-golfers there are tennis courts in the area, and a delightful little village filled with shops, including an array tucked into the old Pinehurst Theatre. Fanning out from the town center are avenues and roads laid out just before the turn of the century by the New York experts in the field of landscaping, the Frederick Law Olmstead firm. Stately homes are shaded by masses of magnolias and tall, tall pines, and there's an overwhelming air of affluence from one end of Pinehurst to the other.

It's the kind of formal informality that characterizes the inn, a place where men are required to wear jackets after six, where guests like to dress for dinner, where the linens are replaced and the beds turned down each night.

PINE CREST INN, Pinehurst, North Carolina 28374. Telephone: (919) 295-6121. Accommodations: 43 rooms, all with private baths, cable televisions, telephones. Rates: inexpensive to moderate; includes breakfast and dinner. No pets. Cards: AE, MC, V. Open year round. *Getting there:* Pinehurst is 59 miles west of Fayetteville and 75 miles southwest of Raleigh at the intersection of State Roads 5 and 2; the inn is a block from the center of the village.

PLANTATION INN
Raleigh, North Carolina

I know it's a local link in a giant nationwide chain, but in setting and substance, in spirit and soul, the Plantation Inn in Raleigh is pure Southern country inn: comfortable, cozy, caring. In an area where preppy has always been popular, the Plantation Inn is the ultimate preppy performer, with a front desk staff straight from the pages of a Brooks Brothers catalogue, and an uncompromising maintenance standard. This is an inn of considerable class, and numerous extras.

I like the attractive furnishings, the clock-radio, a closet I can walk into, the screened door slats allowing for air conditioning by nature, three-way light bulbs, coffee and a morning paper delivered to the room, coffee in the lobby twenty-four hours a day. And I like a management that strives to live up to its logo: Quality Service Hospitality.

Included in the twenty-six wooded acres is a putting green (an eighteen-hole course for inn guests is just a mile away), a playground, and a small fishing pond ringed by old-timey wooden-slat chairs commodious enough to accommodate an Orson Welles. The pool is open from April 1 to November 1, but the Carriage Club Cocktail Lounge and the adjacent dining room never shut their doors. The noon and nighttime buffets alone are worth the trip. During the 5:30 to 9:00 evening spreads there's an organist in attendance, playing golden oldies in the shadow of the American flag.

The Stars and Stripes is a fitting addition to the Southern colonial setting of red carpet and chairs, gleaming brass chandeliers, candles, fresh flowers, and a groaning table of excellent fare: roast beef and fried chicken, stuffed flounder, Yorkshire pudding, French-fried onion rings, all kinds of freshly assembled salads, relishes, cakes, and pies. The food is prepared and served by an unusually friendly staff and

Plantation Inn, Raleigh, North Carolina

complemented with a wine list featuring more splits than are usually found in restaurants these days.

The Plantation Inn is a quiet, gracious retreat, a welcome country inn escape after a busy day visiting the State Capitol area, or working in the famous Research Triangle, or touring such Raleigh sights as the Mordecai House, built in the 1780s seven years before the town was laid out. The house is now the center of Mordecai Historic Park, which has other buildings of historic interest: an old post office, a simple church, the birthplace of President Andrew Johnson. In the 1820s famed Southern architect William Nichols designed a two-story Greek Revival addition to Mordecai House.

PLANTATION INN, 6401 North Boulevard, P.O. Box 11333, Raleigh, North Carolina 27604. Telephone: (919) 876-1411. Accommodations: 108 rooms; singles and doubles; all with private baths, telephones, and televisions. Rates: moderate. Meal service: breakfast, lunch, and dinner; full bar service. No pets. All major credit cards. Open year round.
Getting there: The inn is three miles north of Raleigh on U.S. 1.

THE CAROLINA INN
Chapel Hill, North Carolina

All college towns should have an inn with the class and dash of Dartmouth's Hanover Inn or Chapel Hill's Carolina Inn. "A cheerful inn for visitors, a town hall for the state, and a home for returning sons and daughters of Alma Mater," states the commemorative plaque in the lobby of the Carolina Inn. The plaque honors the generosity of John Sprunt Hill, class of 1889, who built the inn in 1924 and gave it to the university eleven years later.

There's a collegiate look about the inn, built in Southern colonial style of red brick with white pillars, gabled roofs, and multipaned windows; a newer section built in the early 1970s blends harmoniously with the old. Inside, the light and spacious lobbies are ringed by numerous meeting rooms usually filled with one or another university-affiliated activity; while on the comfortable assortment of couches and chairs, grouped together for conversation, there are usually more than a few professors or parents or returning alums holding forth.

There's an established feeling about this inn, a quiet and confident air that reflects the aura of permanence of Chapel Hill. Bedrooms reflect that same spirit; their solidly made reproductions of colonial furniture strike a balance between tradition and modern convenience. The inn was completely redecorated in 1982.

The inn's cafeteria provides good food at budget-stretching prices. But for lunch and dinner I prefer to be served in the Hill Room, which is staffed by students and is thus open only when school is in session. At any time of the year, however, the campus of the university should be seen.

The University of North Carolina is the oldest state university in America. Its first students arrived in 1793, and there are now some twenty thousand of them, enthusiastic boosters of their athletic teams—the UNC basketball team was the NCAA champion in 1982. The Old East Building is the oldest state university building still standing, a National Historic Site. Close by is the Ackland Art Center, the Morehead Planetarium with its sixty-eight-foot steel dome (the Apollo astronauts came here to study celestial navigation), and the five-acre Coker Arboretum with plantings of almost every shrub and tree that grows in the temperate zone. There's a theater and, of course, the football stadium. And if you want to participate in something a bit more vigorous than strolling through the campus or sitting in a stadium, there's the eighteen-hole Finley Golf Course, owned and operated by the university. Now how many colleges or universities, state or private, have their own inn *and* golf course?

THE CAROLINA INN, P.O. Box 1110, Chapel Hill, North Carolina 27514. Telephone: (919) 933-2001. Accommodations: 142 rooms and suites; single, double, and twin beds; all rooms with private baths, televisions, and telephones. Rates: inexpensive to low moderate. Meal service: breakfast, lunch, and dinner in cafeteria; dining room lunch and dinner when school is in session (coats and ties required). Children welcome; pets not allowed. Cards: AE, MC, V. Open all year.
Getting there: The inn is bordered by Pittsboro, Cameron, and South Columbia streets, on Business Route 15–501, at the entrance to the campus.

COLONIAL INN
Hillsborough, North Carolina

Some cities and towns across this land are proud of the fact that they have one or two historic plaques propped into the ground describing an early settlement, the home of some famous townsman or the site of an important battle. Hillsborough, in the Piedmont region of North Carolina, has more plaques, racked up one after another, than any town

I've ever seen. One made of metal was rescued from the *U.S.S. Maine*: it marks the spot in Court House Square where on March 17, 1778, Daniel Boone departed with his band of frontiersmen. "They marched away solemnly as if going to the ends of the world," to blaze a trail that became the Wilderness Road leading from North Carolina to Kentucky. Near that plaque two governors, two chief justices, and a signer of the Declaration of Independence are buried.

Hillsborough was founded in 1754 on an old Indian trading path, and it was named to honor the British Secretary of State for the American Colonies, the Earl of Hillsborough. For a time during the Revolution it was the state capital, and in 1778 the site of the Constitutional Convention. The old Orange County Courthouse—the fourth in town—dedicated in 1845, is a gem of a Greek Revival building whose cupola houses a clock said to have been the gift of George III; the county museum now occupies the second floor. The Presbyterian Church dates from 1820, the Episcopal from 1824, the Black A.M.E. Church from 1845, the Methodist 1859, and the First Baptist 1870.

In the midst of all these old and honorable buildings stands the Colonial Inn, which traces its genealogy back to 1759, and the oldest part of its present two-story white wooden structure to ten years before the Declaration of Independence. Cornwallis used the inn as his headquarters and had his men pave with flagstones the muddy roads leading to it. Delegates to the Provincial Congress and Constitutional Convention stayed at the inn, and a few years later, Aaron Burr was a guest.

Seventy years later, the Yankee "bummers" of Sherman's ravaging forces trooped through town and ransacked the inn until the widow of the innkeeper waved her Masonic apron out the window. Her husband had been the grand master of Masonic Eagle Lodge No. 19, housed in a red-brick Greek Revival building just across the street. A Union sergeant who was a Mason ordered his men to cease and desist and to return their loot to the widow.

The inn has had numerous owners throughout its long history. In the 1960s, just as it was entering its third century as an inn, Pete and Lois Thompson took over, making modern improvements and sprucing up the small, simply furnished bedrooms and the meeting and banquet rooms. Just as in Revolutionary times, the inn is the gathering place in the area. The Thompsons added antiques here and there—an old grandfather's clock, spinning wheels, a deacon's bench—but while renovating and restoring they kept intact the spirit of the historic setting.

Their appreciation of tradition is especially apparent in their presentation of solid Southern food drawn from their collection of old recipes. They put out excellent meals in a grand dining room with the atmosphere of an old tavern. There are creaking wide plank boards underfoot, brass chandeliers overhead, and ladderback chairs surrounding bare wooden tables filled with such Southern specialties as Brunswick stew, chicken and dumplings, fried okra, tomato pudding, crab in a variety of shapes and forms, corn pone, yam buns, and green tomato pie. The Thompsons have published these old recipes in a useful little booklet so that you may enjoy the specialties of the Old South long after leaving the Colonial Inn.

COLONIAL INN, 159 West King Street, Hillsborough, North Carolina 27278. Telephone: (919) 732-2461. Accommodations: 16 rooms, all but one with double beds, one with twin beds, all with private baths; no telephones or televisions. Rates: inexpensive. Meal service: lunch and dinner. Bar service: wine only. Children welcome; pets not allowed. No credit cards. Open all year except for two weeks in summer.
Getting there: Take exit No. 164 from Interstate 85 between Greensboro and Durham, proceed 1-1/2 miles to Hillsborough and turn left at King Street traffic light; the inn is a block away, on the left.

TANGLEWOOD MANOR HOUSE
Clemmons, North Carolina

Here is an inn built, furnished, and maintained in the grand manner: a multimillion-dollar, eleven-hundred-acre estate of towering trees, formal rose gardens, stables, bridle paths and steeplechase course, swimming pools, and indoor-outdoor tennis courts. There are lakes for canoeing and paddle-boating, a summer-stock theater, a 165-year-old church, an arboretum and deer park, and a river where Daniel Boone once fished and hunted. There is also a miniature golf course and a championship course where the 1974 PGA tournament was held.

Tanglewood was once the home and estate of tobacco heir William N. Reynolds and his wife Kate. Then in 1954 Reynolds gave it to the people of North Carolina. A tourist park contains a half-dozen cottages, picnic shelters, and campsites, and there is a new motel-like lodge with patios and balconies overlooking the sylvan scene. But overnighting in the Reynoldses' former home is a one-of-a-kind experience. The luxurious colonial bedrooms and sitting rooms will make you feel like a millionaire. There are canopied beds, fireplaces, and furniture that makes it easy to understand why North Carolina is the center of fine furniture manufacturing in this country. This inn is a comfortably elegant experience, as handsome and enjoyable as it appears when you first drive up to the splendidly landscaped home shaded by giant trees. The five intimate dining rooms at the manor house are as colonial in execution as the rest of the house.

Tanglewood is also the perfect base camp for appreciating the other magnificent home deeded to the public by a Reynolds, in this case the late Richard Joshua Reynolds. His Reynolda, a few miles from Tanglewood, was opened to the public in 1965 and is dedicated to the promotion of the arts. The mansion is filled with a priceless collection of American art displayed around a center reception and sitting room large enough to house a basketball court. Close by is the modern, dramatically landscaped Reynolds plant, which is also open to the public.

A few minutes from Reynolda House is historic Bethabara, site of Carolina's first Moravian settlement dating from 1753. (The city of Winston-Salem is a merger of the Moravian settlement they called Salem and the industrial complex that had spread around Winston.) At Bethabara, guides in period dress direct the tourist past a reconstructed eighteenth-century fort, a 1788 Moravian church, and the *Gemein Haus* (German Community Center). Closer to the center of town is the carefully restored and painstakingly preserved village of Old Salem, as impressive in its way as the more-crowded Williamsburg. It is a stimulating experience to walk these village streets, to listen to the unhurried and unspoiled guides, to watch the craftsmen at work, to tour the museum of musical instruments so important to Moravian worship, and to appreciate the contributions made by this disciplined, close-knit congregation.

And it's a pleasure to break the touring with a visit to the old Salem Tavern, dining in an 1816 addition to the 1784 tavern where George Washington slept and ate. Then after eating black bread and apple dumplings, pumpkin soup and sauerbraten, you can walk only several hundred feet to the outstanding Museum of Early Southern Decorative Arts, an uncrowded and detailed crash course conducted by knowledgeable, interested guides.

TANGLEWOOD MANOR HOUSE AND LODGE, Highway 158, Clemmons, North Carolina 27012. Telephone: (919) 766-6461. Accommodations: 11 rooms in manor house, 18 in lodge; single, double, and twin beds; private baths, televisions, and telephones. Rates: inexpensive to moderate. Meal service: breakfast, lunch, and dinner. Bar service: wine and beer and setups. Children welcome; pets not allowed. Cards: AE, MC, V. Open all year.

Getting there: Clemmons is eight miles south of Winston-Salem via Interstate 40 (exit at the Lewisville-Clemmons Road) or U.S. 158; the Manor House is south of Clemmons on 158 by the Yadkin River.

MAPLE LODGE
Blowing Rock, North Carolina

Here's an inn that looks like it's been air-lifted directly from a suburb of Chicago, Cleveland, or Columbus: a two-story white frame vintage-1946 house complete with a side chimney, an overhanging front entry, shutters, a manicured lawn, trimmed shrubbery, magnificent maple trees, a community parlor with a fireplace, and a Florida room out back. Owned and operated by Jack and Rheba Crane since 1979, it's a cozy headquarters for mountaineering in the area, and for learning the legend of Blowing Rock.

Located on U.S. Highways 221 and 321, Blowing Rock is an immense cliff jutting 4,090 feet above sea level, looking down on Johns River Gorge 3,000 feet below. The craggy walls of the gorge form a flume through which the northwest wind swoops with such force that objects cast down are quickly blown right back up—Ripley called it the only place in the world where snow falls upside down.

There's a visitor center and an elevated walkway at the rock for viewing Hawksbill Mountain and Table Rock to the southwest, and Mount Mitchell—highest peak east of the Rockies—and Grandfather Mountain to the west. Grandfather Mountain is the highest peak in the Blue Ridge, all 5,964 feet of it, reached by a twisting road rising to the summit, where there are bears and deer, a swing bridge for the adventurous to cross from peak to peak, the Highland Games and Gathering of Scottish Clans the second weekend of July, and "Singing on the Mountain," a gospel sing-in the last Sunday in June.

Not far distant is the Linville Gorge with its waterfalls and caverns, and midway between Blowing Rock and Boone is the Tweetsie Railroad attraction: a three-mile trip on iron rails behind a huffing and puffing steam locomotive, complete with an Indian raid and hold-up. There's also a Mouse Mine ride, panning for gold, and a petting farm, along with various rides, snackeries, and sweeteries to please children of all ages.

The Crane's base camp is neat as the proverbial pin, and out back there's a two-bedroom cottage, ideal for a family or couples traveling together.

MAPLE LODGE, P.O. Box 66, Sunset Drive, Blowing Rock, North Carolina 28605. Telephone: (704) 295-3331. Accommodations: eight rooms in the house, all with private baths; no televisions or telephones; two bedrooms and two baths with sitting room in cottage. Rates: inexpensive; includes complimentary Continental breakfast. No pets. No cards.

Getting there: Sunset Drive is off Main Street; the lodge is about 100 yards from Main, next to the Blowing Rock Elementary School on the right side of the road. There's a sign out front.

BEECH ALPEN INN
Banner Elk, North Carolina

Crowning the summit of Beech Mountain a couple hundred feet from the Top of the Beech Mountain Inn is the aptly named Beech Alpen Inn. It could have been fabricated in the Austrian Alps and shipped to this recreational area with its high-in-the-sky eighteen-hole golf course, tennis courts, Olympic-size swimming pool, hiking trails, and ski slopes.

The inn is under the same management as the Top of the Beech, and that means Barry and Ute Wolfgang with daughter Heidi as assistant manager. They've been in place since Christmas 1981, working their wonders, repairing, restoring, reviving—just as they had done earlier at the Top of the Beech.

The Beech Alpen Inn has a more rustic feel to it. There are ground-floor game rooms that serve as popular rallying points after a day on the slopes. Four of the bedrooms, located on the corners of the rambling structure, have steam baths and fireplaces, and they're usually claimed by honeymooners.

BEECH ALPEN INN, Route One, Beech Mountain Parkway, Banner Elk, North Carolina 28604. Telephone: (704) 387-2261. Accommodations: 25 rooms, all with private baths, color televisions, and telephones; four singles; four rooms with fireplaces and steam baths. Rates: moderate; includes Continental breakfast. Pets not permitted. Cards: AE, MC, V. Open all year.

Getting there: The inn is 3-1/2 miles from the center of Banner Elk on clearly marked parkway roads, next door to the Top of the Beech Mountain Inn.

TOP OF THE BEECH MOUNTAIN INN
Banner Elk, North Carolina

It's billed as "Eastern America's Highest Inn in Eastern America's Highest Town," scraping the clouds at fifty-six hundred feet, and it was reborn when a diligent duo, Ute and Barry Wolfgang, arrived on the scene the end of March 1980.

They are innkeepers *extraordinaire*, and in the past two years they have scrubbed each of the inn's two dozen rooms, restoring them to sparkling brightness in good German *gasthaus* fashion. Barry, a former Bell Helicopter consultant in Iran, serves as general manager of both this and the neighboring Beech Alpen Inn, which the Wolfgangs took over in December 1981. Daughter Heidi serves as assistant manager, and she's as perfect in that position as her parents are in theirs.

There's a European air about the inn with its large lobby–sitting room, dominated by a massive stone fireplace and a giant chandelier made from half a dozen skis. The ski slopes are only five minutes from the inn, and Barry, a former ski instructor at Beech Mountain, is well qualified to give advice on which of the area's eleven slopes are most suitable for the beginner or the expert. There's a ski school as well as equipment rentals.

Barry can also advise his guests on the many marked nature trails that twist around the seventy-two hundred acres of the mountain, which has the highest golf course east of the Mississippi. There's also an Olympic-size pool, eight hard-surface tennis courts and an open-air ice-skating rink. The pool is open from June through Labor Day, the championship eighteen-hole golf course from April until October.

A Continental breakfast is served in the inn's lobby each morning. For heartier fare there's the Beech Haus down the mountain, open for breakfast daily until 11:30 am and for dinner from 5:30 until 9 pm. The steaks are super and the fresh mountain trout alone worth the trip to Banner Elk—but then the Haus has had the same owner and the same cooks since 1972. They proudly proclaim on their menu that "We're Not Gourmet, But Neither Are We Ordinary."

TOP OF THE BEECH MOUNTAIN INN, Route One, Beech Mountain Parkway, Banner Elk, North Carolina 28604. Telephone: (704) 387-2252. Accommodations: 24 rooms, all with private baths, televisions, and telephones; some with steam units; some with queen-size beds, others with double beds. Rates: moderate; includes Continental breakfast. One night's lodging is required as a deposit when making

reservations. During ski season a two-night minimum weekend reservation is required. Pets not permitted. Cards: AE, MC, V. Open all year.
Getting there: Beech Mountain and the inn are 3-1/2 miles from the center of Banner Elk on clearly marked roads. There's a large sign in front of the inn that looks as though it was transported directly from the Alps.

APPALACHIAN INN
Minneapolis, North Carolina

If ever there were an isolated country inn, this two-story white frame slowly settling into the ground of North Carolina qualifies. Sitting behind a white rail fence and built as a farm house in the 1890s, the Appalachian Inn is in a mountain community close to the Tennessee border, only a few miles from the Appalachian Trail. The town is not even a sleepy crossroads; it is merely a few hundred yards of ground between two 55 MPH signs.

And the Appalachian Inn, with its back-to-the-farm-simple breakfasts and dinners included in the daily tariffs, is a slowing down from the fancier accommodations in the Western North Carolina mountains and valleys. It's ideal for outdoors types eager to avoid the more expensive hostelries, those who want a vintage old-time experience.

APPALACHIAN INN, U.S. 19E, P.O. Box 24, Minneapolis, North Carolina 28652. Telephone: (704) 733-4070. Accommodations: ten rooms, seven bathrooms; no telephones or televisions. Rates: inexpensive; includes breakfast and dinner. No pets. No cards. Open June 15–October 31.
Getting there: Minneapolis is in the northern reaches of the state, about midway between Blowing Rock and Burnsville, on U.S. 19E between Cranberry to the north and Plumtree to the south. The inn has a sign out front.

ESSEOLA LODGE
Linville, North Carolina

Summer vacationeers seeking a touch of class in the heart of the Carolina mountains have been heading for this spot since the 1890s. Today golfers, tennis players, and guests wanting all the modern conveniences plus mountain air continue to check into the Esseola, built in two stages some fifty years ago on the site of the original inn.

Chestnut bark was used for the siding, poplar for the supports of the many porches—each room has its own porch—and locally quarried stone for the massive fireplaces in the double lobbies. In 1982, before opening for the season, the lodge was subjected to a thorough renovation, and all the guest rooms were painted and papered.

The dining room is the setting for country breakfasts and dinners that are considerably more ambitious than most mountain hostelries offer—prime rib, veal, poached salmon—but then the Esseola chef is Swiss. What other inn sets forth a cheese tray as a *coup de grâce* to a six-course meal?

To burn off the calories guests head for the neighboring Donald Ross-designed eighteen-hole golf course, clay tennis courts, a heated swimming pool, a putting green, trout fishing streams, or riding stables. Others concentrate on the natural wonders of the Blue Ridge Mountains, enraptured by the blooming azaleas, rhododendrons, and mountain laurel. Minutes away by car is one of the main attractions in the Carolinas, Grandfather Mountain, one of the oldest rock formations in the world and at six thousand feet the highest peak in the Blue Ridge Range. Grandfather Mountain is the site on the fourth Sunday each June of the "Singing on the Mountain" religious event. The second weekend in July there's the annual Highland Games and Gathering of Scottish Clans, and all during the season, April 1–November 15, the Visitor Center at the summit is open. Inside are museum exhibits, a snack bar, a gift shop, and an aquarium filled with brook, brown, and rainbow trout. Close by is the mile-high swing bridge with panoramic viewing up to a hundred miles.

Under Humpback Mountain, at the head of Linville Valley on U.S. 221, are the Linville Caverns. Discovered a century ago, the caverns have such formations as the Frozen Waterfall and the Franciscan Monk, and an underground stream filled with trout who through years of swimming in the dark have lost their sight.

ESSEOLA LODGE, Route 221, P.O. Box 98, Linville, North Carolina 28646. Telephone: (704) 733-4311. Accommodations: 28 rooms, all with private baths; no telephones or televisions. Rates: expensive; includes breakfast and dinner (modified American Plan). No pets. No cards. Open early June to early September.
Getting there: The lodge with its distinctive peaked entryway of stone and log is in the center of the crossroads town of Linville, on Route 221 a mile west of the Blue Ridge Parkway.

NU-WRAY INN
Burnsville, North Carolina

The Nu-Wray is all nostalgia, a three-story white-frame echo of the past, with black shutters, neatly trimmed hedges, and vine-hidden pillars. It faces a peaceful little town square whose namesake stands primly on his pedestal: Otway Burns, hero of the War of 1812.

The food at Nu-Wray is exceptional—hickory-smoked ham and fried chicken, hot biscuits and fresh-baked breads, corn pudding, cooked apples and baked beans—platter after bowl after platter of home cooking, some of it prepared on a wood-burning stove. Meals are served at tables seating twenty-two people, with the diners passing dishes boardinghouse style.

For guests staying in the hotel the day starts at 8:00 sharp with the ringing of an old farm bell out back; thirty minutes later it's rung again, summoning you to breakfast. Suppers start promptly at 6:30, but instead of the booming bell, a Reginaphone, a marvelous old music box with flat metal discs, is cranked up and played.

The Reginaphone is but one antique from a museum-quality collection casually scattered around the Nu-Wray. By the entrance a massive, elaborately carved cuckoo clock ticks away the time, and it's usually so quiet here that it's the only noise that can be heard. There is an ancient long rifle over the stone fireplace. There are spinning wheels and aged pianos, time-worn prints and pastoral scenes and portraits of the previous owners. Newspaper clippings about the inn and its town fall in disarray from an old scrapbook.

Built in 1833 of locally cut logs, the original inn had a large dining room and eight bedrooms, four upstairs and four down. It was enlarged in the 1870s by Rush T. Wray, the grandfather of the present owners, and his sister, Mrs. Annie Wray Bennett. Other than the installation of certain modern conveniences, it's hard to believe that the inn has changed much in the past three generations of Wrays.

The Nu-Wray is meticulously maintained and filled with furnishings not found in any furniture catalogue for many decades, least of all one used by hotels and motels. My favorite room is No. 22, just past the second-floor sitting room filled with antiques. This bedroom has a giant claw-footed tub, a pair of double beds, and four windows giving it a light and airy feeling. One window faces the church, and the other three face the town square.

Burnsville is a mountain-lover's paradise. Plan to visit Litiville Gorge in the heart of the Pisgah National Forest, often called the most rugged wilderness in the eastern United States. Also nearby is Mount

Nu-Wray Inn, Burnsville, North Carolina

Mitchell, the highest mountain east of the Mississippi at almost sixty-seven hundred feet. At the summit is a state park.

NU-WRAY INN, Burnsville, North Carolina 28714. Telephone: (704) 682-2329. Accommodations: 35 rooms; single, double and twin beds; five rooms without baths, others with private or connecting baths; no televisions or telephones. Rates: inexpensive to moderate, with special weekly rates for modified American plan. Meal service: breakfast and supper. No bar service. Children welcome; pets not allowed. No credit cards. Open all year.
Getting there: Burnsville is 37 miles northeast of Asheville via Route 19 and Route 19E; the inn is in the center of town facing the square.

ROCKING CHAIR INN
Burnsville, North Carolina

A half mile from the village green and the imposing, impressive Nu-Wray Inn is this far more modest hostelry, with a simple setting and namesake rockers. Some of the comfortable rooms are small enough to be almost overwhelmed by the new king-size beds. When I made my inspection tour in the spring of 1982, the dining room was serving three solid, home-cooked meals a day. A few months later a reader informed me there was no longer a restaurant. It's of little importance: the food at the Nu-Wray is too good and too plentiful to miss.

And down the road a piece, down twisting, winding Route 80 south, there's Albert's Lodge for lunch and dinner. It's a sensational drive, through woods and alongside creeks, with endless picnic possibilities, whether in a springtime shower of delicate greens or autumn blazes of color. The highest point in the eastern United States, Mount Mitchell (6,684 feet), is en route, as is the Blue Ridge Parkway—one enters that beauteous boulevard at an elevation of 3,322 feet, on the Eastern Continental Divide.

ROCKING CHAIR INN, West Main Street, Burnsville, North Carolina 28714. Telephone: (704) 682-2112. Accommodations: 14 units, each with a private bath and entrance; color televisions; no telephones. Rates: inexpensive. No pets. Cards: AE, V. Open year round.
Getting there: Burnsville is 37 miles northeast of Asheville via Routes 19 and 19E; Main Street runs directly from the village square.

FLINT STREET INN
Asheville, North Carolina

In January 1982 Lynne and Rick Vogel, natives of New Orleans who had amassed a quiet little collection of antiques over the years, opened that collection to the public in a home completed in 1915 and listed in the National Registry of Historic Homes. After a half-year of bone-weary work they converted that home to an inn, one in which, in the best traditions of the trade, they also live.

But it's really a mini-museum, as well as a vibrant testimony to the exquisite taste and imagination of the Vogels. In one of the rooms an old Singer sewing machine serves as a dressing table; in another there's a vintage triptych dressing table graced with three antique hats in what could pass as an altar to Lilly Daché. The bedsteads have been around longer than the house, and nowhere have I seen such a stunning collection of Art Deco. Out back there's an old fishpond and patio; in front a grand old porch for looking out at all the non-action on a street with many other period houses in the process of being lovingly restored by their new owners.

The Flint Street Inn is a marvelous base camp for exploring the Asheville area, which is rich with interesting one-of-a-kind attractions. First and foremost is the overwhelming Biltmore estate, a breathtaking bit of Gilded Age bravado that took George Vanderbilt's thousand workers five years to build. From 1895 until his death in 1914 the 125,000-acre empire was Southern headquarters for the Vanderbilt clan. It was also the site of the country's first forestry school, established by Gifford Pinchot, the man Vanderbilt recruited to oversee his thousands of acres. At Vanderbilt's death most of those acres were given to the government and now form much of the Pisgah National Forest.

On Spruce Street in town is the twenty-eight-room Victorian boardinghouse once run by the mother of Thomas Wolfe and named Dixieland in *Look Homeward Angel.* It's now a memorial to the genius who immortalized his boyhood town as "Altamont" and so rudely characterized its citizens. There are guided tours of the home, which features a display of Wolfe memorabilia. Also in town is the Wall Street experience—not a financial tycoon's rendezvous, but intended for strollers and shoppers. A few blocks distant is the Lexington Park area, an assemblage of grand old brick structures that have been restored to house still more shops and snackeries.

On a hill north of Asheville is the Grove Park Inn and Country Club, built by Edwin W. Grove, a patent-medicine millionaire who developed Bromo Quinine and Grove's Tasteless Chili Tonic. The hotel is an attraction in itself with its 230 rooms, its gigantic lobby, its sloping roof, its spectacular views and high ceilings. Behind the Grove Park Inn is the Biltmore Homespun Shop, producing what many claim to be the finest hand-woven wool cloth in the world. The tours are free and there are weavers in residence—only a few of the once-thriving trade still survive—working their wonders.

A different kind of handicraft from the mountains is on display at the easy to-recommend Folk Art Center of the Southern Highland Handicraft Guild, located at the entrance to the Blue Ridge Parkway.

And there's more, much more, in the Asheville area. The Vogels can provide the details, then listen to your enthusiastic reports when you return to their inn among the oaks, the dogwood trees, the rhododendron, and the mountain laurel.

FLINT STREET INN, 116 Flint Street, Asheville, North Carolina 28801. Telephone: (704) 253-6723. Accommodations: three double rooms, one with twin beds, two with double beds; two shared baths; no televisions or telephones. Rates: moderate; includes Continental breakfast. Only well-behaved older children permitted; no pets. No cards, but personal checks are welcome. Open year round.
Getting there: The inn is three blocks from the Asheville Civic Center on Haywood Street. Haywood becomes Flint Street as it goes over the 240 Expressway. Continue on Flint past Cherry and Starnes streets, each with a traffic light; the inn is the fourth house on the left past the intersection of Flint and Starnes.

PISGAH VIEW RANCH
Candler, North Carolina

Ever since George Washington was President this forested land has been in the hands of the Cogburn clan (as in Rooster Cogburn!), and the first log cabin the founders built still stands—a 1790 tribute to the past. There are other historic and rugged reminders of the pioneers, as well as an antique store and other log cabins of newer vintage. Duplexes and A-frames also dot the landscape, along with a barn used for evening entertainment highlighted by the ranch's championship square dance and clogging team. A swimming pool and wading ponds, a lake stocked with rainbow trout, tennis and shuffleboard courts, and a wide variety of hiking and riding trails provide other outlets for exercise on the seventeen-hundred-acre ranch with its sensational view of mile-high Mount Pisgah.

Cottage accommodations and the choice of activities make the ranch ideal for family groups eager to get away from it all, to summer fun and family-style feed-ins featuring generous portions of rib-sticking chicken and ham, picked-fresh vegetables, and the house special of oatmeal pie, regarded in these parts as "the poor man's pecan pie."

Among the many cottages I like the Toll Gate House, but my favorite is the one down Possum Trot off Tobacco Road: the Chickadee with its stone fireplace, its cozy front porch with a swing and rocker, its braided rug and total sense of privacy.

The Chickadee cabin, along with so much else in the Pisgah View Ranch, provides the traveler with a great sense of place. How grateful we are that the present keepers of the flame, Ruby and Chester Cogburn, are dedicated to the preservation of that sense, that reassuring feeling of security in the heart of the Blue Ridge Mountains.

PISGAH VIEW RANCH, Route 1, Candler, North Carolina 28715. Telephone: (704) 667-9100. Accommodations: 52 cottages, all with private baths; no telephones or televisions. Rates: inexpensive to moderate; includes three meals a day (picnic lunches available at noon for hikers); full American plan. No bar service. No pets. No cards. Open May 1–December 1.

Getting there: Six miles west of Asheville take the Enka-Candler exit (No. 44) from Interstate 40 and drive south almost three miles to Candler; turn left on Route 151 and continue six miles to the ranch sign and follow the road two miles to the ranch.

STONEHEARTH INN
Bat Cave, North Carolina

Since 1980 Ellen and Don Staley have been in charge of this mini-inn holding down the rocks between river and road. Built in 1940 and as romantically rustic inside as out, the Stonehearth greets its guests with a merry blaze crackling in the namesake fireplace and, from April through Thanksgiving, a feast of solid North Carolina country fare: baked ham and pork chops, stuffed steak, fried chicken, fresh rainbow trout dredged in cornmeal and sautéed in butter, and some of the best side dishes in the South—coleslaw that is really a hearty cabbage salad, dumplings, spiced applesauce, whipped baked sweet potatoes, and stewed tomatoes with the zing of okra, the crunch of celery, and a touch of green pepper. On the side are triangles of marvelous iron-skillet corn bread, and for finishers a selection of Ellen's made-out-back desserts:

Stone Hearth Inn, Bat Cave, North Carolina

buttermilk pie and something she properly labels "sinful," made with chocolate and cream cheese spiked with rum.

There's no wine or beer but there is an array of interesting teas: cinnamon rose, country apple, spicy orange, and something called Mo's 24 featuring two dozen different spices and a touch of mint.

Wooden paneling frames the single dining room; off to a side is a small shop featuring the creations of local artisans. The Staleys, in the best tradition of innkeeping, live upstairs. Guests are housed downstairs in a quartet of rooms cooled by mountain breezes and serenaded by the ceaseless splashing of the rocky Broad River a few feet away.

Maintenance is faultless, and the care and concern of the Staleys is personal but non-interfering. And not far distant is that unique formation above Lake Lure known as Chimney Rock. Asheville, Flat Rock, Tryon, and Hendersonville are also close to this Bat Cave base camp.

STONEHEARTH INN, Route 74, P.O. Box 9, Bat Cave, North Carolina 28710. Telephone: (704) 625-9990. Accommodations: four rooms, all with private baths; no telephones or televisions. Rates: inexpensive. Meal service: dinner April–Thanksgiving; no bar. No pets. Cards: MC, V. Open all year.

Getting there: Bat Cave is 20 miles southeast of Asheville via Route 74, and 15 miles northeast of Hendersonville via Route 64. The inn is on the town's main street, Route 74.

ESMERALDA INN
Chimney Rock, North Carolina

The origins of the Esmeralda go back to 1891 when Colonel Tom Turner built an inn on the old stagecoach route over the mountains from the Piedmont Plateau. The town was then known as Esmeralda, but as the fame of nearby Chimney Rock Park grew, and more and more visitors came in summer months to marvel at the Hickory Nut Gorge and Waterfalls, and Moonshiner's Cave, the name was changed to honor that massive, monumental tower of granite christened Chimney Rock.

The inn retained the name of the town, rebuilding on the original foundations in the early years of the century. It was extensively restored in the mid-1970s and has survived intact from its Hollywood heyday, when stars such as Fairbanks and Gable, Mary Pickford, and William S. Hart flocked there. In the twenties the silent movies *Esmeralda* and *In the Heart of the Blue Ridge* were made in the area, and

94

in room No. 9 of the inn Lew Wallace finished the screenplay for the spectacular, *Ben Hur.*

Today the inn is vintage mountain home, a rugged retreat with the simply furnished rooms, unpeeled log railings, a heavy stone fireplace, back porches leading from the rooms and providing a quiet escape from the bustle of the highway in front. The high-ceilinged lobby was constructed with locally cut tree trunks and is decorated with a variety of natural artifacts from Chimney Rock and paintings by area artists.

The dining room is a real stunner, with a menu that's hard to believe in these parts: fresh Maine lobster, poached salmon, oysters and scallops, red snapper and grouper, veal sautéed or given the schnitzel or cordon bleu treatment, filet mignon. All this along with the usual country ham, rainbow and gold mountain trout, and a brace of Carolina quail.

ESMERALDA INN, U.S. 64 and 74, P.O. Box 57, Chimney Rock, North Carolina 28720. Telephone: (704) 625-9889. Accommodations: 13 rooms, some with a private bath, others with a shared bath; no telephones or televisions. Rates: inexpensive. Meal service: dinner every night except Monday. No pets. Cards: MC, V. Open mid-March to October 31.
Getting there: Chimney Rock and the inn are 25 miles southeast of Asheville on U.S. 64 and 74, State Route 9.

ECHO MOUNTAIN INN
Hendersonville, North Carolina

Scraping the sky at thirty-one hundred feet, overlooking an affluent spread of homes known as Laurel Park, and blessed with the most sensational panoramas of any inn in this book, Echo Mountain Inn is a sheer delight. This mountaintop country inn is run by a thorough-going professional with years of experience operating oceanfront hotels in Florida. When Cooper Smith and his wife Elizabeth purchased the inn in July 1981, they dove into their new challenge with great gusto, replacing all the beds and bedding, restoring the stonework, painting the wooden trim, laying carpet, sprucing up the dining room, adding a tennis court to the grounds.

The original building of the inn dates from 1896, and in the seven years before the arrival of the Smiths no fewer than five owners struggled for survival atop Echo Mountain. The Smiths, with their talents and treasure, reversed the trend and have been swimming in success, making the landmark one of the most popular destinations for

95

dining in the greater Hendersonville area. On cool nights the fireplace in the dining room blazes its merry warmth, and there's another hearth in the sitting room. The middle table in the bay window overlooking the majesty of the Blue Ridge Mountains—due east—is reserved weeks in advance, and there's a small alcove of tables that's usually reserved for parties.

In addition to Smith's new tennis court, there's another court for shuffleboard, and a swimming pool. Eight miles distant is the Etowah Valley Golf and Country Club, one of the loveliest clubs in the land and popular with Echo Mountain Inn guests. Another eighteen-hole championship challenge is the Crooked Creek Golf Course where inn guests also have golfing privileges. And a few hundred feet farther up the mountain road from the inn is Poplar Lodge, a rustic assemblage of poplar logs. The lodge has no accommodations, just food (prepared by a chef who hails from Miami), but with the Echo Mountain Inn now sparkling with the results of the Smiths' ceaseless efforts, no other accommodation in the area need be considered.

ECHO MOUNTAIN INN, 2849 Laurel Park Highway, Hendersonville, North Carolina 18739. Telephone: (704) 693-9626. Accommodations: 35 units, nine suites; each unit has a private bath and a television; no telephones; seven of the rooms have fireplaces. Rates: moderate. Meal service: breakfast and lunch daily; dinner nightly except Sunday; full bar service. No pets. Cards: AE, MC, V. Usually open year round (but inquire as owners might be closed during a period in January–March). *Getting there:* The inn is five miles from Interstate 26, reached by U.S. 25 South through Hendersonville; turn right at Fifth Avenue, which becomes Laurel Park Highway and leads directly to the inn 2.8 miles away.

HAVENSHIRE INN
Hendersonville, North Carolina

Approaching this multilevel mansion in the rolling farmlands of western North Carolina, I had the distinct feeling of opening a Thomas Hardy novel. Workers were out in the fields, there were horses nuzzling near a rail enclosure, and the brooding stone and wood house with its chimneys and gables dominated the landscape.

The English manor house, built by one George Holmes, an Englishman who led a group of settlers to the area, celebrated its centennial in 1882. Holmes was a man of substance and he built well, using native cedar and redwood, mortaring large blocks of fieldstone into outer walls and foundations, spreading his home over Bowman's

Bluff overlooking the rolling French Broad River and a small pond, good for canoeing.

The innkeeper is the attractive, retiring Cindy Findley, who spends her winter months at Miami's Jockey Club. She entered into her new avocation almost by chance. After buying Havenshire she was invaded by Florida friends who never wanted to leave the mountain air and the relaxed atmosphere of a country home set in the midst of majestic pastures and tranquil, beckoning forests. She decided to share the wealth by establishing a rate schedule.

The revenues help compensate for the expenses incurred when Cindy worked a total restoration of the grand century-old house. She has filled the rooms with well-preserved antiques, has revitalized the magnificent double dining rooms, and has put in brightly patterned drapes and spreads. The minute one enters Havenshire, the darkness of a Hardy mood is dispelled, and the first impression is happily changed to one of comfort and friendliness.

HAVENSHIRE INN, Cummings Road, Route 4, Box 455, Hendersonville, North Carolina 28739. Telephone: (704) 692-4097. Accommodations: six rooms, two with private baths, four that share baths; no televisions or telephones. Rates: expensive, including Continental breakfast. Well-behaved children are acceptable, but prefer none. No pets. No cards. Open May 1–October 31.
Getting there: The inn is 20 miles from Asheville, reached via Route 64 and Cummings Road; it is 2.4 miles from Route 64 on Cummings.

WOODFIELD INN
Flat Rock, North Carolina

In the decade preceding the War Between the States, a group of local and Low Country Carolinians, including the governor of South Carolina, banded together to build a hotel to accommodate the increasing number of travelers coming to the mountains. Their plans were ambitious, and it took two years to construct the three-story structure— the first turnpike stop south of Asheville and one of the most elaborate. Foundation timbers were hand-hewed and secured with oversize wooden pegs; the exterior siding was finished with white pine, the inside walls with oak; and twenty-two fireplaces were fitted with black walnut.

In 1853 Henry T. Farmer, a furniture manufacturer and one of the original shareholders, purchased the hotel outright, named it after himself, and ran it until his death thirty years later. In the fall and winter

97

Woodfield Inn, Flat Rock, North Carolina

months, he hosted hunting parties, roasting whole animals in the huge kitchen fireplaces out back; in warmer months, he held barbecues on the grounds. Farmer created an atmosphere that gave the town the satisfaction of being labeled "Provincial Charleston" and "The Little Charleston of the Mountains."

During the last six months of the Civil War, a company of Confederate soldiers took up residence in the Farmer Hotel, providing protection from marauding bands for the townspeople and a measure of stability for the surrounding community. When the long and bitter war came to an end, the hotel was returned to Farmer safe and intact, and the citizens of Flat Rock reclaimed the valuables they had entrusted to the safekeeping of the Confederate detachment.

No wonder Carl Sandburg paused on entering this inn and declaimed in that dramatic, on-stage manner of his—"These walls talk to me." The poet and famed Lincoln biographer spent the last twenty-two years of his life in this area. His 240-acre homestead, Connemara, is now a National Historic Site open to the public; visitors park at the (summer-stock) Flat Rock Playhouse, two blocks from the inn, and take a shuttle bus to the house.

When Sandburg was a regular visitor to the inn, it had been renamed Woodfield by new owners. Mr. and Mrs. Joseph N. Clemons bought the building in 1939 as a summer retreat and a place to house an ever-growing antique collection. The Clemonses ran the successful Grandma's Kitchen restaurant in Miami and were very active in National Restaurant Association affairs; he was NRA president and one of the founders of the Florida Restaurant Association.

After Clemons' death his wife and son took over, and in July 1981 they sold the twenty-five acres and what is generally considered to be the oldest operating inn in the state to the Levins, a hotel family originally from Philadelphia but with extensive properties in Florida. Innkeeper David Levin, now in charge at Woodfield, is the third generation in the business. And he supervised the ten-month period of total restoration and revitalization.

Levin installed a thoroughly modern kitchen—and a chef with international credentials in charge of an ambitious menu—replaced all the beds, stripped decades of paint from the black-walnut mantels, modernized the bathrooms with new fixtures including gleaming brass piping reminiscent of the Victorian era, and brought in the curator of Philadelphia's Athenaeum to consult on colors authentic to the period: Roger Moss, noted for the historic shades he researched and developed for Sherwin-Williams.

It was a careful and, I'm sure, rather costly endeavor, and the finished results are a joy to experience in the pair of formal dining rooms, in the sitting rooms with their elegant antiques, in the manicured gardens and along the trails, and of course in the bedrooms. Among my favorites are No. 20 with its cherry twin beds, and No. 22 with its pineapple-crowned four-poster and a pair of overstuffed chairs in front of a fireplace. Most of the rooms have fireplaces, and they all have ceiling fans and beautifully coordinated colors, right down to the thirsty towels, the bedspreads and pillows, even the stationery.

WOODFIELD INN, Highway 25 South, P.O. Box 98, Flat Rock, North Carolina 28731. Telephone: (704) 693-6016. Accommodations: 18 rooms, half with private baths, some with television, all with telephones. Rates: expensive; includes Continental breakfast. Meal service: breakfast, dinner, Sunday brunch; no bar service but brown-bagging (BYOB) permitted. No pets. Cards: AE, MC, V. Open year round.
Getting there: Flat Rock is 1-1/2 miles from Interstate 26, and three miles from Hendersonville via Highway 25 South. The inn, two blocks from the Flat Rock Playhouse, is clearly marked.

ORCHARD INN
Saluda, North Carolina

In November 1981, Ann and Ken Hough from Charleston realized their dream of many years: they bought a country inn. Built originally as a summer home for employees of the Southern Railway Company, the structure had fallen on hard times since its life as the White Stag Inn. The two-story frame house with its wide, wide wraparound porch was totally renovated by the Houghs, who wore their knuckles to the bone gutting, scraping, sanding, painting their dream into a stunning reality. They furnished the rooms with appropriate pieces to create a mountain inn atmosphere, scattering about a wealth of plants reflecting Ann Hough's previous career as an interior landscape designer, and a wealth of books reflecting Ken's past as private school headmaster. There are libraries upstairs and down, a marvelous fireplace in the spacious sitting room with its bright, airy feeling, and a window-filled dining room with a fantastic view of the Warrior Mountain Range.

The eighteen acres of the inn's own range catch the mountain breezes at twenty-five hundred feet, while chef Ken catches the gastronomes of the area with his cooking, preparing mountain breakfasts for inn guests, and opening to the public for lunch and dinner. At noontime there are one or two entrées, such as beef Stroganoff, fettuccine Alfredo, or a light chicken salad with walnuts and white grapes. At dinner Ken prepares a five-course meal Thursdays, Fridays, and Saturdays and four courses the other days (except Sunday). Among his specialties are pâté and South Carolina caviar (he buys a case a year of the not-so-easy-to-find millionaire's marmalade), Cornish hen, lamb prepared in a variety of ways, tenderloin of beef in a rich mushroom-sprinkled sherry sauce, and fresh mountain trout, broiled simply with a bit of clarified butter. "It presents on the plate so well," Ken proudly told me.

The Orchard Inn is in a dry county, but there are package stores in nearby Tryon and Hendersonville, and brown-bagging is permitted.

ORCHARD INN, P.O. Box 725, Highway 176, Saluda, North Carolina 28773. Telephone: (704) 749-5471. Accommodations: eight rooms and three cottages, all with private baths; no telephones or televisions; queen or twin beds. Rates: moderate; includes complimentary breakfast. Pets allowed in cottages only. No cards, but personal checks are welcome. Open year round.
Getting there: The inn is one mile from Saluda on State Highway 176, and two from Interstate 26; Saluda is midway between Tryon and Hendersonville.

MILL FARM INN
Tryon, North Carolina

In March 1982 Chip and Penny Kessler, Chicagoans with experience in real estate and apartment rental and management, opened this quiet little retreat a mile and a half from the heart of Tryon. They were thus responsible for the rebirth of an inn built in 1939 but converted to a private home fifteen years later. The most recent occupants before the Kesslers were interior decorators, and signs of their talents were left behind in carefully coordinated colors and patterns of carpets, curtains, wallpaper, paint trim, and furnishings.

The guest rooms are upstairs on the second floor of the all-stone structure, which is sturdy enough to withstand the most severe weather. Downstairs is a cheerful dining room, a large living room with a fireplace, and a fully stocked kitchen cleverly equipped for do-it-yourself Continental breakfasts: dry cereals, juice, coffee makers, tea, milk, jams, pumpkin or other specialty breads, English muffins. There's a refrigerator for storing guests' bottles, ice, and other necessities.

The kitchen is ultra-modern, and the inn is spotlessly maintained. Outside, there are 3-1/2 acres of manicured landscaping, and the Pacolet River flowing along the boundary of the property.

Travelers who want to be in Tryon can contact the Kesslers, who also own and operate a series of apartment units at 319 Melrose Avenue, across from the Episcopal Church. Studios and one- and two-bedroom accommodations are available, and each has a fully equipped kitchen; one unit has a fireplace, and several have patio decks overlooking the garden and forest behind the building. It's called L'Auberge of Tryon, and reservations for what the Kesslers refer to as "innpartments" are made at the same address and telephone number as the Mill Farm Inn.

MILL FARM INN, Highway 108, P.O. Box 1251, Tryon, North Carolina 28782. Telephone: (704) 859-6992 or (704) 859-9630. Accommodations: eight rooms, 6-1/2 baths; when inn is full, two rooms share a bath. Rates: moderate; includes Continental breakfast. No pets. Open mid-March–December.
Getting there: The inn is 1-1/2 miles northeast of Tryon on State Highway 108.

PINE CREST INN
Tryon, North Carolina

If ever there were a happy and harmonious meeting of mind, spirit, and personality with setting, a proper pairing of innkeeper and community, it is the perfect match of Bob Hull and the Pine Crest Inn of Tryon.

A former high-pressure corporate executive, Hull wanted to avoid what he calls the "pathed-out pattern of splitsville and heartsville" so many of his colleagues seemed doomed to. Bob and his wife Fran, a former nurse and now chef extraordinaire, left their suburban comforts in the North, migrated to the South, and became innkeepers. They found a rundown rambler of an old building with a variety of cottages spread around the grounds just a few minutes from the center of the town of Tryon—a very special spot in the Carolinas.

Tryon is in the heart of the so-called Thermal Belt region of the state, in the valley of the North Pacolet River with an elevation of 1,000 to 1,200 feet. Spurs of the Blue Ridge Mountains form barriers up to 4,000 feet, the Blue Ridge proper and the Great Smoky Mountains barriers up to 6,000 feet, blocking the cold winter blasts that sweep down from Canada across the Great Plains to the south. In the past half century there's been only one zero reading recorded, and even in the

Pine Crest Inn, Tryon, North Carolina

coldest months of the year the temperature rarely fails to go above freezing during the day.

Tryon, a stable and settled community with many families living on pre-Revolutionary land grants pioneered by their ancestors, is the hunt country of the Carolinas. Large estates provide the needed acreage for the fox hunts, and the Tryon Riding and Hunt Club sponsors a series of events in the spring, including the Horse and Hound Show and the well-known Block House Steeplechase—held where there used to be a Cherokee Indian trading post.

Tryon also is home for "The World's Smallest Daily Newspaper," the fifty-five-year-old *Tryon Daily Bulletin*, and the site of the state's last private subscription library, a twenty-thousand-volume collection named for poet Sidney Lanier, who spent the last two months of his life in Tryon.

And now Tryon has something else to make it special—a totally refurbished, crisply maintained, and professionally run Pine Crest Inn. Set back off the road, it is far from the noises of even a small town, yet close enough to walk to the action and the stores. The carefully landscaped inn combines the best of a history that goes back to the turn of the century (for a brief period a team of doctors ran it as a tuberculosis clinic) with the most modern conveniences, swathed in super-solicitous service. Ice is brought to the rooms promptly at five every evening, wood to those cottages with fireplaces, and the food in the rustic dining room is served by a staff that's been in place forever.

The dining room is as appealing in spirit and atmosphere as the splendid little hunt lounge, which could have been transplanted from an olde taverne in England. The rugged wooden dining tables are made to look old by a process known to antique dealers for years and which the Hulls will be happy to explain. The chairs have bottoms woven from corn husks—an almost extinct art. Beamed ceilings and stuccoed walls provide a comfortable setting for the joys that stream from Fran's kitchen. She didn't really intend to take over the back room; during their first Thanksgiving at Pine Crest the cook walked out. Fran has been behind the burners ever since, when not playing golf. Her handicap has gone from fourteen to twenty-four, but inn guests are hoping she'll get rid of the clubs altogether and stay in the kitchen. It is difficult, however, to ignore the nine holes at the Tryon Country Club and the beautifully laid out eighteen at the Red Fox Club.

While Fran has been cooking up a storm, Bob has not exactly been idle. That's never an innkeeper's lot in life, and Bob has discovered skills he didn't know he had: tiling bathrooms, resetting stone, wallpapering, painting, landscaping, matching marvelously the

104

old and the new, providing a variety of accommodations from singles to suites. It's hard to pick a favorite among the cottages: the rustic stone and log cabin, the modern Cape Codders, the one called the Swayback which was F. Scott Fitzgerald's favorite. I find it hard to believe he ever experienced the comforts enjoyed today by any guest at the Pine Crest. Under the Hulls this has become a *ne plus ultra* of inns.

PINE CREST INN, P.O. Box 1030, Tryon, North Carolina 28782. Telephone: (704) 859-9135. Accommodations: three rooms in main building, nine cottages, all with private baths; televisions but no telephones. Rates: inexpensive to moderate. Meal service: breakfast, lunch, and dinner. Bar service: beer, wine, and setups. Children welcome; pets allowed only in cottages. No credit cards. Open all year except for January.

Getting there: Tryon is a mile from the South Carolina border and three from Interstate 26 via state Route 108. Take 108 to town where it intersects with Route 176, which is Trade Street; take Trade to New Market Road to Pine Crest Lane and the inn.

STONE HEDGE INN
Tryon, North Carolina

Innkeepers Lucille and John Weiner came to this special slice of the South all the way from New Hampshire and the Snug Harbor Inn in North Conway. They met at the CIA—not wearing trenchcoats in Washington, but whisking sauces in Hyde Park, New York, at the Culinary Institute of America.

Their training shows in the handsomely appointed dining room of this ever so solidly built mansion of stone. The soups are brewed fresh daily; the mushroom caps are stuffed with duxelles and crab meat; the veal sweetbreads are sautéed swiftly and served on a bed of spinach noodles kissed with a champagne sauce; the scallops are gently baked in a casserole with a light sherry sauce and served with spinach; the veal piccata is christened with mushrooms and shallots, then lightly laced with lemon and sherry; and the Weiners work wonders with beef Wellington, christening it with a light sauce spiked with port.

It's a super menu and a super setting: a stone fortress of a country home built in 1935 on a thirty-nine acre estate complete with swimming pool and a namesake hedge of stone. There's a rustic cottage on the grounds available for overnight guests, as well as four beautifully furnished and spacious rooms in the main house. My favorite is the suite with twin beds, a great sofa, a large television, and a stereo; but I also like the room with the wagon-wheel chandelier, the four-poster, and the richly patterned matching drapes, bedspread, and oversize chair. The guest rooms are as spotlessly maintained as the dining room.

STONE HEDGE INN, Howard Gap Road, Tryon, North Carolina 28782. Telephone: (704) 859-9114. Accommodations: one cottage, four rooms in main building, each with a private bath; televisions but no telephones. Rates: moderate; includes full breakfast. Meal service: breakfast daily, dinner Wednesday–Saturday, lunch Sunday. No bar but you can bring your own. No pets. Cards: MC, V. Open year round. *Getting there:* Howard Gap Road is 1-1/2 miles northeast of Tryon on State Highway 108, and the inn can be seen from 108, where there's a sign.

PINES COUNTRY INN
Pisgah Forest, North Carolina

Innkeepers Mary and Tom McEntire, natives of Georgia, arrived in this isolated retreat via Florida, where they operated a used-furniture store a decade ago. The furniture they had on hand, and more that they had collected over the years, was put to good use in the buildings rambling over some dozen acres of woodland on Hart Mountain, overlooking the Little River Valley. The functional furnishings, reminiscent of summer camp, were put into the four cottages and the two-story log cabin as well as the main building, a two-story white clapboard inn that celebrates its centennial in 1983. The other buildings in the complex were put up at the turn of the century.

The wood-paneled dining room is where inn guests gather for breakfasts and dinners, which are included in the rates and served family style; and on cool summer nights there's a cozy fire in the living room to rally around. The atmosphere is strictly informal, the setting mountain rustic, and the sense of escape total.

PINES COUNTRY INN, Hart Road, P.O. Box 7, Pisgah Forest, North Carolina 28768. Telephone: (704) 877-3131. Accommodations: five rooms in main inn, eighteen in four cottages, one log cabin; all rooms with private baths; no telephones or televisions. Rates: inexpensive; includes breakfast and dinner. No pets. No cards. Open from first week in May to last week in October.
Getting there: The inn is four miles east of the town of Pisgah Forest on Hart Road leading from U.S. 64 to Hart Mountain and Little River. Pisgah Forest is a mile east of Brevard.

COLONIAL INN
Brevard, North Carolina

This tall, handsome building is a real eye-catcher. With a magnificent Greek Revival two-story portico and walls of popcorn "rubble" stucco, it looks as though it had been imported directly from Natchez, Mississippi. But the mansion is not antebellum: it dates only from the turn of the century, when it was built by a prominent local attorney who was mayor of the town and state senator, William E. Breese. In 1911 he hosted in his home a reunion of the Confederate troops who had served under Gen. Stonewall Jackson. In the 1940s, when his heirs sold the building, it was converted to an inn.

In September 1981 David Chotiner took over as innkeeper and started working the wonders of restoration, applying gallon after gallon of white paint to the exterior walls, installing new bedding, collecting antiques for furnishing the two bedrooms on the second floor of the main building and the public rooms downstairs, then sprucing up the ten rooms on the side of the inn, a sort of motel-like afterthought. On a former open-air porch he built his dining room, where guests are served a full Carolina mountain breakfast. When I toured the property in the summer of 1982 he had just opened for lunch and was hoping to be open for dinner as well in the not-too-distant future.

Chotiner is no stranger to the business of innkeeping. His family built the Sands Harbor Inn on Florida's Gold Coast in 1965. Three years later they sold the Pompano Beach building with its marina on the Intracoastal Waterway, and David, a graduate of Florida Atlantic University, has been itching to get back into the business ever since.

He chose an exciting location: Brevard and Transylvania County with thousands of acres of Pisgah National Forest, and over two hundred miles of mountain streams for trout fishing and numerous lakes full of bream and bass. There's an abundance of golf courses and hiking trails, camping and hunting sites, and an endless variety of scenic picnic spots and many stables for the hiring of horses.

The Brevard Chamber of Commerce, a few blocks from the Colonial Inn at 35 West Main Street (telephone: 704-883-3700), has informational brochures on the various activities, along with a handy foldout describing seven scenic driving tours of the area, ranging in distance from ninety-nine to 136 miles. They can also provide information on the annual performance schedule of the Brevard Music Center, a six-week happening in July and August. Included in the 1982 program was a splendid selection of shows, from *Don Pasquale* and *Rigoletto* to *The Mikado* and *The Merry Widow*, from George Gershwin and Jerome

107

Kern nights to chamber music, youth orchestras, wind ensembles, and choral groups. No wonder Brevard claims the title "Summer Music Center of the South."

COLONIAL INN, 410 East Main Street, Brevard, North Carolina 28712. Telephone: (704) 884-2105. Accommodations: two rooms in the main building with a shared bath; ten rooms in the side unit, each with a private bath and black and white television; no telephones. Rates: inexpensive; includes full breakfast. No pets. No cards. Open April–December, but be sure to inquire about exact dates.
Getting there: Brevard is 33 miles south of Asheville via State Routes 191 and 280, and the inn is four blocks from the center of town on its main street.

HIGH HAMPTON INN
Cashiers, North Carolina

Ten miles from Highlands, in the Cashiers Valley of the Blue Ridge Mountains, there's an inn where there's much more to do than sit and rock or keep a tally. It's the High Hampton, given that name by Gen. Wade Hampton who settled into this spectacular country before the Civil War. For eighty-five years the Hamptons called it their summer home; after the war, the bounty of the surrounding land—the game and fowl in the forest, the trout in the streams, the fruit and vegetables grown in their gardens—kept the family alive. In 1890 Dr. William S. Halstead, the general's nephew-in-law, purchased the twenty-three-hundred-acre estate. As chief of surgery at Johns Hopkins, he was the trailblazer who developed aneurysm and gall-bladder surgery, and he brought to his new home the medical greats from around the world to consult, learn, and teach.

After the Halsteads' deaths in 1922, the estate was sold to E. Lyndon McKee, who converted it to an inn. His son William is the present innkeeper, and he has remained loyal to the rustic, relaxed traditions that keep families coming back summer after summer.

They return to play golf on the excellent course laid out by George W. Cobb (it surrounds the inn and has a famous island green, the 137-yard eighth hole), to play tennis on the eight courts, to hike around the grounds. Farther afield they explore the waterfalls in the area—the Whitewater, Silver Run, the Narrows, and Horse Pasture—or Whiteside Mountain, at eighteen hundred feet the highest sheer precipice in the eastern United States. There's an archery range, another for skeet and

High Hampton Inn, Cashiers, North Carolina

trap shooting, and forty acres of lakes and streams for swimming, fishing, sailing, canoeing, and pedal-boating.

Youngsters are carefully looked after at High Hampton. It's organized as a summer camp, with a director of youth activities from the first of June until Labor Day. The children have their own recreational building called Noah's Ark, their own beach, golf and tennis clinics, horseback riding, donkey-cart rides, rock hunts, movies, hayrides, games and stories until nine at night. Teenagers have their own club room in the inn and their own schedule of activities.

In the center of all the summer sport is the great old rustic structure with pine planks on the bedroom walls, and rugged hunting-lodge-style furnishings. The decor is as appropriate to the setting as the siding on the walls of the inn—incredibly durable chestnut bark shingles, cut and shaved at a time when chestnut trees were found in great abundance. Also appropriate are the all-American meals made with vegetables from the inn's own gardens, ham cured and smoked in the inn's own smokehouse, breads and pastries made in the inn's own kitchen.

HIGH HAMPTON INN, Cashiers, North Carolina 28717. Telephone: (704) 743-2411. Accommodations: 120 rooms in main building and cottages, all with private baths, none with televisions or telephones. Rates: moderate; American plan. Ten percent for gratuities added to all bills; no other tipping. Meal service: breakfast, lunch, and dinner. No bar service, but setups are provided anywhere in the inn. Children welcome; pets not allowed, but the inn has a kennel. No credit cards. Open: May 1 to November 1 with full American plan and from December 1 to March 5 with modified American plan.
Getting there: Cashiers is on U.S. 64 between Highlands and Henderson-ville, 65 miles from Asheville; at intersection of 64 and State Road 107, follow 107 south to the inn entrance.

HIGHLANDS INN
Highlands, North Carolina

Miss Helen Major, hostess-manager of Highlands Inn, recalls an incident that truly describes this quiet little hostelry in the southern Appalachians. Several years ago a harried businessman rushed up to the desk, nodded "I'm here," and signaled his wife to hurry to their room to turn on the ball game.

"We do not have television sets in the rooms," Miss Major

politely informed him. "There is only one set, in the second-floor sitting room."

"What kind of place is this? No television?" he responded gruffly, asking for the key. There were no keys in the inn, Miss Major told him; doors locked only from the inside. "Ye Gods! What about my briefcase? Wait until I call the office and tell them about this place."

Miss Major replied that he would have to use the phone in the lobby because there were no phones in the room. The would-be guest sputtered a few oaths not often heard among the quiet antiques. At that point a little old lady appeared from an adjoining room and sweetly asked that he be a bit less noisy, for he was disturbing a bridge game. Fuming, he shouted to his wife that they were leaving; he would never stay in such a place. Miss Major, a fairly patient, stalwart type, calmly bet him ten dollars that if he stayed just one day, he would want to stay more. You know the punch line: After he unwound, he loved it, tried to extend his original reservation, and made plans to return the next year.

The Highlands is a quiet, restful place with porches running the length of both floors, a pink-accented dining room that features good food, and a lobby with an inviting fireplace. Rooms are comfortably furnished, but not elaborate. It's an old-fashioned, white-frame structure of a style and vintage that they just don't build anymore. And it's been sitting proudly on the corner of the main streets in this town ever since 1881.

Miss Major owned the inn for some twelve years, but she recently sold to an absentee owner in Miami—with the proviso that she stay on for a few years as manager. We hope it's forever, to ensure that there are no changes in the pace and laid-back patterns that keep guests coming back year after year.

What do people do in Highlands? "Nothing," was the answer a big-city journalist received from resident after resident a few years ago when he was doing a story on this resort town. The guests at Highlands Inn love to do just that—nothing. "Most of my guests are between eighty and one hundred," Miss Major declares with a twinkle of exaggeration, "and they run this place from May to October; they tell me what to do."

There is more to do, however, than rocking on the porch and watching the main-street goings-on, more than tiptoeing through the card room, attending auctions, and browsing in the local antique stores. A half mile east of town the Highlands Botanical Gardens shelters sixteen acres of Appalachian wild plants in their natural habitat, and a museum organized and maintained by the University of North Carolina. Fifteen miles away is Dillard, Georgia, gateway to the wilds of Rabun

County; to the north is the Nantahala National Forest and the Blue Ridge Parkway, a Cherokee Indian Reservation, and spectacular scenery. It is not surprising that Carolinians call this area the "Land of the Sky."

HIGHLANDS INN, Highlands, North Carolina 28741. Telephones: (704) 526-9380 (May 1 to October 31) and 526-2949 (November 1 to April 30). Accommodations: 30 single and double rooms, all with private baths; no televisions or telephones. Rates: moderate; American plan. Meal service: breakfast, lunch, and dinner. No bar service. Children discouraged; pets not allowed. No credit cards. Open mid-May through October 31.
Getting there: Highlands is at the intersection of U.S. 64 with two roads coming out of Georgia, 28 and 106. The inn is in the center of town, at the crossroads.

OLD EDWARDS INN
Highlands, North Carolina

The year 1983 marks the centennial of a grand old lady of a landmark that was revived just in time by Rip and Pat Benton. They took a wood and brick structure that had stood empty for eighteen years and spent months and a reported half million dollars to breathe life back into it.

Émigrés from St. Simon's Island in Georgia, where they had converted an old garage into a popular restaurant, Blanche's Courtyard, the Bentons brought their own crew to Highlands, relying on the same craftsmen who had performed so well in St. Simon's. How ably they succeeded here in the Carolina mountains is apparent as soon as one enters the inn, after passing that special sign which proclaims "21 Good Rooms for Ladies and Gentlemen."

The ground-floor Moose Room has a moosehead affixed firmly to the wall; nearby is the inn restaurant, called the Central House and still in the process of renovation as we go to press, but scheduled to open in 1983. The rooms are tastefully appointed in carefully coordinated colors. Some rooms have quilted bedspreads, some lace with dusters; beds are made of brass, iron, and wood; the chests of drawers match the beds; and those rooms without closets have armoires.

The wallpaper and paints have been carefully researched by the Bentons, and they used the talents of master stenciler Brenda Kellum to further decorate the rooms, basing her designs on patterns found in European homes, where the fine art of stenciling on walls reached its peak of popularity in the seventeenth and eighteenth centuries. Potted ferns in the rooms add a homey touch, and I like the liberal use of wicker and the strategic stationing of more greenery on the front porch and on the balconies.

OLD EDWARDS INN, Main Street, Highlands, North Carolina 28741. Telephone: (704) 526-5036. Accommodations: 21 rooms and suites, each with a private bath; no telephones or televisions. Rates: moderate; includes Continental breakfast. No pets. Cards: MC, V. Open May–November.
Getting there: The inn is across the street from the Highlands Inn.

POOR RICHARD'S SUMMIT INN
Franklin, North Carolina

High atop the highest hill in the little (pop. 22,000) town of Franklin, this inn, thoroughly revitalized by Minnie Hays and Lloyd Woosley, draws visitors and residents alike in droves—all through the spring, summer, and fall. They come to partake of the inexpensive all-you-can-eat dinners from Poor Richard's Country Kitchen, dinners that always include chicken, beef, pork, endless round trips to the salad tub, vegetables of the day, home-baked biscuits and French bread, brown and wild rice. Or to order the house specialties from the à la carte menu: the Maryland crab cakes, the fresh mountain trout baked with a bit of butter and lemon then showered with toasted almonds, wine-glazed Cornish game hen, country ham—hickory-smoked and served with red-eye gravy—steaks and farm-fresh chicken accompanied with dollops of excellent homemade stuffing. The sweet potatoes with marshmallows are marvelous, the dumplings with gravy good enough for the fussiest of grandmothers. At Easter time, roast rabbit is the delicacy of the day.

During the height of the season, the hungry diners line up early in the evening—and the nine dining rooms with their ten-foot ceilings and profusion of plants can handle some 110 people.

When Minnie Hays first opened the inn in 1979 she operated only the restaurant, quickly establishing a reputation with her recipes and her honest, down-home approach to preparation and presentation. She used the profits to make improvements, buying soothing-to-the-eyes blue and white napery, continuing the tasks of restoration, giving new life to the upstairs rooms, making lace curtains and quilts, using her experience as a one-time antique dealer to acquire turn-of-the-century furnishings: brass beds, rockers, marble-topped dressers, and rocking chairs.

Operated as a country inn since the 1920s, the summit-straddling yellow-poplar ramble of rooms was built in 1898 by Franklin resident S.L. Rogers, and it's the atmosphere of that era that Minnie and Lloyd have captured so well.

Among my favorite rooms is No. 15, a corner wraparound with four windows, a fireplace, a heavily carved massive headboard, and an oversize marble-topped dresser with a mirror. It's a grand room to return to after working through one of the inn's meals, bringing to life the inscription on the menu: "Ye tables groan before ye feasts; Ye feasters groan thereafter." Or after a day riding the Franklin trails or canoeing on the Little Tennessee River—horses and boats are available at the Franklin Riding Stables four miles from the inn. Or after a day exploring the Cullasaja Gorge on U.S. 64 E, hiking along Cliffside Lake, or joining the rockhounds about eight miles north of the inn searching for amethysts and rutiles, sillimanites and moonstones, garnets and sapphires (Cowee Valley on State Highway 28 is the largest source of pigeon-blood rubies outside of Burma). The Franklin Area Chamber of Commerce publishes a detailed sketch map of the mines and can provide information on locations, fees charged, and procedures to be followed. It's located at 180 Porter Street, which is also U.S. 441 Business Route.

No matter what the activity pursued, it's always a pleasure to return to the summit, to breathe in the invigorating air at twenty-three hundred feet, to stay where the innkeepers work hard to implement what is written on their brochure:

> Not everyone enjoys the touch of another time but are comfortable only in the luxurious, if anonymous, accommodations of today. . . . We wish them well and suggest they look elsewhere for they would not enjoy the Inn—and after all, the Summit Inn is our home we share with friends.

POOR RICHARD'S SUMMIT INN, P.O. Box 511, East Rogers Street, Franklin, North Carolina 28734. Telephone: (704) 524-2006. Accommodations: 14 rooms, three with private baths; no televisions or telephones. Rates: inexpensive to low moderate. Meal service: breakfast for inn guests only; lunch and dinner for public; brown-bagging permitted. No pets. No credit cards. Open year round, but limited operation during off-season.
Getting there: Franklin is 70 miles from Asheville, 20 from Bryson City and Highlands; East Rogers Street is one block east of U.S. 441 Business Route, and the inn is clearly visible from the road.

SNOWBIRD MOUNTAIN LODGE
Robbinsville, North Carolina

High in the heart of the Nantahala National Forest is a marvelous Shangri-la of a mountain lodge. Nestled among the trees at an elevation of nearly three thousand feet, the Snowbird offers spectacular views of cloud-scraping mountain peaks misted by the blue haze that gave one of the oldest ranges on earth its name, the Great Smokies. Built of native stone and chestnut logs, the lodge opened in the early 1940s as a strategic stopover for Chicago bus tourists making a week-long circuit of the Smokies. It's the epitome of rustic charm, constructed with an appreciative eye and an understanding of the surroundings. The bedroom walls are paneled in native woods; the lounge-sitting room with its wall-dominating stone fireplace is paneled in butternut; the dining room, with another huge fireplace, in cherry; the terraces and observation decks are constructed of flagstone and heavy timber.

From the lodge there are numerous trails winding through old Cherokee Indian hunting grounds—there are still some thirty-five hundred Indians here—and almost 450,000 acres of national forest. For the beginner there's a shortie of only a quarter mile and for the experienced hiker, or just the more energetic and enthusiastic, there are other trails that cover up to twenty miles. Then there's the Joyce Kilmer Plaque trail, weaving through a fitting memorial to the author of the poem "Trees": thirty-eight hundred acres of forest primeval— forest with virgin hardwoods, giant hemlocks and tulip poplars, rhododendron thickets, bushlike ferns and delicate wildflowers blooming beside splashing streams—a gently rolling land where the Unicoi range joins the Cheoah and Snowbird mountains. At the end of the trail, in the Joyce Kilmer Forest, is a bronze plaque with his famous poem and another plaque commemorating the poet.

In the heart of the Nantahala National Forest is the fifty-thousand-acre Cherokee Indian Reservation. Those who want to find out more about the Cherokee culture should visit the carefully re-created Indian village of Oconaluftee. Here you can observe Indian crafts and skills firsthand: pottery-making, basket-weaving, the burning out of a dugout canoe, and the chipping of flint for arrowheads. In one corner of the reservation there is an amphitheater where *Unto These Hills* is performed under the stars each summer. It's the tragic tale of the removal of the Cherokees from their ancestral home, along the "Trail of Tears." There is also an Indian Museum in the town of Cherokee, the main Carolina entrance to the Great Smokies National Park.

For those who would rather drive than walk, there are many circle tours, one more breathtaking than the other. It will take the better part of a day to cover the Great Smoky Mountains National Park, stopping at the highest point—Clingman's Dome at sixty-six hundred feet—and gazing out at fifty-two other peaks more than a mile high.

Closer to Snowbird Lodge is Fontana Village, spread around the great Fontana Dam. Created by TVA flood control and hydroelectric projects, the thirty-mile-long Fontana Lake is the highest in the eastern United States and largest in the southern Appalachians. Closer to Snowbird, Santeetlah Lake was also the product of dam building, by the Aluminum Company of America, which owns the complex of well-tended buildings twenty miles north, in Tapoco.

After a day of hiking and driving, it is a joy to return to the tranquility of Snowbird Lodge and to eat heartily, satisfying an appetite stimulated by exercise in the fresh mountain air; to browse through the lodge library or take a turn at table tennis or badminton; to watch movies and slides showing the awesome beauty that surrounds the lodge on all sides.

And to share in the enthusiasm of the new owners of this classic mountain retreat, the Rhudy family from Maryland: Bob and Connie and their children, teenagers Becky and Bobby. What a wonderful transition they've made from running a florist shop and bait-tackle store to running an inn in the mountains!

SNOWBIRD MOUNTAIN LODGE, Joyce Kilmer Forest Road, Robbinsville, North Carolina 28771. Telephone: (704) 479-3433. Accommodations: 20 rooms; double and twin beds; all rooms with private baths or connecting bath between two double rooms; no televisions or telephones. Rates: low moderate; full American Plan. Meal service: breakfast, lunch, and dinner. No bar service. No children under 12; no pets. No credit cards. Open end of April to the first week of November.
Getting there: Take the Joyce Kilmer Forest Road ten miles from Robbinsville, which is 75 miles south of Knoxville, Tennessee, via U.S. 129, and 98 miles from Asheville via U.S. 19–129.

FOLKESTONE LODGE
Bryson City, North Carolina

A quarter mile from one of the entrances to the Great Smoky Mountain National Park, Irene and Bob Kranich have converted a 1920s stone and wood farmhouse into a charmingly rustic mountain inn.

Fresh flowers and bowls of fruit greet the guests in rooms filled with country antiques; there are handmade crocheted bedspreads and claw-footed bathtubs; and awaiting in the morning is a mountaineer's breakfast served with freshly baked breads and the kind of generous dishing-out one needs to take on the trails of the Great Smokies.

For the visitor who needs some guidance, the Kranichs keep a well-stocked library, and, being avid outdoors people, they are eager to give advice on what to do in this beautiful section of the country. Then there are other activities, starting with midday strolling through the mountain town, attendance at a nearby county auction (a weekly occurrence), a visit to the Cherokee Indian reservation. The Kranichs keep a supply of rental bicycles available for those who want to do more than hike or stroll.

FOLKESTONE LODGE, Route 1, Box 310, West Deep Creek Road, Bryson City, North Carolina 28713. Telephone: (704) 488-2730. Accommodations: five rooms, all with private baths; no telephones or televisions. Rates: inexpensive; includes full breakfast. No pets. Cards: MC, V. Open June through October.
Getting there: Two miles from the center of Bryson City is the Deep Creek Campground entrance to the Great Smoky National Park and a sign pointing the way to the lodge.

FRYEMONT INN
Bryson City, North Carolina

The little mountain settlement of Bryson City, gateway to the Great Smoky Mountains National Park, is somnolent most of the year, but it bustles with summer vacationers and those who rush through during "leaf season." Then there are those visitors who return, year after year, to a unique experience awaiting those who check into the Fryemont Inn, a rambler of rusticity that has hugged a mountainside overlooking Bryson for more than half a century.

Capt. Amos Monro Frye, a lumber baron who made his fortune cutting timber in the Smokies, built this two-story structure along four hundred feet of mountain shelf. He cut poplar bark for the siding; oak for the tremendous lobby floor; maple for the dining room; cherry, walnut, and more poplar for the furniture made by two local master craftsmen. A mountain blacksmith forged the wrought-iron hardware, while other artisans wedged together giant stones to create the huge fireplaces; one in the lobby takes ten-foot logs and another in the dining room can handle logs up to seven feet long. The architect was New Yorker Richard Hunt, whose previous credits included the world's largest private home: Biltmore, the Vanderbilt mansion in Asheville.

Frye's inn opened for business in the summer of 1923, at first under his firm management and later, until 1951, under his widow's. Then came a period of idleness and emptiness for almost a decade until the Dillard family came along and worked a complete renovation. There's still a Dillard in residence and in command: Catherine, aided mightily by husband Jim Collins and a cheerful corps of young college students.

Catherine is a sensational woman who imparts a spirit of informality, comfort, and fun to inn and guests. A young lanky blond striding about in bib overalls, she's an ode to joy and a kitchen wizard. At one moment she's explaining to a guest that there are no weights in the windows so they slide across or swing out—they do not lift. Next she's showing new arrivals to her "Three Bears Room," with its trio of beds lined up along the wall and one of the best views in the inn. Then she's out back cooking: assembling casseroles to provide a challenging variety of flavors to her guests, and doing special things to country ham and chicken to make them taste better at the Fryemont than at twenty-five other places in the mountains. Or she is checking over the vegetable inventory; she's proud of the fact that if a guest stays a week, he will not see the same vegetable twice—though apples in one form or another are served almost every night. Catherine's inn is her kingdom, but the kitchen is her court. At the registration desk is this note:

If thou needeth solace and consolation (or a place to sleep)
Go forth and seek. We ever abideth in the kitchen.

When Catherine does emerge from the kitchen, it might be to provide music in the dining room. An accomplished pianist, she was a music major in college until switching to accounting, fortunately for her present innkeeping responsibilities. A year at Heidelberg's Goethe Institute studying German was not of such direct benefit, although it undoubtedly helped shape in some measure her sparkling personality, her ability to cope so beautifully, and her special talent of combining warmth and sincerity with a hidden efficiency.

At the Fryemont, surrounded by some of the most beautiful country in the world, you can cool off in the pool or rock yourself to sleep on the porch, gazing out at the highest range in the Great Smokies and planning your next excursion. For trout fishermen there is Forney Creek, Noland Creek, Hazel and Deep creeks; for bass fishermen the eastern end of thirty-mile-long Fontana Lake.

118

FRYEMONT INN, P.O. Box 459, Bryson City, North Carolina 28713. Telephone: (704) 488-2159. Accommodations: 36 rooms with single, double, twin, queen- and king-sized beds; all rooms with private or connecting baths; no telephones or televisions. Rates: inexpensive to moderate, with special modified American plan rates. Meal service: breakfast, lunch, and dinner. Beer and wine, and a full-scale wine shop in the inn. Children welcome; pets not allowed. Cards: MC, V. Open first week of May to last weekend of October.
Getting there: Turn right at the first traffic light in Bryson City coming in on Route 19. The inn is by the town square and city hall, a block up the hill and then to the right a quarter mile following the signs.

RANDOLPH HOUSE
Bryson City, North Carolina

This 1895 mansion with almost as many gables overhead as there are rockers on the stone-pillared front porch used to be known as the Frye-Randolph House, in honor of the attorney–land baron who built it, Amos Frye. But a few years ago, Ruth Randolph Adams, the niece of Frye's son-in-law, changed the name. But certainly not its ambience of a lovingly kept country inn. With husband Bill she oversees a happy home that features Carolina cooking, with homemade rolls, freshly plucked vegetables from local fields, stuffed trout, prime rib, and fried chicken among the specialties. Floridians eager for a taste of home will be happy to note that Ruth also has a reliable recipe for Key lime pie, and any guest who wants to take home tastes will be happy to find a selection of Bryson City beauties: jams, relishes, and honey—along with various handicrafts by mountain artisans.

The rooms are comfortable, and scattered here and there are memories of the Fryes and Ruth's aunt and uncle, Lois and John Randolph. For those braving the cold of winter, there's always a cheerful fire to sit around in the living room, relaxing a spell after one of those down-home belt-stretching meals or after a tour of the countryside.

RANDOLPH HOUSE, Fryemont Road, P.O. Box 816, Bryson City, North Carolina 28713. Telephone: (704) 488-3472. Accommodations: six rooms; three rooms have private baths, but when all six are occupied, all rooms share baths. Rates: moderate; includes breakfast and dinner (modified American plan). No children under 12; no pets. Cards: MC, V. Open year round.
Getting there: On Spring Street in Bryson City (Route 19E), turn right on Church and go one block to the library; turn right on Fryemont.

NANTAHALA VILLAGE
Bryson City, North Carolina

The post office address is Bryson City, but this complex is nine miles west of that mountain town. And it's a 215-acre fully equipped resort, complete with tennis courts, a swimming pool, paddle boats, miniature golf and shuffleboard, horseback riding, supervised children's programs in the summer months; not far distant is some of the best whitewater rafting in the country, on the clear, clean, cold (50° F) dam-controlled Nantahala, which roars for eight miles through the Nantahala Gorge.

The affable team at the main desk has all the information on these activities in the shadow of the Nantahala National Forest, some 152,441 acres, of which fewer than 3,000 have been developed. Rental cottages at Nantahala Village are tucked into the trees, and the main lodge, a two-story solid structure of stone mortared together in 1947, has ten rooms furnished in the best country–mountain inn fashion.

Ideal for families or couples traveling together, the cottages, each with a kitchen and ten with fireplaces, are as rustic inside as out, a credit to the architect and the designer. Some are made of logs, others of frame or frame and stone, and there's a special honeymoon cottage, No. 47.

The snack bar in the main lodge is busy most of the day, and the adjacent chestnut-paneled dining room is the scene of breakfast, lunch, and dinner, when the headliners are steaks and prime rib, sautéed shrimp and scallops, roast turkey, mountain-cured ham, and homemade apple pie. Portions are generous, and the kitchen works hard to live up to its boast that they have the "Finest Food in the Smokies."

NANTAHALA VILLAGE, P.O. Drawer J, Bryson City, North Carolina 28713. Telephone: (704) 488-2826. Accommodations: ten rooms in lodge, all with private baths; 36 housekeeping cottages accommodating from two to ten guests, all with private baths and kitchens; no telephones, but television available on a rental basis. Rates: inexpensive to low moderate; lower April 1–June 1 and Labor Day–October 7. No pets. No cards. Open April 1–October 31.
Getting there: The village is nine miles west of Bryson City on State Road 19.

THE JARRETT HOUSE
Dillsboro, North Carolina

Dillsboro's sole reason for being is its proximity to the mountains. The iron rails and wooden ties of the Western North Carolina Railway could not penetrate, ascend, or circumnavigate the heights. While a tunnel was being cut, an enterprising developer, William Allen Dills, laid out a town, started selling lots, and then built a hotel. He named the town after himself, the hotel and mountain after his daughter Beulah. In 1894, when spas were the magic magnet of the mountains, R. Frank Jarrett bought the hotel and rechristened it the Jarrett Springs, to inform one and all that a fine little sulphur spring was right behind the hotel.

Jarrett and his wife set a table that soon brought more visitors than the springs. Up to the time of his death in 1950, the hotel was noted for groaning boards of generous portions, with slices of his specially cured ham and bowl after bowl of vegetables fresh from his gardens.

A succession of owners paraded through in the next several years; then in 1975 Jean and Jim Hartbarger purchased the ninety-year-old inn, starting a new career. Jean used to teach the first grade; Jim had been basketball coach for nearly eighteen years at nearby University of Western Carolina. Today with sons Buzz and Scott, a staff of pleasant young women, and an experienced team behind the burners—one cook has been here for thirty years—the Hartbargers run a most pleasant inn, stamped indelibly with their personalities.

Neither had any prior innkeeping experience, but Jim, after extensive traveling with his basketball team, had a long list of various things he didn't like when eating and overnighting away from the home hearth. He used that checklist to eliminate the negatives when reorganizing the Jarrett House.

The Hartbargers are spotless housekeepers. The inn is sparklingly clean and lovingly maintained. Fresh-cut flowers greet the guest at the reception desk, and tiny baskets of fresh flowers brighten the dining room tables. Flowers also blossom in a Victorian parlor that might have belonged to your great-grandmother—if she was a fussy housekeeper.

In the front of the building, along the three layers of wedding-cake porch with latticed banisters, there are rocking chairs for watching the world go by and looking at that tongue-twister of a Tuckaseigee River splashing its way to the giant Fontana Lake. Just across the river is the Riverwood Craft Shop, where local artisans do wondrous things with pewter, wood, and copper.

The Jarrett House, Dillsboro, North Carolina

The rooms in the Jarrett House have been completely refinished; the Hartbargers stripped away decades of paint and wallpaper, finding in one room no less than five layers of paper, the original dating from 1902. Three of the rooms have showers and eighteen have bathtubs. Among my favorites are room No. 202 with its burled walnut bed and matching dresser, No. 204 with a cherry bedroom suite made locally in the 1920s, and No. 210 with a beautiful cherry Empire bed. Other rooms are filled with oak, and the Hartbargers have taken pains to create an authentic turn-of-the-century Victorian atmosphere by making sure there's a good supply of rockers in the rooms.

In the dining room the Hartbargers work hard to honor the traditions of the Jarrett House. When Frank Jarrett was in command he boasted that if a guest ever had to ask a waitress for more ham, the meal was on the house. No one ever heard of such a thing happening, and today the diner never has to ask for anything. It's served in down-home, back-to-the-farm portions: baked ham and mountain-country cured ham, Southern pan-fried chicken, chicken heaped with creamy dumplings, marvelously fresh vegetables, excellent coleslaw, candied apples, hot biscuits with a pitcher of honey, cobblers and other homemade desserts.

The fame of the dining room has spread far and wide, and since taking over the inn in 1975 the Hartbargers have not lost a cook or chef out back. On one record day they fed some six hundred hungry folks. Recently they opened a Brown Bag barroom on the second floor. Jim's many awards when he was coaching basketball are on display here. He and Jean should be given another award: one for keeping alive a piece of Carolina mountain history—in grand style.

THE JARRETT HOUSE, P.O. Box 219, Dillsboro, North Carolina 28725. Telephone: (704) 586-9964. Accommodations: 22 rooms with single, double, or twin beds; 18 rooms with private baths; no televisions or telephones. Rates: inexpensive. Meal service: breakfast, lunch, and dinner with brown bag (BYOB) license. No pets. No cards. Open April through December.
Getting there: Dillsboro is 47 miles west of Asheville via Interstate 40 and Route 23–19A. The inn is in town at the intersection of 23–19A and 19A–441.

PIEDMONT INN
Waynesville, North Carolina

Three thousand feet above sea level in the Land of the Sky sits this classic, century-old inn, shaded by giant maples and oaks, surrounded by some 250 acres of inn-owned woodland. Hiking trails lead another two thousand feet skyward to the top of Eagles Nest Mountain.

Guests at the inn can make their own nests, snuggling into the weathered old gazebo overlooking the country road, sitting on the arched second-floor balconies or on the shaded old-fashioned swing or behind the railings on the wide, wide wraparound porch. There are other buildings on the grounds including a recreation hall, and some cottages and motel-style units, along with a swimming pool, a tennis and shuffleboard court.

Furnishings are simple turn-of-the-century period pieces, and there are wood-burning stoves in the main lobby and dining room to warm guests on cool days—a homey touch as honest as the table-groaning portions of food served morning and night: stewed apples, grits, and fresh-baked biscuits for breakfast; mounds of freshly picked vegetables and entrées of chicken, pan-fried trout, and pork for dinner, followed by freshly assembled desserts.

PIEDMONT INN, 630 Eagles Nest Road, P.O. Box 419, Waynesville, North Carolina 28786. Telephone: (704) 456-8636. Accommodations: 15 rooms in main building of inn, 13 rooms in motel and cottages; all rooms with private baths; no telephones or televisions. Rates: inexpensive to moderate. Meal service: breakfast and dinner. No bar. Pets allowed only in motel and cottages. Cards: MC, V. Open May 1–November 1, but motel and cottages open year round.
Getting there: From Waynesville take Route 19A–23 South to the Hazelwood exit, which is Eagles Nest Road; turn right and drive just over half a mile to the inn.

THE SWAG
Waynesville, North Carolina

The innkeepers described in this book come from a delightfully diverse assortment of backgrounds, but only the Matthews come from the bosom of the church. Dan Matthews is the rector of St. Luke's Episcopal Church in Atlanta. When he was leading a flock in Knoxville, he and his wife Deener built a retreat a mile in the sky at the very border of the Great Smoky Mountains National Park, using it for church groups in search of seminars and solitude.

From the windows of the inn and the floor-to-ceiling glass walls of the oversize living room, Mount Pisgah and Mount Mitchell, the latter the highest peak in the eastern United States, are on glorious display. Inside and out there's a sense of the past—despite the fact that the inn was built only a dozen years ago. Wisely, the Matthews used stones and timbers rescued from buildings whose origins go back to the founding fathers. Strategically scattered here and there through the inn are antiques, paintings and sculptures, faded photographs, and hand-woven wall hangings that lend an air of old-fashioned authenticity.

The kitchen staff, which provides hearty box lunches for hikers or drivers who want to explore the Smokies, whips up mountain breakfasts that are included in the room rates, as well as dinners for those who make reservations. The inn has an extensive library on the wonders of the neighboring national park, the flora and fauna of the mountains of western North Carolina, the handicrafts of the mountain artisans, and the history of the area.

THE SWAG, Route 2, P.O. Box 280–A, Waynesville, North Carolina 28786. Telephone: (704) 926-0430. Accommodations: 14 rooms, most with a private bath; no televisions or telephones. Rates: moderate; includes full breakfast. Meal service: breakfast, box lunches; dinner by reservation only. No pets. No cards. Open weekends year round; weekdays from mid-May to end of October. For reservations and information during weekdays November–April, contact the Matthews at 178 17th Street NE, Atlanta, Georgia 30309; telephone: (404) 873-5427.

Getting there: Two miles north of Waynesville, just east of the junction of U.S. 276 and U.S. 19A, take Hempill Road north, following the inn signs 2-1/2 miles up the narrow, rugged road.

TENNESSEE

MOUNTAIN VIEW HOTEL
Gatlinburg, Tennessee

When the ten-room Mountain View Hotel first opened its doors in 1916, Gatlinburg was a sleepy little town with a single reason for being—it was the Tennessee gateway to the Smokies, some of the most beautiful country in America. The fortunate few who were able to find and finance their way to this forest paradise with its fast-flowing rivers and streams, its gorges and breathtaking color displays in spring and fall, were no doubt outnumbered by the lumberjacks working the woods and the lumber buyers in the town, as well as a handful of mountain youths in the Pi Beta Phi Settlement School. Started in 1912, the school pioneered the revival of mountain handicrafts. Its superlative crafts shop is in the center of town.

What a change the automobile, excellent roads, and the establishment of the six-hundred-square-mile Great Smoky Mountains National Park have made to the town, whose first settlers came from Virginia and North Carolina in the eighteenth century. There are now close to nine million tourists a year streaming through Gatlinburg, and there's a vast array of multilevel shopping malls, motels, fast-food franchises, side shows, and such Coney Island hokum as a Ripley's Believe It or Not Museum and a Guinness Book of Records Museum, a space needle, a wax museum, and what is advertised as the world's largest cable car and the world's largest artificial ski surface.

Owner Andrew Huff built the original Mountain View Hotel to house lumber buyers. As the town expanded and the number of tourists increased, he added new wings to the hotel. There are now three—a large lobby wing with two floors of rooms, a kitchen wing, and a dining wing. His five children, who still own the hotel, have added a motel unit on some of the remaining thirty acres and have refurbished the original

126

Mountain View Hotel, Gatlinburg, Tennessee

hotel rooms, creating in the process a haven from all the hype and modernity that engulfs this gateway to the Smokies.

There's a wonderful old porch for rocking, surrounded by stone and hand-split shingle siding, a grand old lobby with a merry blaze roaring in the stone fireplace, comfortable overstuffed chairs and couches for reading and visiting, and bedrooms furnished in a rustic manner that does not detract from the natural mountain setting of the town—white pine walls, turned cherry beds, multipaned windows. In short, the Mountain View Hotel offers a comfortable headquarters for expeditions on foot or by car into the national park. The hotel has a pair of swimming pools and can make arrangements for golf outings, fishing, and horseback riding. In the winter, there's skiing nearby on snow or Astro-Turf.

Nearly half of the park is in its original forest state, with native species of trees shading a profusion of wild flowers. In late April there's a three-day wild-flower pilgrimage conducted by the Park Service, the University of Tennessee's botany department, and the Gatlinburg Garden Club. And all through the summer the Park Naturalist Service organizes nature walks through the 515,000 acres of the Smokies, the most-visited of all our national parks, with some sixteen mountain peaks rising over six thousand feet, close to six hundred miles of trout streams, and of course, all those begging black bears.

MOUNTAIN VIEW HOTEL, 500 Parkway, P.O. Box 727, Gatlinburg, Tennessee 37738. Telephone: (615) 436-4132. Accommodations: 76 rooms in the older, hotel section; double and twin beds; all rooms with television, telephone, private bath, and coffee service. Rates: inexpensive to moderate. Meal service: breakfast and dinner. No bar service. Children and pets welcome. Cards: AE, DC, MC, V. Open all year. *Getting there:* Gatlinburg is reached by U.S. 441 or Tennessee Route 73. The hotel is downtown just off the main street, Parkway.

CHOO-CHOO HILTON INN
Chattanooga, Tennessee

Choo-Choo is not in the country and Hilton is not exactly a "li'l ole" innkeeper. But where else in the South, or the nation, can you sleep in your very own railroad car? Chattanooga, Tennessee's fourth-largest city, where the Tennessee River meets the Appalachian Mountains, is known as "The Scenic Center of the South." It also has one of the best-known railroad stations in the country.

The Choo-Choo Hilton Inn, which is located right in Chattanooga's

Terminal Station, has no Pullmans with drapes to draw and ladders to climb. Instead it boasts converted parlor cars, divided down the middle with soundproof partitions and filled with Victorian furniture and color: brass beds, tulip lamps, red carpeting, and drapes. Perfect for someone in satin and lace. Modern conveniences include complimentary coffee, facilities that can be flushed in the station, refrigerators, and a vending machine for ice, beer, soft drinks, and snacks, with charges automatically recorded at the front desk.

There's no clickety-clack, no sudden starts and stops, railyard shouting, rock-a-byes. And when you step outside your own car, you're in Chattanooga's famous terminal, completed in 1909 at a cost of $1-1/2 million and based on a design that won its architect, Donn Barber, first prize in a 1900 competition sponsored by the Paris Institute of Beaux-Arts. The interior was modeled after New York City's fashionable National Park Bank, and today its grand dome of concrete and steel and its sweeping brick arches are all part of one of the largest restaurants in the world. The atmosphere takes you back to the turn of the century. Meals are served in the former main lobby and concourse, not on oak benches but at comfortable marble-topped tables, surrounded by latticework, potted greenery, and arches of light—a Crystal Palace setting straight from Copenhagen's Tivoli Gardens.

You'll find gaslight and splendidly landscaped strips of bloom and green where the chugging giants used to hiss to a stop, a converted station house with red-checkered tablecloths and family entertainment, the old club car of the Wabash Cannonball for pre- and post-dinner refreshment, and another authentic old-timer, a wood-burning Chattanooga Choo-Choo, given that name in the 1880s shortly after the regular route to Cincinnati was inaugurated.

There's more for ferreoquinologists to marvel at—FDR's old railroad car and the Chattanooga Area Model Railroad Club's display, one of the world's largest model railroad systems—with one hundred miles of HO gauge track, one hundred locomotives, and hundreds more passenger and freight cars.

There are other shops in the station complex, along with an oyster bar, a bakery, and a taffy store. Inside the Hilton Inn, which has another couple of hundred rooms, there's a year-round waterfall swimming pool. There are also day-long trips to consider, all close to the city that likes to call itself "The City Next Door to Outdoors." Plan to visit the eight-thousand-acre Chickamauga National Military Park, site of the 1863 Battle Above the Clouds that was so crucial to the Confederacy. On the other side of the city there's Lookout Mountain, with Ruby Falls roaring 145 feet, and a Rock City collection of fun and games for the younger set. There are eight hundred miles of shoreline for fishing, boating and swimming at Lake Chickamauga; and in Sequatchie Valley, sixty miles of geological cleavage, the only such area in the world besides Africa's Great Rift Valley.

CHOO-CHOO HILTON INN, Terminal Station, Chattanooga, Tennessee 37402. Telephone: (615) 266-6484. Accommodations: 48 converted parlor car rooms; king-size beds and sofas that make into three-quarters beds; all rooms with private bath, television, telephone. Rates: moderate; children free. Meal service: breakfast, lunch, and dinner. Full bar service. Children welcome; pets not allowed. Cards: AE, CB, DC, MC, V. Open all year.
Getting there: Follow the many signs and take the Market Street exit of Interstate 24; drive east two blocks to the station.

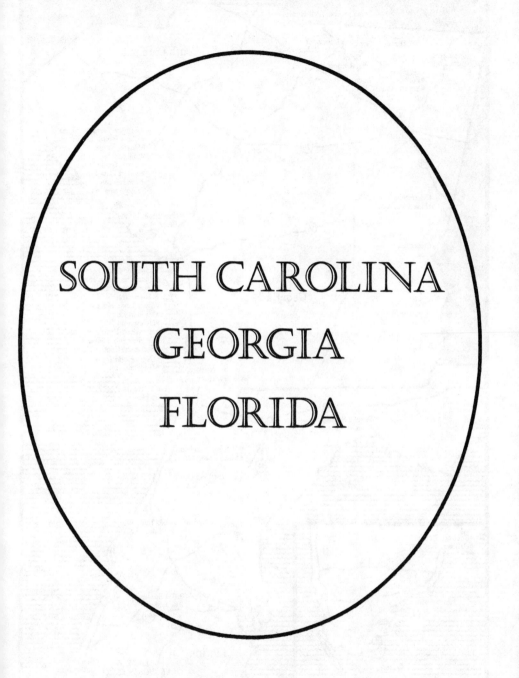

SOUTH CAROLINA
GEORGIA
FLORIDA

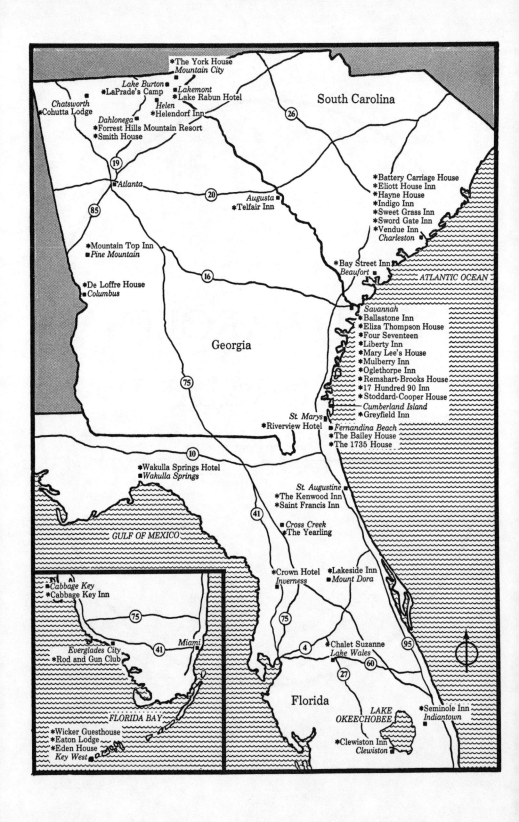

The York House
Mountain City

Lake Burton
*LaPrade's Camp   *Lakemont*
                   Lake Rabun Hotel

Chatsworth
Cohutta Lodge

Dahlonega
*Forrest Hills Mountain Resort
*Smith House

Helen
*Helendorf Inn

South Carolina

26

19

■Atlanta

20

85

Augusta
*Telfair Inn

*Mountain Top Inn
■Pine Mountain

16

*De Loffre House
■Columbus

Georgia

75

10

*Battery Carriage House
*Eliott House Inn
*Hayne House
*Indigo Inn
*Sweet Grass Inn
*Sword Gate Inn
*Vendue Inn
Charleston

*Bay Street Inn
Beaufort

ATLANTIC OCEAN

Savannah
*Ballastone Inn
*Eliza Thompson House
*Four Seventeen
*Liberty Inn
*Mary Lee's House
*Mulberry Inn
*Oglethorpe Inn
*Remshart-Brooks House
*17 Hundred 90 Inn
*Stoddard-Cooper House
—Cumberland Island
*Greyfield Inn

St. Marys
*Riverview Hotel

■*Fernandina Beach*
*The Bailey House
*The 1735 House

*Wakulla Springs Hotel
■*Wakulla Springs*

St. Augustine
*The Kenwood Inn
*Saint Francis Inn

41

■*Cross Creek*
*The Yearling

GULF OF MEXICO

*Crown Hotel
Inverness

*Lakeside Inn
■*Mount Dora*

75

■Cabbage Key
*Cabbage Key Inn

75

41

Everglades City
*Rod and Gun Club

Miami

4

*Chalet Suzanne
Lake Wales

95

60

27

Florida

LAKE
OKEECHOBEE

*Seminole Inn
Indiantown

FLORIDA BAY

*Wicker Guesthouse
*Eaton Lodge
*Eden House
Key West

*Clewiston Inn
Clewiston

SOUTH CAROLINA

CHARLESTON
South Carolina

This gracious city was the South's premier pre-Civil War city, the center of Southern social life and secessionist sentiment (South Carolina was the first state to secede in 1860). The charm, grace, and culture of old Charleston are still evident today: block after block of carefully restored and tenderly preserved houses, bordered by cloistered gardens behind aged brick and wrought iron. Nearly eight hundred acres of historic district shelter imposing churches and graveyards filled with the flower and genius of Carolina's past. Here is the nation's first municipal college and its first proscenium theater. Here are galleries and museums, including the oldest museum in America, the Charleston Museum, founded in 1773.

Charleston is a walker's delight. You can wander from one historic building to another, stepping into secluded and well-tended gardens (but only if the gate is ajar; if it's closed, walk on). You can listen to the bells of St. Michael's resounding across the rooftops just as they've been doing since 1764.

In March and April of each year during the Charleston Festival of Homes, many of the grand old houses are open to the public. Some tours are given in the evening when the owners' treasured possessions are bathed in the soft glow of candlelight. During those magical spring nights there's a very special appeal to this town where the outside world of commerce and bustle never seems very pertinent; where there's more concern about making sure the silver gets polished on Saturday than there is with the headlines in the daily paper; where there's more recognition of family, position, and place than of power and money, especially if the money is the least bit flashy.

While you're in Charleston, plan to explore the historic military bases. Fort Moultrie, built in 1776 and the site of the first major Revolutionary War victory against the British, is ten miles east of town. Fort Sumter, which drew the first shot of the Civil War on April 12, 1861, is on an island in the bay and can be visited only by tour boat.

Charleston is also known for its beautiful gardens. Magnolia Gardens, with its stunning array of azaleas and camellias, is ten miles from town. John Galsworthy once called it "the most beautiful garden in the world." Middleton Place, the oldest landscaped garden in America, is just past Magnolia, and Cypress Gardens is located in the swamps, twenty-three miles distant. Boone Hall Plantation, with its alley of live oaks laden with Spanish moss, and its original outbuildings, is six miles north of town.

Also worth visiting is Charles Towne Landing, a 184-acre park that recreates the wilderness English settlers found when they arrived in 1670. The park opened in 1970 on the occasion of South Carolina's tricentennial. There are bicycle and hiking paths, along with an animal enclosure containing the wildlife that flourished three hundred years ago in these parts. There's also a replica of the colonists' lifeline in those days: a fifty-three-foot sailing vessel.

There is enough to see and do in Charleston to keep any visitor busy at any time of the year—not just during the May–June Spoleto Festival that had its first, and highly successful, season in 1977. And mingled in the midst of all the preservation in what the natives like to refer to as "America's Most Historic City" are seven inns that help mightily to capture that history.

BATTERY CARRIAGE HOUSE
Charleston, South Carolina

The Battery Carriage House is tucked quietly behind the wrought-iron gates of a four-story mansion that dates from 1845. The mansion, planted solidly on an avenue of great houses, has a majestic command of White Point Gardens, which border the point of the peninsula overlooking the harbor and the confluence of the Ashley and Cooper rivers. Two forts once stood on the point: Fort Broughton, built in 1735, and Fort Wilkens, which was erected to defend Charleston against the British in 1812.

The ten rental rooms in the old carriage house combine the best of the old and the new Charleston. There are authentic reproductions of eighteenth-century furniture, canopied beds, and replicas of old Charleston wallpaper and paint colors, but also modern bathrooms, a

Battery Carriage House, Charleston, South Carolina

concealed kitchenette and wet bar with the fridge stocked with setups and a bottle of white wine. And in the morning there's silver-tray service of juice, coffee, and a special kind of cheesecake. This may be served in your room, or in the walled garden under an arbor of wisteria, or off past some hanging geraniums in an arched corner of brick.

In the reception room, there's a decanter of sherry for the weary traveler and information on all the things to do and see in Charleston. You might begin by touring the carriage house itself—it has a fascinating history.

In the 1870s it was a local showplace, the home of Colonel Richard Lathers, a Charleston native who made a fortune in New York and was later named financial chairman of the Erie Railroad. When he returned to the city after the Civil War he added considerably to his house on the Battery, building two stories on one corner, constructing a ballroom and a mansard roof, making a fourth floor that he used as a library. To his home were invited prominent men of both North and South: governors, congressmen, editors, businessmen. Lathers hoped to bring the two warring sides together in new attitudes of mutual cooperation and understanding. But after five years he gave up the cause and returned to New York.

A century after Lather's efforts, the present owners of the Battery Carriage House, Becky and Frank G. Gay, Jr., have succeeded in bringing North and South together, housing visitors from all over the country in handsome surroundings, providing them with overdoses of Southern charm and courtesy, pampering them with morning offerings of Benedict cheesecake from a special family "receipt," bicycles for touring the town, and a small swimming pool for a different kind of exercise.

BATTERY CARRIAGE HOUSE, 20 South Battery, Charleston, South Carolina 29401. Telephone: (803) 723-9881. Accommodations: ten rooms and two suites in the main house available March–September; twin and double beds; all rooms with a private bath, television, AM/FM radio, telephone. Rates: expensive; includes complimentary Continental breakfast, daily wine. Children and small pets welcome. Cards: AE, MC, V. Open all year.
Getting there: Take the Meeting Street exit off Interstate 26, proceed through town to the end of Meeting, and turn right; the house is on the right.

ELLIOTT HOUSE INN
Charleston, South Carolina

Built in the first years of the War Between the States and tastefully, lovingly restored in 1981, the Elliott House Inn is the newest of the special accommodations in Charleston. Furnished with reproductions of eighteenth-century canopied beds, chests, chairs, and armoires (which gracefully conceal television sets), and blessed with a brick courtyard bubbling with a fountain and a Jacuzzi, the Elliott House is a welcome addition to the city's marvelous collection of inns.

There's breakfast service in the morning, a welcoming bottle of wine to greet the guest on arrival, bicycles for touring the town, and lots of friendly advice from the innkeepers, natives of Charleston, about what to do and see, where to eat and be entertained.

They have style—I like the declaration in their eye-appealing little flyer: "At the Elliott House Inn, we request the pleasure of your company. But we think the pleasure will be yours."

ELLIOTT HOUSE INN, 78 Queen Street, Charleston, South Carolina 29401. Telephone: (803) 723-1855. Accommodations: 26 rooms, all with a private bath, telephone, and color television. Rates: moderate to expensive; includes complimentary Continental breakfast and bottle of wine on arrival. Inquire about pets. Cards: AE, MC, V. Open year round.
Getting there: The inn is a block north of St. Michael's Church, and Queen Street is between King and Chalmers, a grand old gas-lighted cobblestone street for strolling.

HAYNE HOUSE
Charleston, South Carolina

The 230-year-old Hayne House is not only the smallest—in terms of rooms—of the Charleston inns listed in this book; it is also the most intimate, providing guests with as much personal contact, information, and advice as they wish from owners Ann and Benjamin Chapman. They bought the venerable three-story frame with its Victorian add-on in the 1970s and shortly thereafter opened to the inn-going public a second-floor suite and a third-floor room behind a pair of dormers.

There's a fireplace in the suite, along with a four-poster and a day bed. The dormer room has twin beds, attractive accessories, and more space than you might guess about a place up there in the dormers. Both accommodations have a fair supply of books—for those who want to learn something about Charleston, and for those who want to relax and read instead of running all over town.

But with the Battery only two blocks away and so many historic homes and well-tended gardens, so many shops and restaurants to check out, I'm sure many of the Chapmans' guests spend little time reading.

HAYNE HOUSE, 30 King Street, Charleston, South Carolina 29401. Telephone: (803) 577-2633. Accommodations: one suite and one double room, each with a private bath and television; no telephones. Rates: inexpensive to moderate; includes complimentary coffee or tea. No pets. No credit cards, but personal checks are accepted. Open year round.

Getting there: King Street, with Meeting, is the main artery of Old Charleston: King runs parallel to Meeting to the west, and the Hayne House is two blocks north of the Battery.

INDIGO INN
Charleston, South Carolina

Opened in 1979, this modern inn is named for one of the most important cash crops of colonial Carolina. Two centuries ago, more than a million pounds of indigo were being shipped annually from Charleston to the mother country. Proclaimed the "King of Dyestuffs," indigo was cultivated in the Low Country in the same manner used by the ancients: the tiny seeds of the *sumatrana* and *arrecta* varieties of the genus *Indigofera* were sown by hand in rows two feet apart, hoed regularly, harvested by hand, fermented in wooden tubs with potash and oil and lime, then dried and formed into bricks for shipment.

The American Revolution closed off European markets, but the Low Country continued producing indigo for domestic use until the 1890s when it was manufactured chemically. Carolina blue provided the original dye for the heavy cotton denim pants sold out West to miners and cowboys by Levi Strauss. So King Indigo continues to reign today, all over the world.

And at the Indigo Inn it rules supreme: in the color of the fabrics and bedspreads of the handsomely appointed rooms filled with excellent mahogany reproductions of Chippendale's finest, including queen-size cannonball beds that are unusually comfortable; in the prints from the famous Mouzon map of indigo planting. The chintz fabric is a reproduction of an eighteenth-century pattern, and there are also some prints by local artists.

Indigo Inn, Charleston, South Carolina

The entrance lobby is a delightful mélange of styles; the interior courtyard, ringed by three floors of rooms, covered with brick and attractively landscaped, is a New Orleans kind of setting for enjoying the hunt breakfast spread out on a groaning table in the lobby, or for relaxing after a busy day in the town.

The Indigo is in the Rhettsborough section of Ansonborough, Charleston's eighteenth-century subdivision. To the west, just off Meeting Street, is King Street, the nineteenth-century shopping district; south and east is the Market Section with its many shops, galleries, and restaurants.

INDIGO INN, One Maiden Lane, Charleston, South Carolina 29401. Telephone: (803) 577-5900. Accommodations: 40 rooms and four suites, all with a private bath, color television, and telephone; there are two ground-floor rooms for the handicapped. Rates: moderate to expensive; includes hunt breakfast. Pets and children permitted. Excellent off-street parking on premises. Cards: AE, MC, V. Open year round.
Getting there: Maiden Lane is a block east of Meeting Street at Pinckney.

SWEET GRASS INN
Charleston, South Carolina

Close by the Vendue Inn is another converted warehouse, one that's nearly two centuries old. A three-story solid structure with heart-pine planking, the Sweet Grass Inn is the brainchild of Joye Meares Craven. From the early-morning complimentary breakfast of orange juice, fruit, cheese, coffee or tea, special fresh-baked breads, and, of course, the daily paper, until the nighttime gathering before the cheerful hearth in the parlor, she sees to her guests' comforts, providing them a cozier, homier setting than that of the super-elegant Vendue. Sweet Grass received its first guests in September 1980.

The rooms are individually furnished, and several of them can accommodate family groups or two couples traveling together. And, of course, the location shares all the advantages of the Vendue in terms of being close to the Market, several easy-to-recommend restaurants, and East Battery with its array of eye-pleasing commercial and residential properties.

SWEET GRASS INN, 23 Vendue Range, Charleston, South Carolina 29401. Telephone: (803) 723-9980. Accommodations: seven rooms and two suites, one of which has a sofa bed in the sitting room; single, double, and queen-size beds; private baths. Rates: moderate; includes complimentary breakfast, candy and fruit in the rooms. No small children or pets. No credit cards, but personal checks are accepted. Open year round.

Getting there: Vendue Range, an extension of Queen Street, is just off East Bay Street, which loops from East Battery along the water.

SWORD GATE INN
Charleston, South Carolina

A few blocks from the Battery Carriage House is another special over-nighting experience in Charleston, the Sword Gate Inn. The lodgings consist of four rooms on the ground floor and a honeymoon suite occasionally available on the third floor in the main house. In between is a 165-year-old grand ballroom with heart-pine flooring, Adam leaf crown molding, and gigantic Victorian gilt mirrors. The quartet of rooms downstairs was once the servants' quarters in a building that was constructed in 1740—as far as can be determined from all the yellowed documents and deeds that suffocate anyone doing a Charleston title search.

Across the cobbled brick courtyard is the kitchen and carriage house. Over the road is a magnificent three-story Stuart home where King George's emissary met clandestinely with Catawba and Cherokee chiefs to plot against the colonists and where, as local legend has it, on certain spring nights a phantom carriage stops before the gate and delivers a visitor in full eighteenth-century regalia.

Behind the inn is a large frame structure that was originally joined to the brick building when it all served as a girls' school before the War Between the States. The whole complex later became the home of the British consul and was subsequently owned by relatives of Lincoln and of Teddy Roosevelt. The entrance to the frame structure is on another street through a famous sword gate, past a row of stately magnolias. Cast in 1830, the gate's design is based on the ancient Roman motif of sword and spear and still stands out as a brilliant artistic achievement.

The inn's rooms are brightly decorated and cozy. You walk through an archway of ivy and potted plants into a private hideaway, insulated from the outside world by twenty-seven inches of brick wall. You'll sleep soundly in a high-standing four-poster covered with crisp sheets, a handmade bedspread, and a gingham comforter. There are comfortable wicker armchairs for reading and relaxing after a long day of sightseeing on tours arranged by the manager or on bikes from the inn's stable. Special touches include fresh flowers, a bowl of fruit, and a decanter of sherry.

Sword Gate Inn, Charleston, South Carolina

Down the hall from your room, through the begonias, azaleas, and ferns, the coffee and tea flows all through the day in a small room where you get your own breakfast. You toast your own English muffin and pour your own orange juice. There are also apple and blueberry tortes and hominy with bacon that can be sprinkled on top. All of it is organized and presented with a restrained flair typical of the Sword Gate Inn—laid out neatly inside an old five-foot fireplace, one of the large, walk-in colonial hearths. Breakfast can be consumed on the spot, back in your room, or outside on a small patio with peppermint-striped chairs and gingham tablecloths.

The innkeepers are the David Redd family—he's a Charlestonian to the core, the organist at the Citadel as well as at the seventeenth-century Old Baptist Church. The family faithfully oversees the treasures that were so carefully restored and revitalized by former owners Kerry Anderson and Eleanor Cain. Eleanor, a bundle of energy with a deep, abiding appreciation for Charleston, had already worked wonders on a late-Victorian mansion on Broad Street before she came to the inn in the early 1970s. At the Sword Gate she found adequate outlet for all her feminine fancies by redecorating the inn, like a giant dollhouse, with each room individually planned and oh-so-carefully coordinated right down to the gingham sachets and gingham-bordered stationery.

SWORD GATE INN, 111 Tradd Street, Charleston, South Carolina 29401. Telephone: (803) 723-8518. Accommodations: four rooms with two double beds, one with a single double bed, all with a private bath, television, and telephone. Rates: moderate; includes self-service Continental breakfast. Honeymoon suite in main house occasionally available—inquire. No small children or pets. No credit cards, but personal checks are accepted. Open all year.
Getting there: Take the Meeting Street exit off Interstate 26 and follow Meeting to the end of road at Battery; turn right and right again on Lenwood Street to Tradd and take another right. Tradd is a one-way street, and the inn is on the right.

VENDUE INN
Charleston, South Carolina

For a crash course in Charleston history plan to spend a couple weeks at the Vendue moving from room to room, each of which is named for a famous figure of the past. John C. Calhoun and Pinckney are, presumably, familiar names, but what about Robert Mills and William Henry Drayton—Vendue rooms 33 and 34 respectively?

Mills, native of Charleston, was the first professionally trained architect in the country. His Circular Congregational Church in town was the first auditorium-type house of worship in America, his local Record Building the first completely fireproof building. In Washington, D.C., he designed the Patent Office, the Post Office, the Treasury Building, and, as capstone, the Washington Monument.

Drayton, also a Charlestonian, moved from staunch supporter of the British cause to fervid opponent. From his undersize schooner, *Defense,* he had the audacity to fire on two British men-of-war in Charleston harbor—and that was before the Revolution! Chief Justice of the South Carolina Supreme Court, he was elected to the Continental Congress. His Drayton Hall Plantation on the Ashley River is open to the public and well worth a visit.

Other rooms at the graciously appointed Vendue are named after other great leaders of this proud city. All rooms have Oriental rugs and antiques; some have four-poster, tester beds of brass and wood; all have ultramodern bathrooms. The multilevel courtyard is bright and inviting, a splendid staging area for the afternoon complimentary wine and cheese.

Mornings at the Vendue begin with a smiling butler cheerfully delivering a silver tray filled with orange juice, coffee, or tea, fresh croissants and jam, the morning paper. Evenings end with turned-down beds and chocolate mints.

The Vendue Inn is a vibrant example of the miraculous transformation of a solid warehouse relic of the past into something with considerable class. Other examples are just around the corner: the Colony House complex of restaurants carved out of another warehouse; the Wine Cellar restaurant, with one of the best wine lists in the South; and Perdita's, a Charleston dining tradition.

VENDUE INN, 19 Vendue Range, Charleston, South Carolina 29401. Telephone: (803) 577-7970. Accommodations: 18 rooms, each with a private bath, telephone, color television. Rates: moderate to expensive;

includes complimentary Continental breakfast, afternoon wine and cheese. No pets. Cards: AE, MC, V. Open year round.

Getting there: Vendue Range, an extension of Queen Street, is just off East Bay Street, which loops from East Battery along the water.

BAY STREET INN
Beaufort, South Carolina

In April 1982 Terry and David Murray opened the perfect inn to grace the little South Carolina town of Beaufort—pronounced BEWfert. And they picked the perfect building on the perfect thoroughfare: the 130-year-old Lewis Reeve Sams House on Bay Street, a three-story, double-porch, columned slice of antebellum wedding cake, a magnificent monument to the glory that was Beaufort's past.

Its neighbors are even more grandiose: the 1814 Marshlands, the 1850 Joseph Johnson mansion known as the Castle, and the 1865 Tidalholm, all constructed in the grand plantation manner by owners who found more space here than in Savannah or Charleston, and a cooler, less humid climate than in the Low Country. The thermal zone around the town means that hot air rises in the afternoon sun and cool air is drawn in from the Atlantic, some ten miles away.

The Murrays quickly fell in love with the lifestyle, the history, and the pace of Beaufort. She's a native of Arkansas, he's from Texas, and together they've adopted this architectural treasure trove, a town that escaped the ravages of the War Between the States. Union forces occupied Beaufort in the first year of the war and used it as base of operations against Charleston to the north and Savannah to the south. The military is still in residence, although Beaufort is anything but a military town: there's a naval hospital not far distant, a Marine Corps Air Station, and the Marine Recruit Depot at Parris Island.

Moviemakers have also discovered Beaufort. *The Great Santini* and parts of Jon Voight's *Conrak* were filmed here. I'm sure there will be other films in the future. Just as I'm sure there will be an ever-increasing number of tourists streaming to a town that was considered before the Civil War "the wealthiest, most aristocratic, most cultivated town of its size in America."

Three hundred and four acres of that town—the entire downtown section—is a National Historic Landmark. Along a gentle curve of the Beaufort River, it has remained blessedly free of the encroachments of modern main-street civilization.

GEORGE KAUFMAN

There has been modern improvement however—a $5.5 million waterfront park complete with a marina, a tree-shaded common, a small plaza, a thousand-seat covered pavilion, and a sunken amphitheater that accommodates three thousand people. The park is the landing site of the annual invasion of a pirate fleet during the last weekend in June. A few weeks later it's the center of activity of the annual Beaufort County Water Festival, with antique shows, concerts, motorboat races, a blessing of the shrimp fleet, a parade, parachute jump teams, and a climaxing Low Country feed-in featuring boiled shrimp, corn on the cob, and watermelon.

There are also tours of the historic homes. Two of the most famous are open year round to visitors: the George Elliot House on Bay Street, a beautifully restored 1840 gem, and the John Mark Verdier House built in 1790—from its balcony Lafayette addressed the townspeople during his grand tour of the United States in 1825. On the ground floor of the house is the Historic Beaufort Foundation. Not far distant is the colonial two-story built by Thomas Hepworth in 1717 on New Street—the oldest in Beaufort.

At the other end of Bay Street from the Bay Street Inn is more architectural history: the 1810 John A. Cuthbert House, the 1790 Robert Means House, the 1786 Thomas Fuller House, and the 3-1/2-story pre-Revolutionary War home of William Elliot, which is now known as the Anchorage House.

It's a haven of superbly prepared and presented food, in a formal setting that's the proudly and oh-so-professionally-run property of a pair of not-so-melancholy Danes, Vagn Nielsen and Stig Jorgensen, former co-owners of Atlanta's famous Midnight Sun restaurant. Nielsen is out back and Jorgensen in the front; together they are creating one of the most memorable dining and lunching experiences in the South.

The Anchorage House is the perfect place to celebrate your discovery of Beaufort. Have a sherry in the Bay Street Inn before you go, and some fruit from the basket Terry Murray stocks, and when you come back to your spacious room with its grand view of the Intracoastal Waterway, put your feet up by the gas fireplace. Or recline in the claw-footed tub, appreciating the modern amenities, admiring the excellent taste displayed by the innkeepers.

The next morning you'll descend the grand center-hall staircase to meet the other guests gathered around the table for a grand breakfast.

BAY STREET INN, 601 Bay Street, Beaufort, South Carolina 29902. Telephone: (803) 524-7720. Accommodations: five third-floor rooms, each with a fireplace, unobstructed waterfront views, a private bath; no telephones or televisions. Rates: moderate; includes full breakfast, sherry, fruit, morning paper, evening chocolates, use of bicycles. Inquire about children; no pets. Cards: MC, V. Open year round.
Getting there: Beaufort is reached via U.S. 21 from Interstate 95 and is approximately an hour's drive north from Savannah and slightly more south from Charleston. Bay Street is on the waterfront.

GEORGIA

THE YORK HOUSE
Mountain City, Georgia

This historic hostelry near the North Carolina state line was a popular watering hole in the good old days before World War I, before the Georgia Power Company turned off the water at nearby Tallulah Falls, diverting it into gigantic pipes powering the equally gigantic hydroelectric generators. Tallulah was then the Niagara Falls of the South, a honeymooner's delight, a bustling tourist mecca with a myriad of hotels and lodges overlooking the gorge. The tourist trade spread to neighboring settlements, and the York House in Mountain City flourished as a result. Before the rail line ran through the county it took the better part of a day to make the round-trip journey by horse and buggy to meet the summer visitors arriving on the Tallulah Falls Railroad from Atlanta.

The York House was originally a log cabin built by Civil War veteran W.T. York returning from the battles. The house was gradually expanded, especially when the siding was laid by the railroad. Train travelers were delivered almost to the door, there to remain most or all of the summer. They came to partake of the bountiful hospitality and the solid, home-style food served by the Yorks.

The same family operated this landmark from 1896 until September 1979. That's when Mrs. Fannie York Weatherly's daughter, Bea Broadrick, sold the inn to Mildred and John Dillon. He's a native of Savannah and a lover of antiques, and he's filled the York House with what he's collected over the years. The Dillons worked a full-scale revitalization of the inn, but did nothing to disturb the tranquility of the setting shaded by giant cedars and hemlocks and a pair of Norwegian pine trees out front. According to local stories, the pine trees were planted by the man who built the house and were sold to him by an

148

The York House, Mountain City, Georgia

itinerant Norwegian who was trying to raise enough money to go back home.

No meals are served now, but there is a refrigerator and a community kitchen for the use of guests.

Plan to visit the observation tower atop Rabun Bald and the thirty-five-hundred-foot-high Black Rock Mountain State Park with its sensational view of the Blue Ridge Mountains and the Little Tennessee River Valley—both are easily accessible from the York House via the paved Herman Talmadge Trail from Mountain City. Railroad buffs will want to search for the remnants, including wooden trestles, of the old Tallulah Falls Railroad—these trestles occasionally collapsed, which caused local wags to translate the "TF" on rail cars as Total Failure.

The Rabun County Welcome Center in Clayton can provide maps and information on the surrounding area. Those who are interested in learning more about the Foxfire phenomenon should visit the Rabun Gap Crafts Shop just north of Mountain City. This famous research and publishing project, which is responsible for reviving forgotten mountain crafts and skills, started in 1966 at the Rabun Gap–Nacoochee School, a preparatory school combining work, worship, and study. Andrew Jackson Ritchie, one of the county's first college graduates (he attended Harvard), founded the school in 1903 for the education of the mountain people. It eventually housed entire families who worked the farmlands while completing their studies. The campus is just across the road from the store, and a drive or walk through some of its sixteen hundred acres is well worth the time.

THE YORK HOUSE, Box 126, Mountain City, Georgia 30562. Telephone: (404) 746-2068. Accommodations: twelve rooms; single and double beds; all rooms with a private bath. No telephones; television only in main-house sitting room. Rates: inexpensive. No meal or bar service. Children welcome; pets discouraged. No credit cards. Open June 1 to October 31.
Getting there: Mountain City is five miles north of Clayton on U.S. 23–441, five miles from the North Carolina border. Turn at the sign on 23–441 and drive east a quarter mile. The house is on the right.

LAPRADE'S CAMP
Lake Burton, Georgia

LaPrade's Camp is not for everyone. The twenty-one cabins along Lake Burton's tranquil little misnamed Wildcat Cove are starkly simple, the light bulbs bare; the walls have scribbles from previous occupants, and the porch is small (but screened); however, if you like canoeing and fishing, there are boats available at LaPrade's marina, and in the area are several stocked trout streams. The Appalachian Trail is nearby, as is a riding stable. If you're on a stringent vacation budget and have a family to feed, LaPrade's should be considered, even if you don't like camping. It has been around since 1925.

Included in the inexpensive rates are all three meals, and that means a bounty of freshness and quality from the owner's own farm: chicken, ham and pork, beef, and a never-ending supply of produce. Tourists and residents of the area start stacking up early in front of the LaPrade mess hall, where the severest cases of the hungries are cured by the plates and bowls of food heaped high on the long tables.

LAPRADE'S CAMP, Route 1, Georgia 197 North, Clarkesville 30523. Telephone: (404) 947-3312. Accommodations: 21 cabins, each with a private bath, two bedrooms, kitchen, fireplace, porch. Rates: inexpensive; includes three meals a day. No pets. No cards, but personal checks are accepted. Open April 1–November 30.
Getting there: The impossible-to-miss collection of cabins is on State Road 197 eighteen miles north of the town of Clarkesville.

LAKE RABUN HOTEL
Lakemont, Georgia

The Lake Rabun Hotel is in *Deliverance* country, where also *The Great Locomotive Chase, Whiskey Mountain, Grizzly,* and a hundred other films have been made. More than half of Rabun County, which was carved from Cherokee territory in 1818, is now in the Chattahoochee National Forest. Almost a tenth of the county is under water in a chain of six lakes—Burton, Seed, Rabun, Tallulah, Yonah, and Tugaloo. These lakes offer white-water canoeing, tubing, kayaking, and some of the best trout fishing in the South. The county is bordered by the Chattooga River on the east, the Appalachian Trail on the west, and the Tallulah Gorge on the south; the gorge is the deepest in the eastern United States and is second in depth only to the Grand Canyon. But in rainfall Rabun County is second to no other spot in the country: more

Lake Rabun Hotel, Lakemont, Georgia

than seventy inches a year, which translates to lush forests and rare wild flowers including orchids.

Barbara and Dick Gray came to this wet and wild setting in 1976, adding their numbers to a county population of some nine thousand residents—that's about one person for every twenty-six acres. The Grays came from Tampa, after answering an ad they had seen by chance about a hotel for sale. They both wanted to start new careers and escape from their rushed lives—he was a traveling salesman for a Florida building supply company and she was a banquet director. Dick is a soft-spoken native of Jonesboro, Tennessee, and Barbara is an effusive native of Tampa. Her sprightliness is as evident in the colorful country curtains and the ruffled skirts she's sewn for sinks and dressing tables as it is when talking with guests. Together the Grays have given new life and spirit to a wood and stone hideaway known as the Lake Rabun Hotel. It is ideal for boating (there's a rental boathouse just across the road), swimming, fishing, hunting, hiking, and driving tours (self-guiding tour maps are at the Welcome Center in Clayton), or just plain "sittin' and a-thinkin'. "

In the years since the Grays took over this rustic retreat, they have poured great doses of tender loving care into their Shangri-la, making friends from all over the United States, providing their own vital definition of the word *innkeeper.*

There's no lunch or dinner served at the hotel, but for sustenance in these hills, the folks stream to the Dillard House just up Route 441 a few miles or they go over to LaPrade's Camp at Lake Burton where the food is served family style: country ham, grits, scrambled eggs, and hot biscuits and sorghum syrup for breakfast, chicken and dumplings for lunch, fried chicken with all the trimmings for supper. LaPrade's Camp has been in business since 1925, three years after the Lake Rabun Hotel was built. The latter was then known as the Crow's Nest—its owner, Everett Crow, used it as mountain retreat and hostelry on the lake the Georgia Power Company created when they cut off the roar of the river in 1913 and constructed power dams. The great ravines at Tallulah Falls were left with only a trickle of a stream where there used to be mighty waterfalls cascading—it was an extremely popular turn-of-the-century resort for honeymooners and many others. But the view of the gorge is still spectacular, and there are other falls in the area, some within easy walking distance of the hotel.

After a day of exploring, what could be better than to return to the warmth of the hotel's great stone fireplace, cozy into handmade rhododendron and mountain laurel furniture, and share the day's activities with the Grays and other guests?

153

The fireplace is again the focal point in the morning, when the guests gather for coffee and one of Barbara's special baked goods that popped out of the oven while you were still sleeping. If you wonder why your morning brew never tastes that good at home, it's not only the charm of the surroundings, your hosts, the stimulation of the other guests, or even all that marvelous mountain air. It's the water, fresh from a cool mountain spring. Rabun County has more than five thousand of them.

LAKE RABUN HOTEL, Lakemont, Georgia 30552. Telephone: (404) 782-4946. Accommodations: 16 rooms; double beds (two of them hand-carved); three rooms with a half bath and four with shared baths; most rooms have sinks. No television in hotel and telephone only in office. Rates: inexpensive; includes self-service Continental breakfast. Children welcome; pets not allowed. No credit cards. Open April 1 through October 30.

Getting there: From Atlanta take I-85 to Gainesville (Exit 6) and Route 23, which joins with 441 at Baldwin. Turn left at the Lakemont/Lake Rabun sign about two miles past Tallulah Falls. Drive two miles, turn left at Lakemont Building Supplies Company, and go two more miles to the hotel on the right side of the road.

HELENDORF INN
Helen, Georgia

The renaissance of this mountain mill town in northeast Georgia began in 1969, when a group of enlightened local businessmen decided something had to be done to change the drab look of their main street, a downtown area as dreary as many others across the country. Local businessman Pete Hodkinson was the spark and local artist John Kollack the instrument. The townspeople provided the time, the talent, and the will to produce *Gemütlichkeit* in Georgia.

Helen was transformed into a town with Alpine ambience, a crossroads of Old World charm with pitched and overhanging roofs, gingerbread trim, arched windows, brightly painted shutters, and murals of town life and history across the buildings. Artist Kollack did the watercolor sketching, drawing his inspiration from memories and sketchbooks from a tour of duty with the army in Bavaria.

In the summer local lasses are outfitted in dirndls, the lads in *Lederhosen*, and there's always some kind of festival going on. In March and April there are canoeing races on the Chattahoochee River which

154

runs through town, in June a clogging convention, and an *Oktoberfest* in mid-September. The Great Balloon Race held in May attracts some thirty hot-air balloonists who race from Helen to the Atlantic. An accident in the 1976 race claimed the life of Pete Hodkinson. But the community resolve did not fade, and Helenites are still expanding their bit of Bavaria, their touch of the Tyrol in the shadow of the southern Appalachians.

Local shops are loyal to the Alpine theme and cater to the tourist—Norwegian and German imports prevail. The town abounds with purveyors of German food: the Wurst Haus, Strudel Haus, the Matterhorn, and Gasthaus zur Schmiede.

The Helendorf Inn, which opened in 1973 on the site of the old sawmill that used to be the town's reason for being, reflects the town's new image. There are flower boxes on galleried balconies, a gate tower, colorful flags, and a *Gasthaus* lobby with an oversize fireplace—ideal for meeting fellow guests. You may find it hard to tear yourself away from your riverfront room with its hand-painted heavy furniture and Kollack prints and its balcony overlooking the splashing Chattahoochee, the changing colors of the Georgia woods, and the rooftops of Alpine Georgia.

The inn is under the diligent management of Richard Gay, a former air force officer assigned to Europe, and his wife Barbara. They run the perfect *Gasthaus* for settling into the town's Tyrolean atmosphere and for exploring the gentle hills of northeast Georgia. Helen is surrounded by 743,000 acres of the Chattahoochee National Forest with its multitude of lakes, streams, and hiking paths—the Appalachian Trail begins a few miles to the west. There's Yonah Mountain to climb; the Chestatee, Chattooga, and Chattahoochee rivers for white-water sports. For detailed information, exhibits, and slide programs check with the Forest Service's Visitor Information Center on top of Georgia's highest mountain, Brasstown Bald, rising to almost forty-eight hundred feet.

Also worth visiting are the Anna Ruby Falls, Duke's Creek Falls, and Tallulah Gorge, in addition to an old covered bridge and the Gold Museum in Dahlonega, Georgia's one-time gold rush town. Nearby is the Old Sautee Store, a century-old collection of memorabilia made into a museum, and next to it the Sautee Inn, an excellent stopover for lunch or dinner. Just north of Helen is the unique Unicoi State Park, with swimming and camping facilities, a conference center, programs on natural resources, folk culture and local history, and a shop with Appalachian handicrafts—toys, dolls, pottery, and the largest display of quilts in the entire Southeast.

155

Helendorf Inn, Helen, Georgia

HELENDORF INN, Post Office Box 305, Helen, Georgia 30545. Telephone: (404) 878-2271. Accommodations: 33 riverfront rooms with kitchenettes, balconies, and two double beds; twelve smaller tower rooms; a two-level honeymoon suite; all with a private bath, television, and telephone. Rates: inexpensive to moderate. Meal service: breakfast only; coffee and rolls available in lobby. No bar service. Children and pets welcome. Cards: MC, V. Open all year.

Getting there: Helen is 90 miles (approximately two hours) from Atlanta and Greenville, South Carolina. From Atlanta take I-85 to Gainesville (exit 6) and then Route 129 to Cleveland and Route 75 ten miles farther north to Helen. The inn is on the right-hand side just as you enter town, by the bridge.

FORREST HILLS MOUNTAIN RESORT
Dahlonega, Georgia

For a forest retreat from all the lore and legend of Dahlonega gold, a Shangri-la Georgia-backwoods kind of getaway, consider this complex of a half dozen rustic cabins deep in the woods near the Amicalola Falls State Park, the highest falls in the state and the starting point of the Appalachian Trail.

It's 140 acres of isolation in cabins solidly built by the Kraft family, refugees from civilization in West Palm Beach. Walking trails and woods abound, and there are a reported nineteen moonshine stills on the property—none of them working, of course—but for those who like to sit and do nothing the porches outside the cabins are perfect.

For inside sitting there's a stove-fireplace assembled from masses of local stone. And there's also a four-bedroom "Executive Retreat" on the premises, a honeymoon cottage complete with a Jacuzzi, a tennis court, and a games room. At last report, there were plans for a restaurant and a swimming pool.

FORREST HILLS MOUNTAIN RESORT, Route 3, Dahlonega, Georgia 30533. Telephones: (404) 864-6456 and (404) 864-3823. Accommodations: six cabins, each with a fully stocked kitchen, private bath, two bedrooms, fireplace; one 2-story cottage with four bedrooms, a fully stocked kitchen, two bathrooms. Rates: inexpensive. Pets permitted. No cards, but personal checks are accepted. Open year round.

Getting there: The resort is four miles east of the Amicalola Falls State Park off State Road 52 on Wesley Chapel Road; there are signs on SR 52.

SMITH HOUSE
Dahlonega, Georgia

The first real gold rush in this country was not in California. It was in Georgia, in the area around the little (pop. 9,000) town of Dahlonega, heart of the one-time richest mother lode of gold ever found in the United States. That was in the 1820s. A decade later the federal government opened a branch mint in Dahlonega, where they coined millions and millions of dollars worth of gold.

The War Between the States closed the mint, and after the war the building was donated to a new college; its foundation now supports a magnificent structure belonging to the land-grant agricultural school, North Georgia College. The dome of that building, Price Memorial Hall, was gilded with Dahlonega gold on the occasion of its centennial in 1871.

Dahlonega gold also gilded the state capitol in Atlanta. The logistics of that operation, as well as exhibits explaining the gold rush, are on display in a marvelous little museum in the center of town, in the 150-year-old Lumpkin County Courthouse, a gem of early Georgia architecture in Greek Revival style that has been used over the years as a jail, a hospital, and a village market.

A few hundred feet from the Gold Museum, past a place where tourists can still pan for gold—a few flecks are guaranteed for payment of a nominal fee—is another Dahlonega landmark: the Smith House.

A century-old structure with eighteen simply furnished, immaculate rooms, it is also the site of one of the best-known pigouts in the South: lunch and dinner extravaganzas with a never-ending parade of plates and dishes overflowing with down-home, back-country food—more than a half dozen vegetables, fabulously crunchy fried chicken, thick and airy beaten-out-back biscuits for dolloping with honey, ham, cobblers, and Georgia ice cream, otherwise known as grits.

It's all served to the starving from 11:30 am to 7:30 or 9 pm depending on the season, and next door is a cafeteria featuring the same kind of food. At 7:30 in the morning the tables begin groaning with country breakfasts. No wonder they have all those rockers on the shaded porch. What else can one do after a stuff-yourself-silly feed-in?

After recuperating, the over-indulgent can stroll the square, looking into the shops with their arts and crafts made by local artisans. On the weekends, there are usually some pickup musicians who will fiddle and strum their way through mountain favorites.

158

SMITH HOUSE, 202 Chestatee Street South West, Dahlonega, Georgia 30533. Telephone: (404) 864-2348. Accommodations: 18 rooms and suites with single and double beds, private baths, no telephones; television in lobby area. Rates: inexpensive. Pets permitted. Cards: MC, V. Open year round.

Getting there: Dahlonega is some 70 miles northeast of Atlanta via State Road 400 and U.S. 19. The Gold Museum is in the center of town, the Smith House two blocks away with a hard-to-miss sign out front.

COHUTTA LODGE
Chatsworth, Georgia

Cohutta Lodge sits majestically on a summit overlooking some of the most breathtaking scenery in the South: the foothills of the Blue Ridge Mountains, in the western reaches of the gigantic Chattahoochee National Forest. To the north is the Cohutta Wilderness Area, a thirty-four-thousand-acre refuge with two of the best trout streams in the state, the Jacks and Conasauga rivers. To the west, as immediate neighbor, is the Fort Mountain State Park, a nineteen-hundred-acre, twenty-eight-hundred-foot-high facility with boating, fishing, picnicking, nature trails, swimming, and an ancient assemblage of rocks that was once a stone fortress. The origin of the ruins is still shrouded in mystery and steeped in legend. Some say the Vikings or the Spanish conquistadors built the fortress; others credit a band of wandering Welshmen in the twelfth century led by a prince named Moduc, and there are Cherokee accounts of moon-eyed white men in the area.

Cohutta is Cherokee country, the heart of their once-mighty nation. In nearby Spring Place there's the two-story mansion of Cherokee Chief Joseph Vann, "Rich Joe Vann" as he was known until forcibly removed from his prosperous plantation by the Georgia militia during those days when all Cherokee land was confiscated and the people sent on their "Trail of Tears."

Twenty miles to the south of Cohutta is the product of a more beneficent and civilized kind of federal activity, the Carters Lake and Dam on the Coosawattee River, the second highest and greatest in volume of any dam east of the Mississippi. It is also the deepest lake in Georgia, and its sixty-two miles of shoreline provide boating, fishing, and swimming activities.

But on cool days you might prefer the Cohutta Lodge pool, which is indoors and heated. The lodge also has lighted tennis courts. A few hundred meters down the mountain there are stables, a general food store, and several artisan shops. It's an artsy-craftsy collection of

Cohutta Lodge, Chatsworth, Georgia

painters, macrame-weavers, and potters; the artists-owners live above their shops. Spring and fall festivals are held in this Fort Mountain mini-village, with street dancing, barbecue, and booths of mountain artists displaying their creations.

The fall-leaf season brings tourists in swarms—many of them reserve at the lodge a full six months in advance. They come to ooh and aah from the lofty elevations, to hike the trails, to pick the berries, to enjoy the solid fare in the lodge, to bask in the smiling hospitality of Julie Franklin and her husband Floyd, an agronomist. What background could be better for an innkeeper in the midst of all this wilderness?

Floyd is also a sportsman who encourages all his guests to get out and hike in summer, and to use the ice-skating rink and toboggan runs in the winter when the fire blazes away in the lodge's stone fireplace. The individual rooms are standard motel in style, but nothing else up this high in the sky suggests a motel.

COHUTTA LODGE, 5000 Cochise Trail, Chatsworth, Georgia 30705. Telephone: (404) 695-9601. Accommodations: 21 rooms; single, double (with two double beds), and suite with king-size bed; all with a private bath, television, and telephone. Rates: inexpensive to low moderate. Meal service: breakfast, lunch, and dinner. No bar service (Murray County is dry, but BYOB permissible). Children and pets welcome. Cards: MC, V. Open all year.
Getting there: The lodge is 110 miles north of Atlanta via I-75. Exit just south of Dalton and take U.S. 76, which goes through Chatsworth and the Fort Mountain State Park 28 miles to the lodge, clearly marked by several signs.

MOUNTAIN TOP INN
Pine Mountain, Georgia

Not all the mountains of Georgia are found in the northern stretches of the state. West of Macon in the foothills of the Appalachians is a seventy-mile ridge in the Lower Piedmont known as Pine Mountain, rising above the Piedmont terrain to just over thirteen hundred feet.

On the slopes of Pine Mountain, in Warm Springs, there's a modest home of wood and native stone known as the Little White House. It was the southern retreat of Franklin D. Roosevelt, the building where he died in April 1945. (An adjacent museum is open daily to the public.) This is where Jimmy Carter launched, with shrewd symbolism, his final campaign push for the presidency in 1976.

The Roosevelt name is also memorialized in the F.D. Roosevelt State Park, nearly five thousand acres of campsites, hiking and bridle trails across the backbone of Pine Mountain. FDR, utilizing the labor and organization of the Civilian Conservation Corps in the 1930s, helped plan the park with its many scenic overlooks, its imposing stone structure of a welcome center, and its scenic parkway along the crest of the mountain—at one time an Indian trail and later a stagecoach road.

The park provides the ideal natural surroundings for the Mountain Top Inn; its immaculately maintained rooms straddle the mountain side and are shaded and encircled by Georgia forest. There's no insult to the environment, outside or in. The rooms are paneled in wood accented with brightly colored floral prints. The dining room is a vintage mountain lodge with a cathedral ceiling of wooden rafters, mounted deer heads, and a large stone fireplace. Two walls of windows offer views of the surrounding six hundred wooded acres, as well as the inn's swimming pool, tennis courts, and miniature golf course.

There's a real golf course eight miles away at the famous Callaway Gardens, a twenty-five-hundred-acre spectacular with thirteen miles of scenic driving trails, swimming, fishing, boating, cycling, and a miniature train. There's also a country store with a restaurant and such home-grown taste tempters as muscadine grape preserves, slab bacon, and country ham.

Other restaurants within easy driving distance of the inn are Bludau's in Hamilton, a dozen miles to the south; it is run by a German who serves a downtown menu—escargots, oysters Rockefeller, beef Wellington—in a house dating from 1870. A dozen miles to the north, in LaGrange, there's an 1893 Victorian mansion decorated to fit the period and converted to a luncheon-dinner restaurant with an American menu.

But the Mountain Top Inn also has excellent food—steaks, lobster, crab, fish, and fowl for dinner, and a variety of sandwiches for lunch, including a "Cuban"—expertly prepared by someone who ought to know. Cuban-born Adalberto Mohar is the inn's general manager, chief chef, and all-around hard worker. He started as chef here in 1972 and has been running things on top of this mountain since 1976. Mohar is another success story of a Cuban who fled Castro to carve out a new career in his adopted country. His Spanish accent isn't exactly what one expects to find in the foothills of the Appalachians, but it gives credibility to the *arroz con pollo,* black beans and rice, and paella on the Sunday buffet.

162

MOUNTAIN TOP INN, P.O. Box 147, Highway 190, Pine Mountain, Georgia 31822. Telephone: (404) 663-4719. Accommodations: 20 rooms; single and twin beds; seven chalet units with three bedrooms and kitchens; all with a private bath and television but no telephone. Rates: inexpensive to moderate. Meal service: breakfast, lunch, and dinner. Bar service: wine and beer only. Children and pets welcome. Cards: V. Open all year except for two weeks in early January.
Getting there: Pine Mountain is about 80 miles southwest of Atlanta, the same distance from Macon, and 27 miles north of Columbus via U.S. Route 27. At Pine Mountain take Route 190 east seven miles to the sign and drive into the woods a mile to the inn.

DE LOFFRE HOUSE
Columbus, Georgia

The pilgrimage of Shirley and Paul Romo, antique dealers with a great respect for the old, took them from Chicago's suburb of Oak Park across the country to Santa Barbara and finally to the heart of the historic district in Georgia's second-largest city, Columbus, the cultural and retail center of southwestern Georgia and eastern Alabama.

In Columbus they found a home for their collection of antiques: an 1863 Italianate two-story Victorian with a wraparound porch, high ceilings, and a beautiful staircase in an entry hall that now looks like the lobby of a mini-museum. Against one wall is a nine-foot-four-inch grandfather's clock that was made in Edinburgh in the 1790s.

There are other clocks strategically situated in the meticulously maintained, faultlessly restored town house, which once belonged to William L. Tillman, head of the Merchants' and Planters' Steamship Line. Paul collects and repairs clocks as a hobby. He and Shirley are in residence on the ground floor of the home they opened to the public in April 1980; their guests are housed in one room on that level and three upstairs.

They can all meet in the mornings, at the candlelight breakfast served in the dining room and including orange juice, coffee, or tea, date-nut bread, and the morning newspaper. Another nice touch at the De Loffre House is the decanter of sherry and the bowl of fruit that greet each guest upon arrival.

And there's no better location for absorbing the past. The house is on brick-paved Broadway, once known as Broad Street, center of the Columbus historic district, a twenty-six-block Victorian residential neighborhood shaded by ancient trees and lighted by gas. A block away, also on Broadway, is the Walker-Peters-Langdon House, the oldest in

town, built in 1828 and restored as a museum with furnishings of the period.

Nearby is the Pemberton House, a cottage occupied by Dr. John Stith Pemberton from 1855 to 1860, during which time he worked on the formula for Coca-Cola. Some thirty years later he perfected the formula in Atlanta, but was unable to market it successfully and sold it for $1,750—when he died, a collection had to be taken so that he could be buried in Columbus.

Behind Pemberton's simple four-room cottage is the kitchen-apothecary, filled with Coca-Cola memorabilia and one of the two remaining silver-plated soda fountains in the country—the other is in the Smithsonian Institution.

Down the road at 527 First Avenue is the only double-octagon house in the country, remodeled in 1862 and known as the Folly. In the other direction, two blocks north of the De Loffre House, is Rankin Square with its striking array of Victorian structures, and the Springer Opera House, constructed in 1871, remodeled in 1903, fully restored in 1965—and for years known as the finest opera house between New

York and New Orleans. Just about everybody who was anybody appeared on its stage: Edwin Booth and Lillie Langtry, Oscar Wilde and Will Rogers, George M. Cohan and Irving Berlin, Victor Herbert, Martha Graham, Agnes DeMille, Irene Dunne, even Franklin D. Roosvelt.

Today the Springer is home of the State Theatre of Georgia and an active children's theater; it's also a National Historic Landmark. Each year during the annual Salisbury Fair, a Columbus happening that includes an arts and crafts festival, the Springer Opera House hosts "Nostalgia Night in the Saloon"—along with something serious such as the Augusta Opera Company's production of *Madame Butterfly*.

The Salisbury Fair, "an urban fair with an 1880s flair," is held in the most ambitious of Columbus's many restoration projects: the revitalization of the giant Columbus Iron Works and its incorporation into a dramatic convention and trade center.

That center is across the street from the De Loffre House, near the new Hilton, opened in 1982. Close by is the Chattahoochee Promenade, an outdoor museum of local history along the river of the same name. Also on the river is the Confederate Naval Museum with the remains of a Confederate gunboat and ironclad, built at the Columbus Naval Yard; and southeast of that is the National Infantry Museum at Fort Benning.

DE LOFFRE HOUSE, 812 Broadway, Columbus, Georgia 31901. Telephone: (404) 324-1144. Accommodations: four rooms, each with a fireplace, private bath, telephone, and television. Rates: moderate; includes complimentary Continental breakfast, morning paper, sherry and fruit on arrival. No small children or pets. Cards: AE, MC, V. Open year round.
Getting there: Broadway is two blocks east of the Chattahoochee River, and the inn on Broadway is four blocks north of Highway 280.

TELFAIR INN
Augusta, Georgia

Of all the dramatic examples of adaptive restoration that have in recent years distinguished so many Southern cities, none are more impressive than those found in Augusta. As expressed by the National Trust for Historic Preservation, "Augusta can be considered the third jewel in the crown; Charleston represents the 18th century, Savannah the early 19th, and Augusta represents the middle and late 19th."

The wisdom of that assessment was recognized by a local entrepreneur who started buying up inner-city properties in 1972.

Peter S. Knox, Jr., now has close to two hundred houses dating from 1860 in the city's oldest downtown residential district, officially known as Olde Town.

Telfair Street is the main thoroughfare of Olde Town. Named for the Revolutionary War patriot and two-time governor, it has an eye-pleasing collection of the greatest number of historic buildings in the town. There's the First Presbyterian Church, completed during the first year of the War of 1812—and designed by the architect immortalized in Charleston's Vendue Inn, Robert Mills. Woodrow Wilson's father served the church as reverend; the home in which he raised his son is across the street. Fully restored, it's open to the public.

Close by is the Greek Revival headquarters of the Augusta Council of Garden Clubs, originally built as Georgia's first medical college. Another first is a few doors away: one of the first public academies in the country, now the Augusta-Richmond County Museum but built in the grand Gothic style in 1783 as the Old Richmond Academy.

Next door is Ware's Folly, a $40,000 extravagance built by U.S. Senator Nicholas Ware in 1818. A superlative example of late Federal style, it's now the Gertrude Herbert Institute of Art. Then there's the Sand Hills Cottage at 456 Telfair, the first house in Augusta to boast electric lights.

At 349 Telfair is the central core of a group of magnificently restored buildings that compose the Telfair Inn. It's an assemblage of eight buildings with a swimming pool and hot tub out back, a short jogging track and tennis court, and a separate restaurant building where the complimentary full breakfasts are served: feasts featuring eggs and grits, baked apples, banana fritters, and fried sweet potatoes. Guests can also take breakfast on the patio.

Each night there are complimentary cocktails, free newspapers, and always and everywhere implementation of the motto posted by the reception-registration desk: "Politeness is a gilt-edged investment that seldom misses a dividend."

The rooms have been beautifully restored, with highly polished hardwood floors, thick carpeting, bared brick walls. Each of the houses has its own character, as do the rooms. The Jack Nicklaus, for instance, has double brass beds; the Jefferson Davis sports a whirlpool tub; and the Oglethorpe suite a grand porch overlooking the street, as well as a Jacuzzi.

Knox and his designers have spared little cost in making the Telfair Inn something special in Augusta, in Georgia, and in the South.

TELFAIR INN, 349 Telfair Street, Augusta, Georgia 30901. Telephone: (404) 724-3315. Accommodations: 54 rooms and suites, all with cable television and telephone, most with woodburning fireplaces, some with wet bars and mini-refrigerators; suites with kitchenettes; 50 rooms with private baths, some with whirlpools; four rooms, appropriately dubbed Scotsman's Roost, share baths. Rates: moderate to expensive; includes complimentary full breakfast and paper, afternoon cocktails. Small pets permitted. Cards: AE, MC, V. Open year round.

Getting there: Telfair is the main street of Olde Town, and it runs parallel, two blocks away, from Broad Street, which turns into Washington Road and then State Road 28 leading to Interstate 20. The inn is clearly marked.

SAVANNAH

Savannah is a paradise for strollers, the premier walking city of the South, a logician's dream with geometrically precise streets leading to landscaped square after landscaped square—twenty-one of them, just as laid out by General James Oglethorpe, who had a royal charter to establish our thirteenth colony.

The two-square-mile district that makes up Old Savannah—the largest district in the Register of National Historic Landmarks—is a vibrant tribute to those who take the history of their beloved city seriously. Beautifully restored, lovingly tended, meticulously kept buildings fill Old Savannah in a dazzling architectural array—early and late Georgian, Federal, Greek and Gothic Revival, Regency—with history seeping from every mossy brick and aged stone, every twist of time-honored wrought iron.

Old Savannah is where Juliette Gordon Low was born; the home of the founder of the Girl Schouts is open to the public, as are other buildings along azalea-lined lanes, including the Green-Meldrim House, a Gothic-inspired dwelling dating from 1853 and designed by New York architect John Norris. Sherman made this house his headquarters when he dispatched a famous telegram to President Lincoln: "I beg to present you, as a Christmas gift, the city of Savannah."

Knowing what Sherman had done to Atlanta and all points in between when they resisted, city fathers wisely met the conquering Yankee general on the outskirts and escorted him into town, surrendering without a fight and leading him to the finest of the mansions. By the end of the war, occupying Union forces were marching in Savannah's St. Patrick's Day parade.

That parade is second only to New York City's and provides still another reason to visit this Southern belle of a city. Other reasons are the annual spring tour of homes the second week of April, the Night in Old Savannah the last week in April, and a garden tour given at the same time: a tour of courtyards and gardens in Old Savannah climaxed by high tea in the antebellum manner. In April there's also an arts festival, held in the old train shed behind the Victorian–Italianate railroad station–Visitors' Center, a memorable achievement of adaptive restoration.

In July there's a blessing of the fleet in the nearby shrimping village of Thunderbolt, complete with street dances, concerts, and flea markets; the second week of February the city celebrates its founding in 1733 with a costumed reenactment of General Oglethorpe's meeting with Indian chief Tomochichi, followed by various pageants and a children's parade. In October there's the annual Designers' Showcase, featuring a newly restored home decorated by interior designers from all over the South. December brings a month-long festival with special home tours, holiday concerts, Christmas trees from around the world, the Savannah Ballet's performance of the *Nutcracker Suite,* and the arrival of Santa by boat on River Street.

Newly revived with $7 million of federal funds and a good deal of local spirit and determination, River Street today is nine blocks of benches and playgrounds; a hundred shops, galleries and eateries; an exciting Ships of the Sea Museum; the old Cotton Exchange on Factors Walk, named for the cotton brokers, or factors, who bartered their bales in the row of red stone buildings perched along the bluff.

Savannah at heart is still the "tranquil old city, wide-streeted, tree-planted" that William Makepeace Thackeray found more than a century ago. In Old Savannah then as now, there's "no tearing Northern hustle, no ceaseless hotel racket, no crowds." Savannahians are among the friendliest people in the South; they take the time to chat, to pass a greeting when crossing in the square, to help a stranger puzzling over a map.

Savannah is not a museum city where costumed guides lock the gates at dusk and retreat to modern dwellings in the suburbs; the residents are already home, and they take delight in doing what they can to make a visitor feel at home too. That's especially true in the ten inns selected for this book.

BALLASTONE INN
Savannah, Georgia

The name stems from those oversize rocks at the waterfront that are so difficult to navigate if one is wearing nonsensible shoes. They were brought to Factors Row by schooners and steamers returning to the docks to pick up loads of cotton.

It's too rugged a name for one of the most exquisite experiences in town. Built by a millionaire merchant in the 1830s, the Inn is a four-story tribute to good taste. Each of its nineteen rooms and suites is furnished with antiques, and each is loyal to a different theme or spirit though most of them are solidly Victorian in style. There's the Gazebo with its spring-bright explosion of color; the China Trader, with Oriental decor loyal to its name; and the Victorian, with its delightfully handsome little love seat and its solid-as-a-ballast-stone mahogany four-poster bed. A pillared side table is the staging area for a complimentary breakfast of freshly baked hot muffins accompanied with pots of jam and marmalade, freshly squeezed orange juice, thermoses of coffee or tea, slices of melon, and the cherriest of "Good Mornings."

In the evening, when guests return from a night on the town to this super-luxe setting, they will find pralines on the pillows and small bottles of cognac on the night stands.

On arrival, there's complimentary sherry in the reception room, which also serves as a rallying point for afternoon tea. On the wall is paper patterned after the famous stained glass in the Cotton Exchange on Factors Row. The colors of papers and paints in the inn recall those in other historic homes and buildings in this most history-conscious city—Lafayette Mauve, Mulberry Silk, Syllabub White, Peach Leather—and the fabrics are straight from the bolts of Scalamandre, the New York firm responsible for so much beauty in Savannah, as well as in the White House and many other museum-quality American houses.

In restoration, in recreation, in rounding up a dazzling array of antiques, the owners have obviously spared little cost. Their ambition must have been to make the Ballastone one of the outstanding inns in the nation. Their success is a great pleasure to behold!

BALLASTONE INN, 14 East Oglethorpe Avenue, Savannah, Georgia 31401. Telephone: (912) 236-1484. Accommodations: 19 rooms, including suites, all with private, ultramodern baths, queen- or king-size beds, telephones, and televisions. Rates: expensive; includes complimentary Continental breakfast, morning paper, fruit, liqueur at

night and sherry on arrival. No pets. Cards: AE, MC, V. Open year round.
Getting there: Oglethorpe Avenue runs east and west between Chippewa and Wright squares.

ELIZA THOMPSON HOUSE
Savannah, Georgia

Innkeepers Laurie and Jim Widman started their innkeeping career by converting five ground-floor garden suites into a highly personalized series of accommodations. The smallest, named the Pulaski, has a fine view of the garden; the remaining four—the Telfair, the Chatham, the Oglethorpe with its walk-in fireplace, and the largest suite, the Savannah—have large double beds.

That was only the start. After a few years of greeting the public and guiding them to the sites and sights of their beloved Savannah, the Widmans really took the plunge and converted the rest of the 1847 three-story home to an inn, continuing to provide a variety of accommodations—from down-home comfy and country simple to more formal and elegant.

Complimentary sherry on arrival, a complimentary Continental breakfast, and use of the first-floor parlor and the tree-shaded garden are all part of the Eliza Thompson experience—and there's a portrait of the beautiful redhead for whom the inn was named (there should also be one of the Widmans). On a tree-lined, quiet brick-paved street in the last of the original colonial wards, they have created a haven of retreat and repose. But the stillness is shattered each and every March 17. That's when the country's second-largest St. Patrick's Day parade comes marching down Bull Street, just a few feet away.

In the other direction, a half-block distant, is the famous Mrs. Wilkes' Boarding House, a trencherman's delight with a parade of plates that just won't quit.

ELIZA THOMPSON HOUSE, 7 West Jones Street, P.O. Box 1921, Savannah, Georgia 31401. Telephone: (912) 236-3620. Accommodations: 26 rooms, including five suites, all with private baths; no telephones but black/white televisions; kitchenettes in suites. Rates: moderate; includes Continental breakfast. No pets. No cards, but personal checks are accepted. Open year round.
Getting there: Jones Street runs east and west, and the inn is just off Bull Street, which runs north and south between Monterey and Madison squares.

Eliza Thompson House, Savannah, Georgia

FOUR SEVENTEEN
Savannah, Georgia

Of all the flyers and brochures I've reviewed in recent years searching for that special state of mind that defines a country inn for me, the one for Savannah's Four Seventeen has been the only one printed in three languages: German and French in addition to English. Four Seventeen owner Alan Fort—he lives upstairs from the ground-level accommodation—handles those languages with ease, and he can also help out when guests speak only Spanish or Norwegian.

But whatever the language, guests here can be at home, rambling through the entire ground-floor level of a private home built in 1872. The front and back entrances are private, and there's a side yard, also private—guests are given their own keys.

The ceilings are high, the windows look out on the garden, and the furnishings are attractive. And Fort can arrange for baby-sitting and catering. The large kitchen has service for eight, a coffeemaker, and a supply of soda and orange juice.

FOUR SEVENTEEN, 417 East Charlton Street, Savannah, Georgia 31401. Telephones: (912) 233-6380 and (912) 233-3408. Accommodations: suite with a full bath, large living room, fully equipped kitchen, dining room, large bedroom with a pair of brass beds, and a queen-size hide-a-bed in living room; black and white television, radio, and telephone. Rates: moderate, with reduced tariffs for weekly or monthly stays. Pets acceptable. No cards, but personal checks are accepted. Open year round.
Getting there: East Charlton Street runs east and west; 417 is a block east of Troup Square.

LIBERTY INN
Savannah, Georgia

Little cost was spared in restoring and refurbishing this three-story, simply designed clapboard-over-brick structure across the street from the Civic Center. After refinishing the exposed beams and interior brick walls, using liberal splashes of historic Savannah Tabby White, the owners installed cushy carpeting, ultramodern bathrooms, all-electric fully equipped kitchens with dishwashers, a laundry center complete with a washer and dryer, and a Jacuzzi in the semi-enclosed courtyard.

Liberty Inn, Savannah, Georgia

Each of the suites has a private entrance to that courtyard and each has a queen-size sofa bed in the living room, along with a fireplace that burns gas logs. And each has some interesting period pieces along with all the modern, super-luxe furnishings.

The Liberty Inn is a brilliant combination of old and new, a happy evocation of the past with all the modern amenities. It's the result of the hard work and dedication of Janie and Frank Harris—she runs the successful Shrimp Factory feedery on the riverfront; he's the man in charge of the Regency restaurant in the Downtowner Motel.

In 1967 they entered into the restoration business—a highly contagious disease in Savannah—purchasing this house built in 1834 for Colonel William Thorne Williams of the Chatham Legion of Militia; he was a publisher and bookseller and served six terms as town mayor. In the 1850s a lawyer from South Carolina, Solomon Cohen, took over. His daughter, Miriam Dent, lived in the home until her death in 1931, when it became a rooming house. When the Harris team signed the deed the building was a derelict. A dozen years later it was reborn as the Liberty Inn.

LIBERTY INN, 128 West Liberty Street, Savannah, Georgia 31402. Telephone: (912) 233-1007. Accommodations: four 2- and 3-room suites, each with a private bath, fully equipped kitchen, living room sofa bed, washer-dryer, telephone, and cable color television. Rates: expensive; includes do-it-yourself Continental breakfast. Inquire about pets. Cards: AE, MC, V. Open year round.
Getting there: Liberty Street runs east and west, and the inn is across Barnard Street from the Civic Center, two blocks from the Visitors' Center.

MARY LEE'S HOUSE
Savannah, Georgia

Across the courtyard from a three-story tabby-over-brick town house built in the 1850s are some of the most delightful accommodations in town. They're the creation of a bubbling blond dynamo named Mary Lee, mother of three, full-time secretary, innkeeper of a trio of garden and carriage house apartments—she and her family live in the town house.

With plants and pillows, guidebooks on her beloved Savannah, menus from local restaurants, and individual touches of her personality, Mary has created a most pleasant home away from home, one that's reached by following the tunnel of an entryway through the downstairs or kitchen gate under the house all the way to the garden and carriage house. This extremely rare architectural feature is an ideal introduction to Mary Lee's retreat, which is the very antithesis of the standard motel kind of setting.

The floors are heart of pine, the brick exposed, the rafters reassuring, and there are fireplaces and refrigerators stocked with orange juice and cola. The kitchens are fully equipped.

MARY LEE'S HOUSE, 117 East Jones Street, P.O. Box 607, Savannah, Georgia 31402. Telephones: (912) 236-7101 and (912) 232-0891. Accommodations: two carriage house suites, one on garden level; each with a private entrance, bedroom, living room, bath, and kitchen; no telephones or televisions. Rates: moderate. No pets. No cards, but personal checks are accepted. Open year round.
Getting there: Jones Street runs east and west; Mary Lee's is between Abercorn and Drayton streets, a few blocks from the famous Mrs. Wilkes' Boarding House with its family-style keep-passing-the-bowls feasting.

MULBERRY INN
Savannah, Georgia

The newest of Savannah's many memorable inns opened its doors in October 1982. Perfectly positioned in the historic district across from the riverfront, the Mulberry is a masterpiece, its public rooms created from a nineteenth-century Greek Revival warehouse that for years served as a Coca-Cola bottling plant. Now it is filled with a stunning array of antiques from the American Federal, Regency, and Victorian periods. At the registration desk are a pair of Ching Dynasty vases, and on the walls are striking portraits—of Jefferson Davis and General Oglethorpe boldly looking down on the guests in the entry lobby.

Beyond is the oversize enclosed courtyard with its fountain and oak trees, potted greenery and bursts of blooms, comfortable chairs and tables. The formal dining room at one end of the courtyard is filled with Empire tables and chairs spread under a wide acanthus leaf crown cornice and lighted by glistening brass and crystal five-tier chandeliers. The fluted columns used to be in the Savannah Cotton Exchange on Factors Row. The handmade doilies on each table match the cloth on the massive mahogany library table in center stage, and the quilted Vermichelli stitch draperies covering the paned windows and French doors are Scalamandre fabric.

There's more Scalamandre in the rooms and suites, the fabrics closely coordinated with the three basic colors found throughout the

175

inn, colors reproduced by Savannah artist Ann Osteen from paint chips from nineteenth-century buildings: Peach Leather, Haint Blue or aqua, and a namesake burgundy of Mulberry Silk.

The bright burgundy-striped awnings and entry canopy recall the efforts of the early colonists—many of them refugees from British debtors' prisons—to cultivate the mulberry tree as a host for the silkworm.

The Inn designers did more than honor history by its decor: they took the unique step of outfitting all members of the staff in nineteenth-century garb conceived by Southern designer Teresa Crabtree. That means maids garbed in long black dresses with gored skirts and puffed sleeves, high collars, white aprons, and tiny white caps. How wonderful to be greeted by a top-hatted doorman, to be ushered into a lobby filled with antiques watched over by a staff costumed as though they have stepped into the present from the past, to have a wing-collared waiter serve high tea, to have a maid straight out of *Upstairs, Downstairs* perform her nightly turn-down duties, placing mints on each pillow. The inn is a total experience, whether you're feasting on Low Country cuisine in the dining room or sipping a drink on the rooftop Riverview Deck with its landscaped Jacuzzi and a dramatic view of the waterfront.

The magnificent Mulberry is the creation of Savannah native Richard Kessler, a descendant of the Salzburgers, who fled from religious persecution in the Hapsburg Empire and settled on land given them by Governor Oglethorpe. In the 1970s, Kessler was responsible for the restoration and reconstruction of that community, New Ebenezer, now known as the New Ebenezer Christian Family Retreat and Conference Center.

President and chief executive officer of the Days Inns of America (which started on nearby Tybee Island in 1970), Kessler has succeeded in creating a place where, as he puts it, "from the time you turn your twentieth-century car over to the valet for parking, you step back in time to Savannah of the late nineteenth century."

MULBERRY INN, 601 East Bay Street, Savannah, Georgia 31401. Telephone: (912) 238-1200. Accommodations: 104 rooms and 29 suites with sinks and refrigerators, telephones, televisions, and private baths. Rates: moderate to expensive. Inquire about pets. Cards: AE, MC, V. Open year round.
Getting there: The inn is on the corner of Bay Street and East Broad, across from the Trustees' Garden and the Pirate House Restaurant.

OGLETHORPE INN
Savannah, Georgia

What better name for an inn in Savannah than Oglethorpe? The great English soldier and member of Parliament founded this city in 1733, bringing with him a group of 120 colonists freed from debtors' prison, planning to create an asylum for Protestants suffering from oppression on the European continent.

Opened in June 1982 in a four-story structure previously known as the William Duncan House, the inn is next door to the home of famed writer Conrad Aiken. It boasts the widest staircase in the city, and its lace-curtained rooms with brass queen-size beds are larger than the norm, each of them with a writing desk and a decanter of sherry for arriving guests. At night, beds are turned down and a chocolate snuggled into your pillow.

The complimentary Continental breakfast is served in the room or in a quiet oasis of a landscaped courtyard. A concierge is on duty from eight in the morning until midnight and is well qualified to make dinner reservations, advise on sightseeing, and offer information on the attractions and enduring charms of this city.

There's an interesting array of rugs and carpets and carefully coordinated period pieces, all of them easy on the eyes and creating an atmosphere of living in an earlier time, maybe all the way back to the year 1883, when the Oglethorpe was built.

OGLETHORPE INN, 224 East Oglethorpe Avenue, Savannah, Georgia 31401. Telephone: (912) 238-0032. Accommodations: 16 rooms and two suites in carriage house, all with a private bath; no telephones or televisions. Rates: moderate; includes Continental breakfast and morning paper. No pets. Cards: AE, MC, V. Open year round.
Getting there: Oglethorpe Avenue runs east and west; the inn is between the Colonial Park Cemetary and the Independent Presbyterian Church—Woodrow Wilson was married in its manse in 1885.

REMSHART-BROOKS HOUSE
Savannah, Georgia

Directly across the street from the wonderful Mrs. Wilkes' Boarding House is this equally wonderful guest house—perfect for those who waddle away from the table at Mrs. Wilkes' and have to rest a bit before taking on the town.

It's the home of Martha and Charlie Brooks, who have converted the ground floor of one of the 1854 Remshart Row structures into a charmingly comfortable garden suite, one that leads out to a walled courtyard, an ideal retreat for starting the day with the complimentary Continental breakfast or ending it with afternoon tea or evening drinks.

There's another kind of haven inside: two fireplaces with a supply of wood, and a collection of books, including many detailing all there is to see and do in Savannah. The Brookses are great boosters of their beloved city.

REMSHART-BROOKS HOUSE, 106 West Jones Street, Savannah, Georgia 31401. Telephone: (912) 236-4337. Accommodations: suite with a large bedroom and queen-size bed, living-dining room with a sofa-bed that could sleep two, fully equipped kitchen, private bath and entrance. Rates: moderate; includes Continental breakfast. No pets. Cards: MC, V. Open year round.

Getting there: Jones Street runs east and west, and the Remshart-Brooks House is a block from Bull Street, which runs north and south.

STODDARD-COOPER HOUSE
Savannah, Georgia

Across from Chippewa Square with its imposing Daniel Chester French bronze of General Oglethorpe is an 1854 brick and stone structure that has been carefully restored by Buffalo émigrés Barbara and David Hershey. A ground-level rambler made with heart of pine and the special gray brick of Savannah, it houses a single suite filled with wicker and American antiques. In front of one of the two fireplaces is a splendid sofa, and in the kitchen is a full service for eight. Out back is a well-tended sunken garden.

Wine greets the guest on arrival, and a Continental breakfast is included in the tariff for this in-town, convenient-to-everything apartment, ideal for a family with children or for two couples.

STODDARD-COOPER HOUSE, 19 West Perry Street, Savannah, Georgia 31401. Telephones: (912) 233-6809 and (912) 234-5305. Accommodations: two bedrooms, one with king-size bed, one with twin beds; large living room, dressing room, bath, and kitchen; telephone and cable color television; large closets. Rates: moderate to expensive; includes Continental breakfast; special rates for weekly or monthly stay; 30 percent required as a deposit when making reservations. No pets. No cards, but personal checks are accepted. Open year round. *Getting there:* West Perry Street is on the south side of Chippewa Square, which is intersected by Bull Street.

17 HUNDRED 90 INN
Savannah, Georgia

German-born Chris Juergensen was one of the pioneers in Savannah's inn revolution, transforming the second and third floors of a pair of Federal-style houses built in the 1820s and 1890s on foundations going back to 1790, utilizing the skills learned during a decade of working in the hotel buisiness in this country and abroad.

There's personalized check-in, and the guest is escorted to the room. A button is pushed, and *voilà!* the gas-fired logs in the fireplace light up (in twelve of the fourteen rooms). Fresh flowers, a green plant, and a bottle of wine are in place, and at night, when returning to the rooms, guests will find the bed turned down, fresh towels, and on the

pillow a delicate little napkin with a chocolate mint and this message:
"The Staff of 17 Hundred 90 Wishes You Good Night."

Before retiring the guest fills out the morning card, placing it
outside the door to indicate wake-up time. Ten minutes after the
appointed hour, the complimentary breakfast of orange juice, pastries,
and coffee or tea is delivered, along with copies of the Savannah
morning paper and the *Wall Street Journal.*

Juergenson and his staff have been pleasing visitors in this
manner since March 1979. That's when they finished the furnishing
and restoration of the two floors, employing local design talents to fill
the rooms with antiques and brass beds and to coordinate the carpet,
wallpaper, and drapery colors using historically documented paints
and Scalamandre fabrics. One of the rooms has a skylight and mirror
cover controlled by a bedside switch—I've been told that's a popular
accommodation for weekenders from Atlanta.

The rooms ramble over the 17 Hundred 90 restaurant, which
Juergenson and his partners, Klaus Jackel and Franz Auer, opened in
mid-1976. It quickly became established as the class act in town,
termed by *Gourmet* magazine "Savannah's most elegant restaurant."
After chef Albert departed to open his own place in town in 1979, the
kitchen had some consistency problems, but at last report those were
solved and the restaurant is once again something to recommend, even
though local competition has become stiffer.

The inn and restaurant are a block from the Davenport House,
the first home restored by the Historic Savannah city-savers. A classic

180

Federal brick structure, it dates from 1820 and is filled with Davenport china and a stunning collection of nineteenth-century antiques. Also a block away is the Owens-Thomas House designed by William Jay in 1816. It's one of the finest examples of English Regency architecture in America. Both houses are open to the public.

17 HUNDRED 90 INN, 307 East President Street, Savannah, Georgia 31401. Telephone: (912) 236-7122. Accommodations: 14 rooms and two suites (each with a living-dining room, kitchen, two bedrooms), all with private baths, telephones, and color televisions. Rates: expensive; includes complimentary Continental breakfast and morning papers. No children or pets. Cards: AE, MC, V. Open year round.
Getting there: East President Street runs east and west between Wright and Oglethorpe squares; the inn is on the corner of President and Lincoln streets.

GREYFIELD INN
Cumberland Island, Georgia

Tucked into a grove of towering, stately oaks is the ultimate inn-escape from the real world: a three-story mansion lovingly tended by the descendants of those who built it at the turn of the century—the Carnegie clan. It originally served as a hunting lodge for the Carnegie estate, which covered most of the 16-mile-long and 3-mile-wide Sea Island, southernmost of the barriers that defend the mainland from New Jersey to Florida.

The Carnegie on Cumberland was Thomas, brother of financial tycoon Andrew, but he died shortly after realizing his dream of a castle home, complete with an indoor squash court and swimming pool. It was built near the site of another mansion, a four-story structure made of the locally quarried tabby and constructed by the widow of Revolutionary War hero Gen. Nathanael Greene. She called her island home Dungeness, the name Carnegie adopted to christen his Victorian ramble of a multilevel mansion. The ruins of the second Dungeness can still be seen, along with the remains of the Dungeness cemetery, once the resting place of Revolutionary War Gen. Lighthorse Harry Lee. He died on the island while visiting his comrade-in-arms, General Greene; in 1913 he was reinterred at Washington and Lee University in Lexington, Virginia—there to lie in a splendid memorial next to his son, Gen. Robert E. Lee.

The ruins and the cemetery are now part of the Cumberland Island National Seashore, established in 1972 and including some 85 percent of the island, which is lush with palmettos, willows, laurels, live oaks, red bays, holly, and longleaf and loblolly pine. The animal population includes raccoons, mink and otter, deer, squirrels, and alligators; terns and sanderlings swoop along the surf, which gently sweeps in across the unspoiled beaches, rich with shells. A variety of ducks make Cumberland one of their migratory stops.

The old Carnegie hunting lodge, known as Greyfield Inn since 1966, still houses occasional hunters who come to bag their limit. The inn has only a half dozen accommodations but tons of history and the aura of another time. Entering the inn after ascending the grand stone staircase, one has the distinct impression that the original owners have just stepped out for a moment, leaving all their books on the library shelves, their paintings and gilt mirrors on the walls, their island mementos—plumes and skulls of loggerhead turtles—scattered here and there.

On one wall is a photo of a young man clad in loin cloth and shooting out to sea; on another is a stunning portrait of a young woman, gypsy kerchief around her head, hunting knife slung at her side. They are Robert and Lucy Ferguson. Robert died a few years back, but Lucy Ricketson Ferguson is alive and well, in her eighties and living in a house not far from the inn.

Lucy is one of the most unforgettable individuals I've ever met. She nurses sick turkeys back to health in one of the rooms in her house. Another room is decorated with oversize rattlesnake skins tacked on the walls. Her outside pens are filled with fowl and a few animals, adding to the total of wildlife on the island, where twenty-six varieties of animals and some 323 species of birds have been identified. She is an indomitable soul who whips around the island on a jeep, standing firm against the encroachments of the National Park Service and overseeing the activities at Greyfield. A granddaughter of Thomas Carnegie, she's lived at Greyfield most of her life, and her spirit permeates the island from surf to salt marsh.

The eight to ten guests who find their way to this Shangri-la come to hike the fifty miles of trails, spotting birds with their binoculars, or just to enjoy the utter solitude, sitting in the shade of a giant, gnarled oak or on the slowly swaying porch swing.

Inn guests are provided with picnic baskets after breakfast. Dinner is a more formal affair, with jackets worn by the men. In the proper season there's a roaring fire in the dining room as well as in the living room. And the food is excellent.

GREYFIELD INN, Cumberland Island, Box 878, Fernandina Beach, Florida 32034. Telephone (radio telephone): (904) 356-9509. Accommodations: five rooms with shared baths, two cottages; no televisions or telephones. Rates: expensive; American plan includes three meals a day. Bar on the honor system. Children 12 and under, 20 percent discount; no pets. One-day deposit required with reservation; one week's notice of cancellation required. No cards; personal checks are accepted. Open all year.

Getting there: The inn is reached by air-taxi from Jacksonville International Airport or by the inn's boat, the *Robert W. Ferguson,* which leaves Fernandina Beach's city dock at 3 pm on Monday–Thursday and 5 pm on Friday and Saturday; there's no boat on Sunday. A private launch can be chartered at Fernandina Beach for the 11-mile, 45-minute trip to the inn's dock at Cumberland.

RIVERVIEW HOTEL
St. Marys, Georgia

Since 1916 the Riverview Hotel has squatted solidly across from St. Marys' waterfront, providing a haven for the occasional tourist, a permanent home for some of the townspeople, and a stopover for businessmen involved with the town's chief industry, the Gilman Paper Company; its kraft mill and bag plant employ some two thousand workers, well over half the town's population. For years the hotel was owned and run by Miss Sally Brandon, who migrated here from North Carolina when her brother George bought some local timberlands. At her side, and eventually succeeding her, were two maiden sisters, Miss Semora, who was also the cashier of the Bank of Camden County, and Miss Ethel, an enthusiastic collector of antiques.

During its long history, the Riverview has welcomed its share of celebrities. Pulitzer Prize-winning author Marjorie Kinnan Rawlings came up from her Florida retreat to enjoy the setting and the hospitality of the sisters. Senator Richard Russell was here during the First World War. And in the 1930s nationally syndicated cartoonist Roy Crane was a long-time guest, immortalizing the hotel and the town's Toonerville Trolley in his Wash Tubbs comic strip; the trolley, built in the 1920s on a model-T truck chassis, was the main means of transportation between St. Marys and Kingsland's rail junction.

When the Brandon sisters retired, a nephew and his wife ran the hotel for a time, but it was a losing proposition, and they shuttered its doors. The Riverview joined the rows of buildings in town needing the care given to other local historic structures such as the Presbyterian

Church, built in 1808, the oldest continuously used church building in Georgia.

A derelict for more than a decade, the Riverview was finally restored and reopened in 1977 by another Brandon, the son of the manager who had closed it. Richard Brandon was raised in the hotel and remembers very well his two maiden aunts. And though he left St. Marys he never forgot the hotel and its special setting across from the shrimp boats; nor did he forget his hometown and its long, sometimes colorful history. The town's origins go back to the Spanish; Yankee gunboats once invaded the settlement, and it claims its own Acadian refugees. Not all of Evangeline's kinfolk who were forced to flee Nova Scotia wound up in Louisiana's Cajun Country, as can be seen by the tombstones in the Oak Grove Cemetery.

Richard Brandon returned to St. Marys as a doctor, with a successful practice in Fort Myers, Florida. He and his wife Margaret made their restoration of the hotel a total labor of love, plunging into the tasks with great determination and energy. They refurbished all the rooms with solid, heavy furniture, modernized the bathrooms, and added a bar, lounge, and restaurant specializing in steaks and fresh seafood. They replastered the exterior so that it looks like that ancient mixture of tabby, seashell, and lime. And they even paid for the landscaping of the median strip in front. Today the hotel with its wide hallways and high ceilings sparkles with Victorian elegance.

Across the street the National Park Service Center runs ferryboats to and from Cumberland Island, 85 percent of which has been a national seashore since 1972. It's the most accessible of Georgia's undeveloped Golden Isles, and also the largest. (The ferry leaves at 9:15 am and 1:45 pm Thursday through Monday, returning at 1 pm and 5:30 pm.) The boats cross the Cumberland Sound to the Park Service dock at the southern end of the island where there's limitless swimming and hiking on an eighteen-mile-long, three-mile-wide stretch of sand covered with salt marsh grass and glens of cedar and oak. The island is the former stamping grounds of ancient Indians (they called it Tacatacaru or "Beautiful Island") and the home of Revolutionary War hero Nathanael Greene. Robert E. Lee's father, Light Horse Harry Lee, died on the island while visiting Greene's estate in 1818. On the foundations of Greene's estate, Andrew Carnegie's brother Thomas built a three-story, thirty-room mansion, Dungeness, in the 1880s, living and entertaining in the grand Gilded Age manner. But all that remains for the hiker to see today are the ruins of walls and chimneys.

RIVERVIEW HOTEL, 105 Osborne Street, St. Marys, Georgia 31558. Telephone: (912) 882-3242. Accommodations: 18 rooms, nine with double beds and nine with two double beds; all with a private bath and television but no telephone. Rates: inexpensive. Meal service: breakfast and dinner. Full bar service. Children welcome; pets not allowed. Cards: AE, MC, V. Open all year.

Getting there: From I-95 take the St. Marys exit, State Highway 40, and follow it nine miles to town. Highway 40 swings into Osborne Street, which goes to the waterfront. The hotel is at the end of the road, on the right-hand side.

FLORIDA

WAKULLA SPRINGS HOTEL
Wakulla Springs, Florida

Wakulla is a nineteenth-century adaptation of a Creek Indian word that means "mystery" or "mysteries of strange water," an apt name for the world's largest and deepest (185 feet) spring. More than 600,000 gallons of water a minute pour forth from its sapphire-blue surroundings and brightly hued limestone heart. Complete skeletons of mastodons and bones from other prehistoric animals who roamed the Southeast during the glacier period have been recovered from the depths of the basin of the springs, where guests now swim and ride around in glass-bottom boats.

There's also a jungle cruise along the Wakulla River that is like no other boat ride in Florida. Hundreds of fish glide past while the shoreline parades a full panoply of the Florida wilderness. There are alligators of all sizes, from the tiny striped babies to the monsters reposing as though long dead; and an abundance of anhingas, that efficient fish-catcher often called the snakebird, who, lacking oil in his plumage, has to perch on shore and hang out his feathers to dry before taking wing. There are cottonmouths coiled on dead logs, turtles, a multitude of white ibis and egrets, purple gallinules, herons, ospreys, and a vast variety of ducks. The brown and white mottled limpkin is found here, piercing the night with its eerie wail, a cry of sadness that sounds like a woman lost forever in the swamps.

By the springs, along the river, in the pine flatlands and hardwood hammocks, the area is a bird-watcher's paradise—there have been 154 confirmed sightings. It's all part of the fenced-in, four-thousand-acre Edward Ball Wildlife Sanctuary, registered by the Department of Interior as a Natural Landmark "possessing exceptional value in illustrating the natural history of the United States." There are another

4,000 acres of sanctuary outside the fence and an additional 80,000 acres of St. Joe Paper Company forest. Ten miles to the south is the 100,000-acre St. Mark's National Wildlife Refuge, and to the west, almost 560,000 acres of the Apalachicola National Forest. These form ideal natural neighbors for a vast virgin forest monument to the late Edward Ball, that sometimes feisty but always gentlemanly practical-minded genius of an entrepreneur. In forty-three years as chief trustee of the twenty-seven-million-dollar Alfred I. Du Pont estate, he turned it into a world-wide empire exceeding $1 billion. In the early 1930s Ball bought Wakulla Springs and built a splendid two-story hotel.

Ball designed the building himself and took no shortcuts. Tennessee marble was used for all the floors, stairs, baseboards, offices and bathrooms. Moorish grillwork and Spanish tiles were installed, and pecky cypress was used for the ceiling of a great porch that faces the springs a few hundred feet away. In the lobby, with its baronial stone fireplace, there are marble tables from Italy and France, including some with checkerboard inlays—a favorite with the younger set who like those oversize checkers. The ceiling was painted in an intricate design honoring the history of the site—designs from the Aztecs and Toltecs who explored the area, the Timucuans and Creeks who lived here, and the Spanish who established their settlement at St. Marks in 1539.

Ed Ball built well. Everywhere in his hotel there is the sense of permanence, of enduring quality. The design is Spanish Mission, but the ambience is European Grand Hotel without the pseudo-elegance and the bustle. At one end of the great lobby is a gift store with a sixty-foot soda fountain made of marble. At the other is the grand dining room, a sea of crisp white napery morning, noon, and night. It is run by a veteran staff who keep busy shucking oysters fresh from nearby Apalachicola, brewing the heartiest of navy bean soups, baking ham and frying chicken with Southern soul, and turning out lemon and pecan pies and special sugar cookies.

Each of the twenty-five rooms has an outside view, a marble bath, a walk-in closet, and furnishings reminiscent of first-class hotels of the 1940s. Flowing from the taps is spring water, the purest of drinks, guaranteed to make your morning coffee taste like some wondrous new blend. It's the perfect beverage to invigorate you for a day of contemplating a setting that hasn't changed much since the Indians first saw it, or walking along the nature trails searching for raccoon, deer, bear, and wild turkey.

WAKULLA SPRINGS HOTEL, Wakulla Springs, Florida 32305. Telephone: (904) 640-7011. Accommodations: 25 rooms; single,

187

double and twin beds; all rooms with private baths and telephones; television only in lobby. Rates: inexpensive. Meal service: breakfast, lunch, and dinner. No bar service. Children welcome; pets not allowed. Cards: MC, V. Open all year.

Getting there: Wakulla Springs and the hotel are 14 miles south of Tallahassee via State Road 61.

FERNANDINA BEACH
Florida

On Amelia Island, at the northernmost tip of Florida, there's a little settlement that is the best of all possible worlds: it has a great sense of history, a time-stood-still assemblage of architecture, a massive military fort, a world-class modern resort, a fishing fleet, interesting restaurants, and thirteen miles of unspoiled shoreline. Fernandina Beach has it all.

Inhabited by Indians four thousand years ago; explored by the French in 1562, three years before St. Augustine was settled; and the only area in the country to have eight different flags flying from its masts—French, Spanish, English, Patriots, Green Cross of Florida, Mexican, Confederate, and United States—Fernandina Beach takes loving care of its thirty-block midtown historic district, bristling with gingerbread reminders of the Victorian era. The old depot, terminal for Florida's first railroad, which ran across the state to Cedar Key, now serves as Chamber of Commerce and Visitors' Center, and a couple hundred feet away, smack on the docks, is Florida's only Marine Welcome Station, which dispenses free orange juice along with informational brochures and maps.

There the visitor can learn the way to the town's twenty-seven-hole golf course, its four lighted tennis courts, and the new fifteen-hundred-foot fishing pier that juts into Cumberland Sound from the jetties in Fort Clinch State Park. The focal point of the park is the massive stone fort, never finished but used during the Civil War, when it was occupied by Yankees, and again during the Spanish-American War, when it was used to train troops heading for Cuba. On certain days park rangers engage in a reenactment of the living, working, and fighting conditions of the 1860s, but on any day the fort is open for touring, and there are nature trails to explore and all that beautiful beach overlooking the Cumberland Island National Seashore.

The Surf, with its fantastic collection of California wines, is a beachfront (across A1A) restaurant, where the specialty is, of course, shrimp. The modern offshore shrimping industry was founded in Fernandina Beach during World War I, and the trawlers still make their rounds, netting a shrimp that is sweeter than most. In the first weekend of May each year there's an Isle of Eight Flags Shrimp Festival, with folk music, arts and crafts shows, and masses of the succulent pink crescents—shrimp boiled, fried, sprinkled in gumbo.

The in-town Crab Trap features roasted oysters, boiled crabs, and broiled rock shrimp. Beef lovers find their land-locked fare at the 1878 Steak House. That's the year Florida's oldest saloon was built. But it was not converted to a tavern until 1903, when beer baron Adolphus Busch supervised the German woodcarvers working their blades on a massive oak-mahogany bar boasting giant caryatids. Those Amazons now look down on lifelike murals of scenes from Dickens and Shakespeare, odd barfellows for all those imbibing their potions and popping fresh-cooked shrimp.

There's far fancier fare at the Amelia Island Plantation at the southern end of the island. Georgia Governor Oglethorpe, on a scouting expedition in 1735, christened the island Amelia, after the daughter of George II, and claimed it for England, although Fernandina Beach marked the Spanish border town south of the English colonies at the time.

There are extensive and expensive accommodations at the Amelia Island Plantation, but for those who want to immerse themselves in the rich history of the area there are two very special places to stay.

THE BAILEY HOUSE
Fernandina Beach, Florida

In the heart of the thirty-block historic district stands this three-story gem of Victorian architecture, replete with turrets and bays, gables and peaks, tightly etched cornices and fish-scale siding. Built in 1895 as a wedding present for Effingham W. Bailey and his bride, the handsome

mansion behind the pristine white picket fence was probably constructed by local carpenters experienced in the challenging trade of building boats. The workmanship inside and out is most impressive, especially in the large ground-floor reception rooms, and the high-ceilinged hall with its mantelpiece inscription: "Hearth Hall, Welcome All."

Diane and Tom Hay are the present owners of the Bailey House (which remained in the Bailey family until 1963), and they have filled their carefully restored possession with a wealth of Victorian period antiques: richly carved furniture, brass beds, marble-topped tables, claw-foot bathtubs, and fringe-filled lampshades.

THE BAILEY HOUSE, 28 South Seventh Street, P.O. Box 805, Fernandina Beach, Florida 32034. Telephone: (904) 261-5390. Accommodations: four rooms, each with a private bath and television but no telephone. Smoking is not allowed inside the house, only in a designated area on the front veranda. Rates: moderate to expensive; includes Continental breakfast. Children under ten and pets not permitted. No credit cards, but personal checks are accepted. Open all year.
Getting there: Fernandina Beach is 32 miles north of Jacksonville via Interstate 95 or U.S. 17 to A1A, and 24 miles from Jacksonville Beach via A1A and 105, the Buccaneer Trail (toll) and car ferry (toll) at Mayport. The inn is in the heart of the historic district, a few blocks from the center of town and the docks. With advance notice guests can be met at the Jacksonville International Airport, the Amelia Island Municipal Airport, or the city marina.

THE 1735 HOUSE
Fernandina Beach, Florida

The name commemorates the year Georgia Governor James Oglethorpe, seeking to protect his colony from the Cherokees and the Spanish, explored the island and named it for Amelia, daughter of his king, George II. Built of tongue and groove Georgia pine in 1928, the two-story seaside structure was converted from rental apartments to an inn in 1981 by a pair of expatriate Philadelphians, Dave and Sue Caples.

They know their trade—Sue was sales manager for Ramada Inns; Dave used to manage a Sheraton. Together they now thrive as live-in innkeepers, working long hours to ensure the comforts of their guests, delivering little baskets of fresh-baked something for breakfasts, furnishing their five suites with antiques loyal to the names they've given them: the Explorer's Cabin, the Patriots, the Scottish Room, and, of course, the Governor's Suite.

The rooms, thanks to a bunk-bed arrangement, can accommodate up to six; in family groups, parents are assured privacy by a separate bedroom. Three of the suites have small kitchenettes. And if you're on a wedding trip, you'll find fresh flowers and a bottle of wine in your suite upon arrival.

A few hundred feet down the beach there's another overnight accommodation, the only one in this book in a lighthouse. It's the very definition of the word "escape," a roundhouse of a getaway guarding Amelia Island's thirteen miles of beautiful beaches.

THE 1735 HOUSE, 584 South Fletcher (A1A), Amelia Island, Florida 32034. Telephone: (904) 261-5878. Accommodations: five suites in main building, another in lighthouse, all with private baths; no telephones or televisions. Rates: moderate, including Continental breakfast and morning paper. Children permitted but not pets; innkeepers will make arrangements with local kennel. Cards: AE, MC, V. Open all year.
Getting there: The 1735 House is reached via A1A from the south or from Fernandina Beach, 2.7 miles from the inn's sign in town. With advance notice guests can be picked up at the Jacksonville or the local airport or at the Marine Welcome Station.

ST. AUGUSTINE
Florida

The country's oldest city is not only getting older, it's getting better! The settlement that celebrated its quadricentennial in 1965 is bristling with more events, attractions, and happenings than ever before. Its streets are the arteries of a living museum; its stones and tiles talk of the British and the Spanish, the Greeks and Minorcans, and the visionary developers such as Henry Morrison Flagler.

St. Augustine was the first Florida stop for its premier developer, who ran his iron rails all the way to Key West, building giant hotels along the east coast. His Ponce de Leon opened in St. Augustine in 1888 after some $2-1/2 million was spent by architects Thomas Hastings and John M. Carrère and interior designer Louis Comfort Tiffany. The style was Spanish Renaissance, and its dominant arches, generous number of towers, quiet little courtyards, two miles of corridors, and 450 rooms today compose Flagler College.

Other hotels have been converted to museum use; the Alcazar and the Cordova were converted to modern utilization. And in the church that Flagler built in 1889, the Flagler Memorial Presbyterian, there are still afternoon organ recitals. The family crypt is in a small chapel of the church.

Across town, flanking the Plaza de la Constitucion, laid out in accordance with a decree by the Spanish King Philip II, are two other churches of note: the beautiful cathedral of St. Augustine erected in the eighteenth century, and Trinity Episcopal, the first Episcopal church established in the state after the territory was purchased from Spain in 1821.

The Spanish era is recaptured beautifully in the buildings that make up San Agustin Antiguo, the restored eighteenth-century Spanish colonial village. This project is sponsored by the local Preservation Board, which oversees the staffing of the various homes and shops where guides and artisans carefully explain the lifestyle of the pioneers and demonstrate net-making, cabinetmaking, weaving and spinning, and the crafts of silversmith and blacksmith. Small gardens are planted with the same kind of produce and tended with the same kind of tools as were used by the Spanish.

St. Augustine is full of delights for strollers: walking across the magnificent Bridge of Lions, watching the boat parade on Matanzas Bay, making a pilgrimage to the site of the first Mass celebrated in this country (now marked by a giant cross), visiting the massive stone fortification where Geronimo was once held captive, window-shopping along the main street of the old town, St. George.

St. George Street leads to the Saint Francis, one of the two inns of St. Augustine. The other, the Kenwood Inn, is only a few blocks away, also in the historic district. Both provide the traveler a special experience in the nation's oldest city.

THE KENWOOD INN
St. Augustine, Florida

In 1980, after years of search through several states of the South, innkeepers Elsie Hedetniemi and Robert Carr found their dream: a century-old hotel just begging to be restored and revitalized. Built during the years following the Civil War, the three-story structure was operating as a boardinghouse as early as 1886, and by 1911 it was known as the Kenwood Hotel.

That's the name Elsie and Bob adapted for their new endeavor, one which quickly began showing the signs of their dedication—and talents. They started with the spacious downstairs rooms, filling them with period antiques, repairing and repainting. Then they turned to the eighteen bedrooms, finishing the first in January 1981. As we go to press, eleven rooms have been completely redone, and that means Victorian antiques lovingly restored by Elsie's father or Bob, and color-coordinated linens, sheets, and afghans selected by Elsie, who displays her skill as an interior decorator in every room.

A former realtor in the suburbs of Washington, D.C., Elsie is the very definition of the word *ebullient,* singing as she works, chatting with her guests, a few of whom are permanent residents, organizing the Continental breakfasts served on ironstone dishes in the parlor, resting a few moments by the swimming pool. A lover of the old and honorable, she believes that, as she puts it, "inning is a terminal malady." We're grateful she caught the fever.

THE KENWOOD INN, 38 Marine Street, St. Augustine, Florida 32084. Telephone: (904) 824-2116. Accommodations: 19 rooms, 11 of which are restored and have private baths; two with king-size beds, five with double beds; other rooms, in the back of the inn, share baths. Rates: inexpensive to moderate; includes Continental breakfast. No small children or pets. Cards: MC, V. Open year round.
Getting there: The inn is on the corner of Marine and Bridge streets, a half block from the waterfront.

SAINT FRANCIS INN
St. Augustine, Florida

A block from the famous "Oldest House" is a white stucco, stone and brown-trim building that goes back to the year 1791. That's when Gaspar Garcia started building his new home—using locally quarried coquina, a soft limestone composed of crushed shell and coral that was mined by Spanish prisoners on nearby Anastasia Island.

In 1838, after a series of other owners moved in and out of the Garcia home, Thomas Henry Dummett purchased the property. He was a former plantation owner in both Barbados and Florida. After his death his daughter, Anna Dummett-Hardee, operated the house as an inn. Married to a one-time commandant of West Point who was later a general in Lee's army, Anna was the indomitable damn-the-Yankees spirit who chopped down the flagpole where occupying northerners were flying the Stars and Stripes. That was in 1862, and there's a plaque honoring the bold deed in the town plaza where the Yankees were foolhardy enough to replace the Stars and Bars.

Another special woman is now in charge of Anna's inn, which in the 1880s was heightened by the addition of a more or less English-style third story wedged on to the original Spanish structure. Elizabeth Davis has been the innkeeper since 1976.

An indefatigable antique collector, she has filled the inn with an extensive array of antiques and collectibles. Much of it is for sale, especially those pieces in the living room, where there's a television set and homey chairs and a sofa for sitting after a day of absorbing all there is to see in St. Augustine.

There's also a small swimming pool and a splendid little courtyard with balconies overlooking street and patio. Rocking chairs provide additional comfort for those who want to relax amidst bougainvillea and banana trees. Behind the inn the old slave quarters has been converted to a separate cottage.

SAINT FRANCIS INN, 279 St. George Street, St. Augustine, Florida 32084. Telephone: (904) 824-6068. Accommodations: one cottage, two rooms, and six suites, all with private baths; cottage and suites with kitchenettes; cottage with two bedrooms and two baths, living room, and Florida room. Rates: inexpensive to moderate; includes morning coffee. No pets. No cards, but personal checks are accepted. Open year round.

Getting there: The inn is on the corner of St. Francis Street and St. George Street, the main artery that runs straight through the heart of the historic district.

THE YEARLING
Cross Creek, Florida

"Cross Creek is a bend in a country road by land and the flowing of Lochloosa Lake into Orange Lake by water. We are four miles west of the small village of Island Grove, nine miles east of a turpentine still, and on the other sides we do not count distance at all. ... Cross Creek belongs to the wind and the rain, to the sun and the seasons, to the cosmic secrecy of seed, and beyond all, to time. ... "

Those are the words of Pulitzer Prize-winning author Marjorie Kinnan Rawlings, and Cross Creek was where that very special woman did most of her writing. Her home, a beautifully preserved assemblage of authentic cracker cottages, is now a state museum, where the spirit of the author of *The Yearling* survives; in fact, thrives.

And a short distance away there's a restaurant and cottage complex honoring that book, providing visitors with such back-country fare as soft-shell crabs and quail, cooter (otherwise known as soft-shell turtle), even alligator tail—one of Miz Rawlings' favorites. She provided precise instructions for its preparation in her book, *Cross Creek Cookery*.

The Yearling is the happy domain of Pat and Herbert Herman, and they've built their seven cabins on the banks of the creek, a free-flowing stream connecting the lakes of Lochloosa and Orange, both of them superior fishing sites for largemouth bass, bream, and speckled perch. Towering oaks shade the comfortable cabins, and there's a screened-in area for cleaning fish.

Fishing guides and rental boats are readily available, and two miles away there's a state wildlife management area for hunting, photographing, or just watching rabbits, wild turkeys, whitetail deer, raccoons, squirrels, and a multitude of birds.

195

THE YEARLING, Route 3, P.O. Box 123, Hawthorne, Florida 32640. Telephone: (904) 466-3033. Accommodations: seven units, five with full kitchens including dishes and utensils, one with three bedrooms; all units with private baths, color televisions, and air conditioning. Rates: inexpensive. Children and pets permitted. Cards: AE, MC, V. Open all year.

Getting there: Cross Creek is 30 miles southeast of Gainesville on the road to Ocala. Take the Gainesville exit from Interstate 75 and follow State Road 20; at the intersection with Route 325, turn south (right) by the Lochloosa Wildlife Management Area, driving eight miles to Cross Creek and the Yearling.

CROWN HOTEL
Inverness, Florida

There's a 1910 red Albany double-decker from London parked out front, a large-size lobby display case filled with glittering reproductions of the crown jewels, portraits of reigning royalty, a Fox and Hound Pub complete with a dartboard, cribbage sets, and skittles, and the menu features steak and kidney pie, roast beef and Yorkshire pudding, and cullen skink, a soup made with smoked haddock.

How very, very British can a hotel be in the heart of citrus country, or in the middle of nowhere, as some would have it? There's even a Churchill's restaurant, a brass and white-wood room with formal but friendly service and such Continental dishes as veal chasseur; sirloin steak stuffed with freshly chopped mushrooms, onions, and ham; chicken in riesling; tournedos paprika; pork Dijonnaise; lobster bonne femme.

That's not exactly standard fare in Inverness, but the English conglomerate that invested some $2 million in the total restoration of an old ramshackle ramble of wood wanted to go the whole way. And they succeeded, right down to the Stilton cheese.

The century-old Crown started its west central Florida life as a general store next to the Main Street Court House. That was when the crossroads was known as Thompkinsville. But an expatriate Scotch settler renamed his new home Inverness, after the ancient capital of the Highlanders. That name proved more permanent than the location of the hotel, which was moved twice. It also added two stories and changed its name. In the 1920s it was called the Orange Hotel; in the late 1950s it was renamed the Colonial Hotel. When the Lincolnshire-based company bought the property in 1980, they put their crown on the building by naming the meeting–banquet rooms Buckingham and

Windsor and affixing a namesake crown on the front canopy, etching one into the handsome cut-glass entry doors, painting one across the top deck of that grand old bus.

There's a swimming pool out back, and the rooms are furnished in the style named for Britain's longest-reigning monarch. There are Victorian brass beds, lacy spreads, tufted chairs, marble-topped tables and chests, gilt bathroom fixtures, luxurious drapes, light fixtures resembling those that burned gas, and fresh flowers.

THE CROWN HOTEL, 109 North Seminole Avenue, Inverness, Florida 32650. Telephone: (904) 344-5555. Accommodations: 34 rooms, all with private baths, color televisions, and telephones. Rates: moderate. Pets not permitted. Full bar service; the restaurant serves three meals daily. Cards: AC. Open all year.
Getting there: Inverness is 67 miles north of Tampa and 16 miles from the toll plaza termination of the Florida Turnpike at Wildwood. From Wildwood drive 4.7 miles north on Interstate 75 to the State Road 44 exit and then west to Inverness. The hotel is across the street from the police station and the lighted shuffleboard courts.

LAKESIDE INN
Mount Dora, Florida

A short drive from all the hectic happenings in Orlando, proclaimed by local boosters as the Action Center of Florida, is this sleepy chunk of New England known as Mount Dora, named after the lovely little lake in town—one of fourteen hundred in the county. The lake itself was named for a local woman who was kind to an 1848 surveying team. From dockside at Mount Dora, from the town marina, or with one of Lakeside Inn's boats, there's access to 145 square miles of boating through a chain of lakes and canals, all the way to the St. John's River and the Atlantic.

Then there are the twenty antique stores scattered in the revitalized downtown of this settlement of six thousand, which ranks as the second wealthiest community in the state, after Palm Beach, with which it has absolutely nothing in common other than money. Mount Dora has often been called "The Antique Center of Central Florida" and "The Rose Capital of Central Florida." But the description that seems most appropriate is "The New England of the South," characterizing the hilly terrain 184 feet above sea level—unusually high for pool-table Florida—the lakes, and the surrounding forests of citrus. It is truly a place to get away from all the growth and development that

197

exploded on this area with the arrival of Mickey and his minions at nearby Disney World.

Mount Dora is an oasis of serenity, an easygoing spot for strolling the tree-shaded streets and the lantern-lit Lake Shore Drive while studying the variety of architecture. Of special interest is a Charles Addams mansion, an 1893 gem of Steamboat Gothic that now serves as the Masonic Lodge. Stop in at the Welcome Center, which also serves as the Chamber of Commerce and town meetinghouse. It's located across the tracks from the Lakeside Inn in the restored railroad station, a model of adaptive restoration for small cities.

Back at the inn you can rock on the porch, looking out over the swimming pool, watching the glorious sunset, and looking forward to the solid American fare served in the dining room. Dinners offer lots of fresh Florida vegetables from the winter-garden center of the nation, with entrées of omelets, pot roast, chicken, fish, and hot fresh-baked breads.

To work off these hearty meals guests use the shuffleboard courts at the inn or in town, where they are the center of the local action. Or they head for the croquet courts in Gilbert Park or to the Mount Dora Lawn Bowling Club in Evans Park, second largest in Florida with fourteen Rubico surface rinks, eight of them under lights.

Mount Dora is not the place for swingers of any age. The main evening entertainment is found at the Ice House, where the players pack them in with a repertory that runs from *Irene* to *Androcles and the Lion.*

But if you enjoy bridge and lawn-bowling, leisurely chats with fellow guests and antique-store owners, the Lakeside Inn is the place to be. It's expertly run by experienced innkeeper Richard Edgerton— Lakeside Inn has been in his family since the mid-1920s. The previous owner added the three-story section of the main building and the dining room and kitchen wings to the core of the structure, built in the 1880s.

LAKESIDE INN, Mount Dora, Florida 32757. Telephone: (904) 383-2151. Accommodations: 110 rooms; single, double, and twin beds; all rooms with private baths; large corner room or bay-windowed double room connecting through bath to single room. Telephones in each room, television only in room off lobby. Rates: American plan only; moderate. Meal service: breakfast, lunch, and dinner. Full bar service. Children and small pets welcome. Cards: MC, V. Open mid-December through mid-April.
Getting there: Mount Dora is 25 miles northwest of Orlando via U.S. 441. The inn is directly on Lake Dora three blocks from the center of town—turn left on Donnelly Street. A hotel car will meet incoming flights at Orlando airport and trains arriving at Sanford or Wildwood.

CHALET SUZANNE
Lake Wales, Florida

In the early years of the Great Depression a little wisp of a woman, recently widowed and the very definition of the word *indomitable*, decided to open a restaurant to support herself and two small children. Bertha Hinshaw was determined that her restaurant would be the best in the state, even though it was located in a sleepy little town in the heart of citrus country.

To spread the word in those free and easy days of roadside advertising, she painted a pile of signs with the name she had chosen—Chalet Suzanne (after her daughter)—and the name of the town. She then packed the kids in the back of the car and drove north along the highways and byways leading into the Sunshine State, hammering into place her homemade advertisements wherever she thought the tourists would be sure to see them.

Bertha Hinshaw is gone now, but right up to the age of ninety-four she was still making plans for her chalet and the complex that grew up around it in that seventy acres of orange groves. The Chalet Suzanne is a one-of-a-kind collection of buildings that could have popped up from the pages of Hans Christian Andersen or J.R.R. Tolkien, an architectural assortment that should house gnomes and leprechauns, princes and fairy godmothers. No two rooms are alike. Ceramic tiles of museum quality are everywhere—some ring a swimming pool, some are casually embedded in the walls or are used to form a tub or shower enclosure, and others are displayed in and around the dining room.

Here the stained glass and the marvelous collection of chairs and tables, lamps and lanterns from all over the world are as original as the recipes Bertha perfected over the years. You start with an appetizer of broiled grapefruit, sprinkled with cinnamon and topped with a chicken liver. Her special soups (cucumber, chive, watercress, and romaine are favorites) are served in Norwegian ceramic dishes. Even in her wildest dreams Bertha wouldn't have imagined her soups going to the moon. But the cannery at Chalet Suzanne, in addition to shipping cases of canned soups and sauces to gourmet shops all over the country, developed a dehydrated version of Bertha's soup recipes for Apollo flights to the moon.

Meals at Chalet Suzanne are far more expensive than the highland country norm, but considering the quality of the food, the originality of the dishes and the setting, the prices are not at all out of line. Their fillets and lamb chops are as prime as can be found, their chicken browned and baked to a golden shade suitable for a sultan,

Chalet Suzanne, Lake Wales, Florida

their luncheons as bountiful as they are beauteous, and their rum pie as scintillating as their crêpes Suzanne. The restaurant reflects the talent and dedication of those who now so ably run Chalet Suzanne: Bertha's son Carl, his wife Vita, and their children.

Chalet Suzanne makes a unique base camp for enjoying the surrounding countryside. Bertha Hinshaw was not the first person to put Lake Wales on the map. President Coolidge visited the town in 1928 to dedicate 130 acres of highland hummock on Iron Mountain. The park was the work of the dean of America's landscape architects, Frederick Law Olmstead, who created New York's Central, Riverside, Prospect, and Morningside parks and Chicago's Jackson and Garfield parks. A thousand oaks, 20,000 azaleas and ferns, 300 magnolias, and 100 palms were planted along with orchids, primroses, and jasmine. The mountain sanctuary was the inspiration and gift of Edward Bok, Pulitzer-Prize-winning author, publisher, editor of the *Ladies' Home Journal,* and winter resident of Lake Wales.

Bok was following the precept of his grandmother who had told the family, "Make you the world a bit more beautiful and better because you have lived in it." He crowned his achievement with a soaring two-hundred-foot singing tower filled with fifty-three bells. From December 1 until April 30 and again from June 20 through Labor Day there are three live concerts a week, on Monday, Thursday, and Friday. On other days quadraphonic recordings are played, a single number after the striking of the chimes each half hour.

Easter is also the time when another Lake Wales phenomenon takes place: a full-scale passion play, performed in a thirty-five-hundred-seat auditorium fragrant with the blossoms of thousands of surrounding orange trees.

CHALET SUZANNE, Post Office Drawer A.C., Lake Wales, Florida 33853. Telephone: (813) 676-1477. Accommodations: 27 rooms; single and twin beds; three suites; all rooms with private baths, televisions, and telephones. Rates: moderate. Meal service: breakfast, lunch, and dinner. Full bar service. Children and pets welcome. Cards: AE, DC, MC, V. Open all year.
Getting there: Lake Wales is in the geographic center of Florida on Route 60. The chalet is five miles from 60, four from the center of town, between U.S. 27 and 27 A. There is a private 2,450-foot airstrip: Unicom 122.8.

SEMINOLE INN
Indiantown, Florida

It's only thirty miles northwest of Palm Beach, but in spirit and setting it's light years away, a one-street (Warfield Boulevard) town in the heart of citrus and cattle country. Settled by the Seminole Indians early in the nineteenth century, the dry lands of the area they found ideal for hunting and camping are just fourteen miles south of the site of the last battle of the Seminole War, the last major Indian engagement east of the Mississippi.

White settlers followed in the 1890s, and during World War I the Corps of Engineers dug the St. Lucie Canal running from Lake Okeechobee through the town to the east coast; but it was not until the arrival of Baltimore banker S. Davies Warfield in the 1920s that Indiantown was really put on the map.

Warfield planned to make Indiantown the southern headquarters of his Seaboard Airline Railroad (now known as Seaboard Coastline), then stretching from Central Florida to West Palm Beach. He laid out streets, built a school and houses, and constructed the Seminole Inn, which he envisioned as a hunting lodge, a wayside stop for travelers on his rails.

Wallis Warfield, his niece, who was later to become the Duchess of Windsor, was there for the gala opening of the inn, and, according to local lore, she worked as waitress in the inn's dining room and later honeymooned at the inn.

Eddy Arnold and Burt Reynolds, who filmed part of *Smokey and the Bandit II* there, are among more recent celebrities who appreciate the isolation of the area and the uniqueness of the Seminole Inn with its Spanish colonial facade, its tiled front porch with rocking chairs, and its high-ceilinged foyer with bronze chandeliers and a pecky cypress ceiling.

Thoroughly restored in the 1970s when air conditioning was installed and the plumbing modernized, the rooms are plainly furnished, but the revitalized dining room is a spring-burst of green and white, with comfortable wicker chairs. Three meals a day are served, and the luncheon buffet is a budget-stretching specialty with beaten-out-back biscuits, fried squash, mashed potatoes, slaw, and mixed salads accompanying such entrées as roast pork tenderloin.

There's full bar service and usually a full house on the weekends. That's when the locals stumble in after a night of bar-hopping—the street in front of the Seminole Inn is then one long row of pickup trucks.

THE SEMINOLE INN, Warfield Boulevard; P.O. Box 625, Indiantown, Florida 33456. Telephone: (305) 597-2526. Accommodations: 28 rooms, each with a private bath (with Therma Sol, whirlpool steam baths), television, and telephone. Rates: inexpensive. Cards: AE, MC, V. Open all year.

Getting there: Indiantown is 30 miles northwest of West Palm Beach and 30 miles southeast of Okeechobee on State Road 710. The inn is on 710 in the center of town on the east side of the street.

CLEWISTON INN
Clewiston, Florida

Clewiston and its inn have long been favorite stopping-off places for travelers crossing Florida north of the famous Tamiami Trail and Alligator Alley. They stop for Sunday dinner or a quiet drink in the inn's Everglades Lounge, where a wall mural depicts the wildlife found in these parts. Or they plan for a longer stay to take advantage of the central location and the proximity to Lake Okeechobee, the nation's second-largest freshwater lake; the name was derived from the Indian words *oki* and *chobi,* meaning "big water."

Clewiston, known as "America's Sweetest Town," is surrounded by rich mucklands with row after row, mile after mile of sugarcane. On the outskirts of town is the longest raw-sugar mill in the continental United States. The inn is owned by the United States Sugar Corporation, which also owns the herds of Brahman and Charolais cattle grazing in the nearby fields.

The Clewiston Inn was built in 1938 in Southern colonial style, with steel-lined walls to withstand the worst weather that might sweep across the hinterland. Ten years before the inn was built, hurricane water overflowed Lake Okeechobee, drowning thousands and destroying farms and homesteads.

The inn was refurbished in 1964, and solid hotel-like Spanish Provincial furniture was installed. In 1977 the dining room was completely redone with admirable results—a fresh, airy, sparkling place with white tablecloths and ladderback chairs. Friendly local women with Southern drawls serve well-prepared specialties: broiled Florida lobster, Okeechobee catfish, steaks, and pecan pie.

The inn will make arrangements for boat rentals and fishing guides for those eager to try their luck with the lake's speckled perch, bass, and catfish. Box lunches are provided, along with courtesy transportation to the marinas. The inn also provides transportation to

Clewiston Inn, Clewiston, Florida

the town's golf course and to the airport. Tennis courts and a public
pool are located across the street from the inn.

CLEWISTON INN, Royal Palm Avenue, P.O. Box 1297, Clewiston,
Florida 33440. Telephone: (813) 983-8151. Accommodations: single
and double rooms with twin beds, six suites and four efficiencies, four
apartments with kitchens; all units with private baths, televisions, and
telephones. Rates: inexpensive. Meal service: breakfast, lunch, and
dinner. Full bar service. Children and pets welcome. Cards: MC, V.
Open all year.
Getting there: Clewiston is 90 miles from Miami and 61 from Fort
Myers astride U.S. 27. The inn is in the center of town, a half block from
the highway.

CABBAGE KEY INN
Cabbage Key, Florida

"Cabbage Key does not intend to meet the needs of all vacationers." So
declares the brochure for this six-room inn and restaurant sitting
astride thirty-eight feet of Indian shell mound, a hundred-acre holdout
against modernity. Mystery writer and playwright Mary Roberts
Rinehart had a hand in its construction in the late 1920s, and until her
death in 1958 she called this outpost in the subtropical jungle home.
Today it's home to Rob and Phyllis Wells, who discovered their
Shangri-la in the 1970s, escaping from careers elsewhere—she was an
elementary school teacher, he was admissions director at High Point
College in North Carolina.

They now oversee the inn with its pine-paneled walls, rocking
chairs, and fireplaces. The oversize zinc tubs are fed by an elaborate
rainwater system. Thousands of gallons of water are stored in a heavily
reinforced concrete structure, which is supplemented by a tank
towering lighthouse style over the grounds and providing panoramic
views of the island and the sea.

There are five porches, awning-crowned picnic tables, and conch-
lined paths leading to cottages hidden by lush overgrown thickets. A
marina accommodates overnight visitors or those who come over for a
lunch from nearby Captiva, Sanibel, or Useppa. On the weekends
commercial fishermen congregate here, and there's usually a lot of
action late into the night as still more dollar bills are tacked onto the
walls of the bar. There's an estimated $8,000 now decorating the
hideaway, where one expects Bogart or Laughton to come around the
corner any minute.

Hearty hash browns and grits accompany the morning eggs, while cheeseburgers and shrimp salads are the featured attractions at noon. Nighttime means fresh grouper, man-sized steaks, and stone-crab claws. But at any time, Rob and Phyllis Wells work hard to preserve this clapboard sentinel of the past, to honor those "simple, basic values which we believe make life so dear!" A visit to Cabbage Key will convince the most sceptical guest of their sincerity.

CABBAGE KEY INN, Cabbage Key, Florida 33924. Telephone: (813) 283-2278. Accommodations: six rooms, each with a private bath; no telephones or televisions. Rates: inexpensive. Children welcome, but inquire about pets. Cards: AE, MC, V. Open all year.
Getting there: Cabbage Key is off the coast of Fort Myers between Useppa and Pine islands, by Intracoastal Waterway Marker 60. It is reached only by water. The well-marked channel runs parallel to the key, and there's dockage for boats up to 55 feet. Nonboaters can take a ferry at Twin Palm Marina in Bokeelia at the northern tip of Pine Island—telephone the inn for schedules and additional information. Rental boats are available at Trispar Marine Charters, Captiva Island; telephone (813) 472-5111.

ROD AND GUN CLUB
Everglades City, Florida

The first settlers in these parts were the Mound Builders. They were followed by the Caloosa Indians, the Spanish, and the Seminoles. When the braves retreated into the wilds of the Everglades after the Seminole War, a trading post was established at the site of Everglades City. In the 1920s wealthy industrialist Barron G. Collier swept into southwest Florida and bought up everything in sight. He carved out Collier County and planned to make Everglades City into another Miami. One of his first purchases was the old Allen House, built on the foundations of the first home put on the south bank of the river. The Allen House had been gradually enlarged over the years to house the fishermen, hunters, and yachtsmen who came through the city. Collier converted the building to a private club, where he entertained the mighty and the wealthy, including a few presidents—Eisenhower was the last.

The atmosphere of a private club still exudes from the dark brown wood, the pecky cypress dining room, the mounted grouper and tarpon trophies, the deer and 'gator skins, the pillared front porch, the casually appointed registration desk. There's wicker furniture along a grand old screened porch, which is ideal for watching the pelicans perched on the pilings and for checking on the river traffic. Off to the side there's a screened and heated swimming pool, and tennis and shuffleboard courts. At dockside, charter captains and guides pick up guests for a day of fishing the flats and backwaters of the glades. Skiffs and canoes can also be rented here.

The Rod and Gun Club is tucked into a waterfront corner of a town that time has not disturbed much since the grand old schemes of Barron Collier. A brief flurry of post-World War II revitalization was brought to a breezy halt with Hurricane Donna in 1960; the dreams of still another Florida developer now echo hauntingly around the oversize buildings, far too grandiose for a swamp hamlet with barely six hundred residents. But once a year for two days during the first week in February that figure explodes to some ten thousand as the city holds its annual Seafood Festival. Tons of mullet, shrimp, hush puppies, corn on the cob, baked beans, and beer are dispensed to the flocks Collier once hoped would settle here. There are also stone-crab claws, that special Florida delicacy taken from the hundreds of traps in nearby waters. It's also a specialty of the Rod and Gun Club dining room.

The club will also prepare whatever you bring in after a day with rod and reel, serving it to you with style in the dining room just off the lobby. Guests are lodged in the cottages scattered under the trees, rustic and comfortable hideaways with simple furnishings. It is pleasant to return here after a day of boating, driving, or exploring the western gateway to the Everglades: the Ten Thousand Islands, a sea of grass sprinkled with hummocks—a place of special appeal for naturalist and nature lover. At the Everglades City Park Visitor Center there's information on various programs, hiking and driving trips, canoes and bicycles for rent, and a two-hour boat ride into the glades.

The Rod and Gun Club will arrange a box lunch for your expeditions, but if you're heading for Marco Island, forty miles distant, don't take any food but plan to eat at another leftover from turn-of-the-century Florida, the Marco Island Inn, built by Nathaniel Currier, partner of James Ives, in 1856. It became an inn in 1884, but no longer has overnight accommodations. The inn's main attraction is a talented German-inspired chef who cooks up a Bavarian storm of wurst, sauerbraten, kraut and red cabbage, schnitzels, and German farmer's soup—hearty stoking for your outdoor exertions in Everglades City and environs.

ROD AND GUN CLUB, P.O. Box G, Everglades City, Florida 33929. Telephone: (813) 695-2101. Accommodations: 18 rooms in separate cottages, two with screened porches, all with private baths; televisions but no telephones. Rates: inexpensive. Meal service: breakfast, lunch,

and dinner. Full bar service. Children welcome; pets discouraged.
Cards: Gulf Oil Company. Open all year.
Getting there: The club is 75 miles west of Miami and 35 from Naples
via the Tamiami Trail (Route 41); at the Carnestown blinker light turn
south on State Road 29 and go five miles to the end of the road—the
club is on the right. From Fort Lauderdale the club is 100 miles via
Alligator Alley (Route 84) and Route 29.

KEY WEST
Florida

There is more history per square Key West inch than in any other
section of the state. It's the last stop, the southernmost city in the
continental United States, with an end-of-the-line mentality that has
attracted the doers and the derelicts, the druggies and the smugglers,
the artists and the writers.

In the early years, after American businessman John Simonton
bought the island from a Spaniard for $2,000—in 1821—the conchs, as
natives of the island are called, lived as wreckers, salvaging ships that
had foundered on the treacherous reefs ringing Key West.

One of the most successful wreckers was Captain John Geiger.
His handsome three-story white frame house was where John James
Audubon stayed in 1832, when painting eighteen of the 435 plates of
his *Double Elephant Folio Birds of America.* Today the building is
known as the Audubon House, and it's been handsomely restored and
filled with the kind of furnishings Geiger would have had: Chippendale
and Queen Anne chairs, Copeland dinner plates, a Regency wine cooler
from 1820, a Sheraton half-moon console table.

The Audubon House, open to the public, is on Whitehead Street,
named for an early trader who once owned a fourth of Key West. Past
the Presidential Gate of the Navy Yard (the navy has been in Key West
since 1823) on Whitehead, past a living catalogue of American
architecture—wide-porch Bahamian and Cuban homes, many of them
imported intact from the islands, and reminders of the Federal and
Greek Revival periods, the influence of the New Englanders—past all
that on Whitehead is the home where Ernest Hemingway lived and
wrote for eight very productive years. In the lofty study, reached by a
catwalk, he wrote *A Farewell to Arms, For Whom the Bell Tolls, Death in
the Afternoon,* and other notable works.

Hemingway was the first writer to find the Rock appealing. Then
came Dos Passos, Robert Frost, Budd Schulberg, Wallace Stevens.
Tennessee Williams started a second wave: novelists Ralph Ellison,

John Hersey, John Knowles, David Kaufelt; poets Richard Wilbur and John Ciardi.

Artists have arrived in like number, and there are numerous galleries on Duval Street where their works are on display and for sale. Another display of note took place in 1982: gold and silver bars, coins, and chains that Mel Fisher and his divers brought up from the Spanish galleon, *Nuestra Senora de Atocha,* some forty miles southwest of Key West in the Marquesas. The most successful treasure-hunter in history, Fisher has continued the salvage traditions that once were the mainstay of the island, making it the wealthiest city, per capita, in the country.

With its massive brick and stone Fort Taylor, Key West was also known as the Gibraltar of the Gulf; during the War Between the States, Union forces used it as a valuable base to intercept Confederate blockade-runners. In the Spanish-American War and both world wars it was an important coastal installation.

The navy and its air wing are still in place, and there's also been an invasion of restaurateurs, creating for the Keys a wide range of dining possibilities: everything from the thoroughly informal Half Shell seafood bar at the shrimp-boat docks to the formal Henry's, which graces the Casa Marina complex.

The Casa Marina is a beautifully restored hotel, originally built by the Flagler interests after Henry Morrison Flagler took his railroad to sea, island-hopping 160 miles from Miami across bridges and causeways. With its magnificent lobby and carefully landscaped grounds the hotel is a quiet retreat from the bustle and hustle found in the trendier Pier House in town.

There are other special hostelries in Key West, a total of thirty-three smaller places to stay. As we go to press, twenty-eight of them cater to a gay clientele. Here are two that do not, and one that is mixed.

EATON LODGE
Key West, Florida

If you arrive by air and have your reservations in order at this century-old architectural gem, the owner will pick you up in a black British taxi straight from London. And when you enter the pecky cypress doors of the crisply maintained three-story inn, you'll find more reminders of merrie old England: carpets and fabrics, some art works.

The garden is the very definition of lush, a subtropical paradise with winding walkways, a coral-rock-surrounded Jacuzzi, and a quiet

209

Eaton Lodge, Key West, Florida

little lily pond—a splendid terrace for sitting and contemplating the special feeling that is Key West.

The old coachhouse has been restored to provide double-level guest suites with patios and verandas. In the main house there's a ground-floor living room for guests to gather, watch television, exchange Key West stories. Off in one corner is an ancient L. C. Smith Typewriter, used by the innkeeper. Overhead are paddle fans that, with the placement of windows to capture island breezes, help compensate for the lack of air conditioning.

Eaton Lodge takes seriously the pledge in its tastefully designed little brochure that their "Traditional Inn of distinction is designed for those who appreciate personal attention and dignified comfort, like staying with friends at their island retreat in the sun."

EATON LODGE, 511 Eaton Street, Key West, Florida 33040. Telephone: (305) 294-3800. Accommodations: two rooms with double beds or twins, one with verandah; studio with double bed, kitchen, and patio; two suites of two rooms each with double beds and verandahs, one with kitchen; all units with private baths/showers. Suites and studio can accommodate a third person. No telephones or televisions in rooms. Rates: moderate to expensive; includes complimentary Continental breakfast. No pets. Cards: AE, MC, V. Open year round. *Getting there:* Eaton Street is between Duval and Simonton, across from the Episcopal Church.

EDEN HOUSE
Key West, Florida

Lovers of the colors green and white should consider the Eden House Mecca. Outside and in, this neatly maintained retreat is a soft, pleasing-to-the-eyes symphony of bright bold green and pristine white, the perfect colors for this special Key West hotel.

Built in 1924 to take advantage of the ferry traffic to and from Cuba and the islands, the Eden House, under the watchful eye of Mike Eden, has been revitalized, its simply furnished rooms scrubbed clean, its wicker-filled lobbies and porches painted and repainted. Out back is a swimming pool ringed by Rich's, a garden-patio restaurant that specializes in breakfasts of eggs Benedict and blueberry-spiked whole-wheat pancakes, with sandwiches and salads for lunch and charbroiled seafood and meats at night. Beer and wine are available at the outdoor bar, a popular rallying point after an evening of sunset-watching at the Mallory Docks—a Key West ritual attended by various and sundry,

211

including jugglers and magicians, banana-bread salesmen, and the local panoply of characters and tourists.

EDEN HOUSE, 1015 Fleming Street, Key West, Florida 33040. Telephone: (305) 296-6868. Accommodations: 31 rooms, seven with private baths, the remainder semi-private with a bath shared by two adjoining rooms or what they call European: bath and shower down the hall. There are sinks in each room. No telephones; television in lobby lounge. Rates: inexpensive. No pets. Cards: AE, MC, V. Open year round.
Getting there: Fleming Street is between Frances and Grinnell streets, five blocks from Simonton and two from the docks.

WICKER GUESTHOUSE
Key West, Florida

John Moore, a veteran of the hospitality business with both Howard Johnson and Ramada, has now realized his dream of being an innkeeper. With partner Jerry Robertson, in 1982 he took over this quiet little retreat next door to a wicker workroom and store. Both men work hard to live up to their promise that this is "The Conch Republic's Friendliest Guesthouse"—a reference to Key West's 1982 "secession" from the Union over the issue of federal officials setting up roadblocks to search for drug smugglers and illegal aliens.

It is friendly, and it is vintage Conch style, neatly restored and immaculately kept, with a tropical garden, a twenty-four-hour Jacuzzi, sunning decks, and a second-floor porch for watching the endless Duval Street parade. There's always something special for the complimentary breakfast, such as cranberry muffins.

The Wicker Guesthouse caters to both straight and gay guests, and I like their out-in-the-open placard about respecting individual lifestyles in their quiet little haven of an inn.

WICKER GUESTHOUSE, 913 Duval Street, Key West, Florida 33040. Telephone: (305) 296-4275. Accommodations: ten rooms including the Honeymoon Suite with private bath, garden, and patio. No televisions or telephones or air conditioning; paddle fans. Rates: inexpensive to low moderate; includes complimentary "Island Breakfast." No children or pets. Cards: MC, V. Open October 31–April 16.
Getting there: Follow U.S. 1 into town to Duval Street, turn right, and proceed a few hundred feet to the wicker sign.

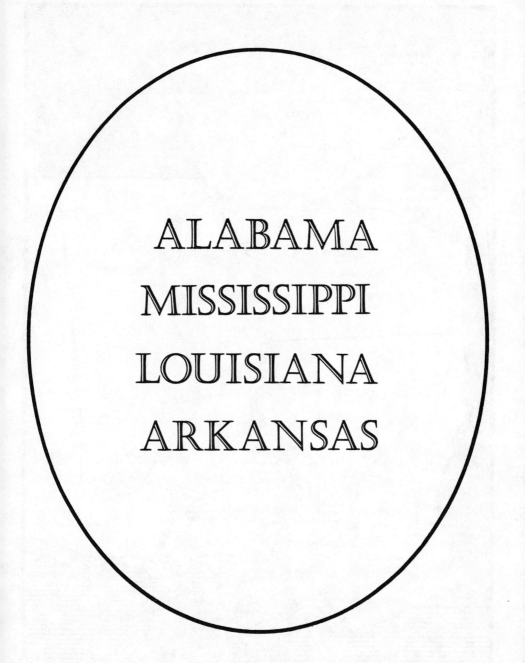

ALABAMA

MISSISSIPPI

LOUISIANA

ARKANSAS

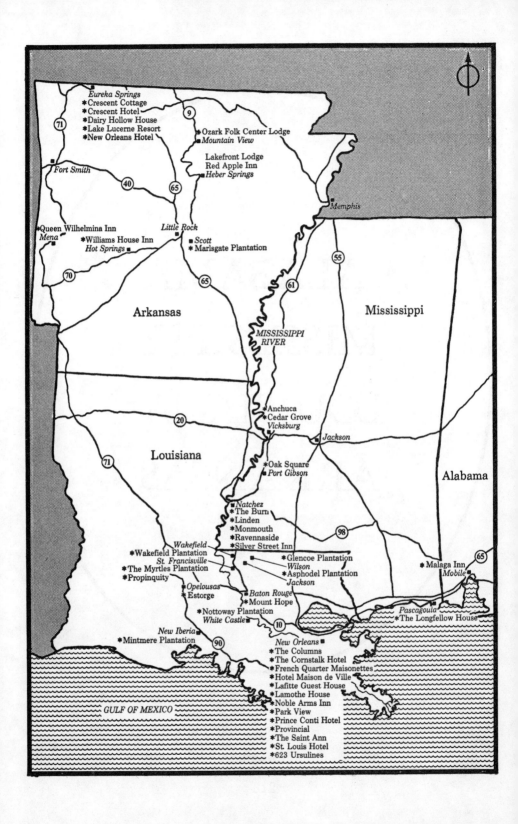

Eureka Springs
✳ Crescent Cottage
✳ Crescent Hotel
✳ Dairy Hollow House
✳ Lake Lucerne Resort
✳ New Orleans Hotel

71

9

■ Fort Smith

40

65

✳ Ozark Folk Center Lodge
■ Mountain View

Lakefront Lodge
Red Apple Inn
■ Heber Springs

■ Memphis

Queen Wilhelmina Inn
Mena ■
✳ Williams House Inn
Hot Springs ■

Little Rock ■

✳ Scott
✳ Marlsgate Plantation

55

70

65

61

Arkansas

Mississippi

MISSISSIPPI
RIVER

20

71

Louisiana

✳ Anchuca
✳ Cedar Grove
Vicksburg

Jackson ■

Alabama

✳ Oak Square
■ Port Gibson

98

65

■ Natchez
✳ The Burn
✳ Linden
✳ Monmouth
✳ Ravennaside
✳ Silver Street Inn

Wakefield
✳ Wakefield Plantation
St. Francisville
✳ The Myrtles Plantation
✳ Propinquity

✳ Glencoe Plantation
Wilson
✳ Asphodel Plantation
Jackson

✳ Malaga Inn
Mobile ■

■ Opelousas
✳ Estorge

Baton Rouge ■
✳ Mount Hope

Pascagoula ■
✳ The Longfellow House

✳ Nottoway Plantation
White Castle ■

10

New Iberia
✳ Mintmere Plantation

90

New Orleans ■
✳ The Columns
✳ The Cornstalk Hotel
✳ French Quarter Maisonettes
✳ Hotel Maison de Ville
✳ Lafitte Guest House
✳ Lamothe House
✳ Noble Arms Inn
✳ Park View
✳ Prince Conti Hotel
✳ Provincial
✳ The Saint Ann
✳ St. Louis Hotel
✳ 623 Ursulines

GULF OF MEXICO

ALABAMA

MALAGA INN
Mobile, Alabama

Mobile's Malaga Inn enjoys one of the most strategic locations of any inn in the South. It sits in the shadow of a multimillion-dollar auditorium and convention complex and is across the street from the Spanish Plaza, with its colorful tiles and commemorative statuary honoring Mobile's sister city of Malaga in Spain. A block away is the city's Welcome Center, a converted servants' quarters dating from 1856. Also close by are a pair of free city museums, which are open daily: the Phoenix Fire Museum in an 1859 station house and the City Museum, housed in a rambling two-story town house built in 1872. The City Museum contains portraits of early area explorers and settlers, historical documents, and maps, as well as other artifacts relating to Mobile history.

Malaga Inn is in the midst of the Church Street historic district with its rich variety of nineteenth-century American architectural styles, from Federal and Greek Revival to Victorian and Gulf Coast raised cottage, from neo-Classical to Creole. You'll also find three of the most historically interesting of the area's five hundred churches: the Government Street Presbyterian dedicated in 1836, the oldest church in town; the Cathedral of the Immaculate Conception, one of seventeen minor basilicas in the nation; and Christ Episcopal with its beautiful stained-glass windows. The pair of five-by-twenty-foot Tiffany windows are fascinating specimens of the iridescent genius of the glassmaking master.

Church Street leads directly to the docks, bristling with the masts and cranes of oceangoing freighters, coming and going just as they have since the first load of cotton sailed out of Mobile Bay. It's also the location of Fort Condé, a two-million-dollar Bicentennial reconstruction

215

of the French fort built from 1724 to 1735. The fort is now surrounded by the gaslighted Fort Condé Village with its Vieux Carré atmosphere and tiny shops sandwiched into century-old dwellings. Close at hand is the Mobile Tour Train, a trackless trolley that makes hour-long daily trips carrying footsore travelers in canopy-covered comfort around the highlights of the city.

In the courtyard of the Malaga Inn, gaslight softly illuminates the brick and tile, the splashing fountain and carefully tended plants and flowers. There's more brick in the lobby with its two-story ceiling, glistening gold chandelier, and giant, gold-leaf pier mirrors.

The inn was built in the 1860s as twin town houses by two brothers-in-law and business partners, William Frohlichstein and Isaac Goldsmith. The so-called left-hand/right-hand plan was popular in Mobile at that time, and there were twin parlors with matching marble mantelpieces and frescoes done by artists brought all the way from Chicago.

In the late 1960s the two houses were converted to an inn. A three-story galleried addition was built out back around a courtyard in the style so popular in New Orleans, and the ten high-ceilinged rooms in the twin houses refurbished. No two rooms are decorated alike—some reflect a Spanish style, some old Mobile, and some, such as room 205, Victorian, with a brass headboard and an oversize chest of drawers.

And on the ground floor in one corner of the addition, the owners installed a restaurant. The bar and lounge are strictly Spanish bullfight motif, but the dining rooms with their hand-hewn rafters, wrought-iron lanterns, and heavy furniture suggest the ambience of a *parador*. It's one of the best restaurants in town, with an ambitious, well-executed menu. Entrées include shrimp remoulade, sautéed fresh trout, and stuffed crabs for lunch; steak Diane, snapper Veronique, shrimp Dijon, and steaks for dinner.

MALAGA INN, 359 Church Street, Mobile, Alabama 36602. Telephone: (205) 438-4701. Accommodations: 41 rooms, ten in original buildings (including two suites); twin, double, and queen-size beds; all rooms with a private bath, television, and telephone. Rates: inexpensive to moderate. Meal service: breakfast, lunch, and dinner, except Sunday when restaurant is closed. Full bar service. Children welcome, but pets discouraged and inquiries are necessary. Cards: AE, DC, MC, V. Open all year.
Getting there: Take Interstate 10 to Canal Street exit and Canal to Government Street (Route 90) to Claiborne Street; turn left to Church Street and the inn.

Malaga Inn, Mobile, Alabama

MISSISSIPPI

THE LONGFELLOW HOUSE
Pascagoula, Mississippi

Compared to the majesty of Natchez, Vicksburg, and Port Gibson with their rich antebellum past, the Gulf town of Pascagoula is a booming modern metropolis with deep-water ports, grain elevators, oil refineries, paper mills, and the gigantic Litton-Ingalls Shipyards, the state's largest industrial employer. The shipyard complex dominates a great stretch of the skyline; since their specialty is the construction of destroyers and nuclear submarines, however, there are no public tours of the sprawling facilities. But there are other attractions in the area, especially an old Spanish fort, recently reconstructed to look as it did in 1718, when Pascagoula was founded by three hundred German colonists.

In April there's a spring pilgrimage of houses and gardens along the coast from Bay St. Louis to Biloxi, where many homes of the early French and Spanish settlers remain. There is also swimming, boating, fishing from shore, pier, or charter boat, and gigging for flounder by lantern. You can watch the oystermen tong for the succulent bivalves in the country's second-largest oyster bed and view the shrimp boats coming in. March through Labor Day there's a trackless touring train that departs from Biloxi and covers forty-six points of local interest. And from April through Labor Day the *Southern Belle* (departing from Biloxi) cruises along the Gulf shoreline providing a waterborne view of the sights.

All of these points of interest are easy to reach from Longfellow House. It was built in 1850 on the shorefront, and its past has been wrapped in mystery and legend. Various owners and occupants have included notoriously cruel slave traders, a renegade priest who ran a girls' school, a drunkard from Maine, a ship's captain lost at sea, and a manager who fell down an elevator shaft. In 1902 W.A. Pollock, a

The Longfellow House, Pascagoula, Mississippi

banker and plantation owner from Greenville, Mississippi, bought the house. He devoted thirty-six years to restoring it—both its reputation and its structure—turning the place, which he called Bellevue, into the belle of the coast. It's been an inn since 1939.

Why the name Longfellow House? The once-popular poet from Portland, Maine, wrote about "Pascagoula's sunny bay" in his "The Building of the Ship," supposedly while staying at this very house. The importance of Longfellow's idyll "Evangeline" to Louisiana's Cajun country to the west and the fact that Ingalls Shipbuilding Corporation owned the house for a time probably have much to do with the assignation of the name.

There's not a whit of similarity between this mansion and Longfellow's famed Craigie House in Cambridge, but that doesn't detract from the grandeur of this white three-story antebellum home behind a grand old iron fence. The building now serves as lobby, lounge, and dining room for a complex of outlying units spread across a portion of the fifty-three-acre grounds complete with tennis courts, swimming pool, and a par-three golf course. It's a mini-resort, with mostly one-level units hidden in the landscape. All rooms are constructed of brick, stucco, and raftered wood; the furnishings, however, are typical motel.

But the dining rooms with their great crystal chandeliers are Old South. For breakfast there is excellent homemade sausage and biscuits; for dinner, red snapper topped with a mini-mountain of lightly sautéed crab meat, shrimp de Jonghe, and freshly shucked bay oysters are among the specialties. The Poet's Nest Lounge with live entertainment is a popular watering hole for the locals through the cocktail hour. And for a wider sampling of the thirty-five thousand people who now call Pascagoula home, head for Miss Farmer's, a boardinghouse-style eatery (lunch only) behind Stone's Grocery on Canty Street. From eleven to two it's filled with shipyard workers, businessmen, and local trenchermen stuffing themselves and then sitting out front to rock a spell.

THE LONGFELLOW HOUSE, 3401 East Beach Boulevard, Pascagoula, Mississippi 39567. Telephone: (601) 762-1122. Accommodations: 63 rooms; queen and double queen beds; all rooms with a private bath, television, and telephone; suites and executive cottages with four bedrooms, kitchen, dining and living rooms. Rates: inexpensive to moderate. Meal service: breakfast, lunch, and dinner. Full bar service. Children welcome; pets discouraged. Cards: AE, CB, DC, MC, V. Open all year.

Getting there: Pascagoula is halfway between Mobile, Alabama, and Gulfport on U.S. 90, which runs along the coast. In Pascagoula turn south on Market Street, which leads directly to Beach Boulevard. Turn left, to the east; the house is on the left.

VICKSBURG
Mississippi

Civil War buffs have long known of the charms of the town laid out in 1819 by the Rev. Newit Vick along the shore of the Mississippi River, but others are now learning that there's more than a national military park to visit in Vicksburg. The city that Jefferson Davis called home, the city that withstood a forty-seven-day siege after responding to Union bombardment with the declaration "Mississippians do not know how to surrender," has a marvelous blend of old and new. Its waterfront bustles; there's an active downtown redevelopment centering around the Washington Street Pedestrian Mall with its sprinkling of new restaurants; and strategically scattered here and there are grand old Victorian mansions, a fair number of antebellum homes, a couple of museums.

The Old Court House Museum on Court House Square, built by slave labor in 1858 and now in the National Register of Historic Places, is a must stop for anyone visiting Vicksburg. The city's history is on display, from its earliest beginnings when pioneers tamed the canebrake along the muddy river and cut down the walnut trees on the bluffs. Settled by Americans but claimed by the English as part of their West Florida territory and controlled militarily by the Spanish, Vicksburg after the end of the Civil War was occupied by Union forces until 1877—it was the 4th Military District Headquarters.

The Court House Museum boasts the largest collection of memorabilia from the War Between the States. Nearby Balfour House, on the corner of Crawford and Cherry streets, built in 1835 and open to the public, served as headquarters of the Union general in command. It was also the site of a colorful Christmas Eve ball for Confederate officers, one that was abruptly interrupted by the news that Union forces were approaching along the Mississippi.

The McRaven House, at 1445 Harrison, was built in three different periods: frontier cottage, Creole, and Greek Revival; the last named was the style of the final addition in 1849. The owner of the house was shot dead in his front yard by Yankee troups.

Of later vintage is the Upton Young House, at 913 Crawford Street, built by a Yankee lawyer who married into a prominent local

221

family after the war; and Grey Oaks, at 4142 Rifle Range Road, which was constructed as recently as 1940 but in a style modeled after Tara in *Gone With the Wind,* with materials salvaged from a century-old home in Port Gibson.

At the U.S.S. Cairo Museum the results of another salvage operation are on display: the skeletal frame of a Civil War gunboat rescued from the Yazoo River after more than a century. The museum is near the National Military Park, which is distinguished by its lack of commercial encroachment. The Visitors' Center details the history of the battle for Vicksburg with life-size exhibits and an eighteen-minute film, the latter a necessary prologue to the sixteen-mile self-guided driving tour through the park, to be taken with or without the aid of a rented cassette player.

In town there's a much smaller salute to the past: the Biedenharn Candy Company Museum at 1109 Washington Street. That's where pharmacist Joseph Biedenharn became the first person to bottle Coca-Cola. A few blocks away there's the *Jefferson Davis* cruise boat, which runs from mid-April through September, taking passengers on afternoon rides and weekend moonlight trips.

Farther afield are two other attractions: the U.S. Corps of Engineers Waterways Experiment Station, with scale models of the Mississippi and free guided tours Monday through Friday at 10 and 2; and the Springfield Plantation, on the road to Natchez. The plantation dates from the Spanish era and was built in the 1780s, one of the first houses in the country to have a full colonnade across its entire facade.

Springfield is open year-round from 10:30 to 5:30 daily. And in Vicksburg some dozen other homes open their doors to visitors, but only during the three-week Spring Pilgrimage, held the last days in March and first weeks of April. But throughout the year two of the city's most magnificent mansions are open—for touring and for accommodations.

ANCHUCA
Vicksburg, Mississippi

The name is Indian in origin and it means, quite simply, "happy home." As today's guest will quickly learn, luxuriating in the pool or taking a turn in the Jacuzzi—both of them tucked into the stunningly landscaped brick courtyard out back—this grand Greek Revival memory of the 1830s *is* a happy home. Whether one overnights in the main house or in the perfectly restored former slave quarters closer to the pool, the total immersion into Vicksburg's past includes a full-scale Southern plantation breakfast served in a grandly formal dining room.

The present owners of Anchuca, the Martin Whites, are responsible for its glorious rebirth and have furnished their happy home with period antiques, four-poster full-tester beds, handsome carpeting, gas chandeliers. From the balcony where Jefferson Davis once addressed his fellow Confederates, the flag of the South still flies.

ANCHUCA, 1010 First East Street, Vicksburg, Mississippi 39180. Telephone: (601) 636-4931. Accommodations: three rooms, one in main house, two in former slave quarters, each with a private bath and color television; gas fireplace in one bathroom. Rates: expensive; includes full Southern breakfast, complimentary wine or mint julep on arrival. Pets permitted, but inquire first. Cards: AE, MC, V; personal checks. Open all year.
Getting there: From Clay Street in the center of town head north on Cherry Street five blocks and turn right (east) on First East Street. The well-marked Anchuca is a few feet from the corner on the south side of the street.

CEDAR GROVE
Vicksburg, Mississippi

Cedar Grove is clearly one of the great homes of America. It was built around 1840 for a family, the John A. Kleins, who spared few costs in constructing and furnishing their two-story Greek Revival mansion. A parlor suite, giant pier mirrors, and cornices were imported from France; the beautiful ballroom has the largest Aubusson carpet to be found in the state, maybe in the South; and there's a magnificent carved rosewood piano made for the nation's centennial in 1876. The library still has the first editions collected by the Kleins, there's a Union cannonball lodged in a front wall, and standing on one of the home's fourteen Italian marble mantels is a mechanized Austrian clock from 1796. Majolica vases grace other corners, along with living room and bedroom furniture crafted by the much-revered cabinetmaker from New Orleans, Prudent Mallard; the back gallery porches look out on the largest magnolia tree I've ever seen. Early morning, pre-breakfast coffee is served in a springtime-gay wicker-filled room overlooking that tree and the well-trimmed gardens, and after this introduction to a day at Cedar Grove, guests breakfast in the formal dining room with its gleaming crystal and silver.

Upstairs, next to a handsomely furnished children's room with a unique pair of half-tester children's beds, and next to the master bedroom with its full-canopied four-poster where U.S. Grant slept after his victory at Vicksburg, are the accommodations for today's overnight guests. Beautifully color-coordinated rooms (down to the color of the hangers and the tissues) in green, blue, or pink are also filled with the genius of Prudent Mallard. Out back, along the upstairs gallery porch is another room, the former school, with a grand old love seat original to the house.

A tour of the home is included in the night's lodging, as is contact with the Robert W. Gibson family, who took over Cedar Grove in 1981. They are the very definition of charm and Southern gentility, ideal guardians of one of the great homes of America—small wonder that a young visitor to Cedar Grove confided to her mother, "I like this better than the White House!"

CEDAR GROVE, 2200 Oak Street, Vicksburg, Mississippi 39180. Telephone: (601) 636-1605. Accommodations: four rooms, each with a private bath; no telephones or televisions. Rates: expensive; includes full breakfast and house tour. No cards, but personal checks are accepted. Open all year.

Getting there: Take the Washington Street exit off Interstate 20 north to Speed Street. At the third traffic light turn left to Oak Street and then right (north). Cedar Grove, which dominates the street, is on the right-hand side of Oak Street.

OAK SQUARE
Port Gibson, Mississippi

Fanning out from the south bank of Little Bayou Pierre, the county seat of Port Gibson was the third town to be incorporated in Mississippi—in 1811—the first to have a library, the second to boast a newspaper, and the third to have a Masonic Lodge. When U.S. Grant stormed through on his way to Vicksburg in 1863, he declared the town was "too beautiful to burn."

The visitor today can be grateful for such Union magnanimity. Most of the original town and its suburb of St. Mary are on the National Register of Historic Places as a multiple-resource district—another "first" for Mississippi. Within a few miles is Rodney, a one-time thriving river town, now reduced to ghost status by a shift in the course of the Mississippi River, and Lookout Point, four miles southwest of town by the Bayou Pierre scenic overlook.

Alcorn State University, between Rodney and Port Gibson, was the first land-grant college for blacks in the country. North of it are the famous ruins of Windsor, considered by many to have been the most palatial mansion of the Old South. It was used as an observation post by the Confederates and, after their defeat in the Battle of Port Gibson, as a Union hospital. It was destroyed by fire in 1890, and all that remains today are twenty-three splendid columns standing in ghostly isolation. A railing and steps from the mansion are in the Oakland Chapel of Alcorn State University.

Ten miles northwest of Port Gibson is the Grand Gulf Military Monument, a four-hundred-acre landmark with a pair of Civil War forts, a cemetery and a museum, campgrounds, picnic areas and hiking trails, an observation tower for viewing the muddy Mississippi and surrounding forest. Its restored buildings recall the prosperous days of Grand Gulf, which suffered a series of calamities: first yellow fever, then a devastating tornado followed by the flooding of fifty-five city blocks—the entire business district—then the final blow, the War Between the States.

But Port Gibson survived, and each year there's a Spring Pilgrimage, a tour of the antebellum homes the last week in March. At other times they are open by appointment. And they are easy to locate.

The Spencer Home, built in 1830 of cypress, is filled with

225

furniture of the Empire period; the Englesing, with the oldest formal garden in Mississippi, has been occupied by the same family since 1850. The 1830 McGregor houses its third and fourth generations of owners; the Gage House, constructed in the 1830s, its fourth and fifth generations. Idlewild is noted for its twelve-foot windows and doors, the 1880 Person Home for its Queen Anne style and its stained glass, and Oak Square (1850–1906) for its namesake massive oaks and its neo-Classical design, with six fluted Corinthian columns soaring some twenty-two feet to the third story.

Oak Square at one time occupied an entire city block. Today, in the loving hands of Bill and Martha Lum, whose Mississippi origins go back two centuries, Oak Square and a neighboring house are country inns. The largest and most palatial mansion in Port Gibson, it's been recently restored by the Lums, who treasure the rich history of their town and are eager to explain its past to overnight guests as well as to those who take the conducted tours.

The Lums are new to the trying tasks of innkeeping, having started in March 1982; but their enthusiasm is contagious, and their knowledge of Port Gibson extensive. They are eager to relate local anecdotes, to explain that the chandeliers in the 1859 First Presbyterian Church came from the famous paddle-wheeler, *Robert E. Lee*, and that the equally famous gilded hand with its five-foot finger pointing to the heavens was put there as "a reverent sign from a people who know and love their God," and as a symbol of the pulpit gesture that was a hallmark of the preacher.

Oak Square is filled with antiques. The double parlor has an 1850 rosewood Victorian suite and French Rococo Revival mirrors, and the library has an Empire Chickering piano and an early Victorian secretary attributed to the great cabinetmaker Prudent Mallard.

Guest bedrooms feature gigantic canopied four-posters, heavy chests, and comfortable chairs or small sofas, and the entry hall is a tribute to the elegance of the antebellum South. The central stairway leads to the Corinthian columns on the second level, transporting the visitor to a more gracious era.

OAK SQUARE, 1207 Church Street, Port Gibson, Mississippi 39150. Telephone: (601) 437-4350. Accommodations: seven rooms in the main house, four in the guest house across a quiet courtyard, each with a private bath with the exception of two that share a bath; color television in each room and a chair lift in the guest house for anyone unable to negotiate the stairway. Rates: moderate, including full

Southern plantation breakfast. No pets, but there's a kennel nearby. Cards: AE, MC, V. Open year round.

Getting there: Port Gibson is on U.S. 61 between Natchez and Vicksburg, just off the Natchez Trace Parkway. Oak Square is on the town's main street, a few hundred yards away from the Chamber of Commerce and Welcome Center, which is a good first stop for picking up maps and brochures of the area's many attractions.

NATCHEZ
Mississippi

For lovers of the antebellum South, Natchez is Mecca. This historic town high on the fertile bluffs of the Mississippi River boasts more antebellum homes than any other city in the South. Its twenty thousand residents are painstaking guardians of that heritage, unanimous in their determination that their Old Dixie will never die, that their Old South will never be gone with the wind. Natchez is a vibrant, living testament to "a way of life and a state of mind that return to us in the soft, delicate fragrance of magnolias, and in the languid whisper of warm, spring breezes drifting through the moss-covered oaks of our stately mansions." That is how the program for the annual Natchez Confederate Pageant puts it.

The pageant is an integral part of the March Natchez Pilgrimage, a tour of thirty homes by day and five by the soft glow of candlelight, when the Southern spring is busting out all over with tulips and daffodils vying for attention among masses of camellias and azaleas. The event started in 1932 when the women of the local garden club started hoopskirting tourists through their homes; since 1977 there's been a fall pilgrimage as well, with thirty-two homes on display during the first two weeks of October.

For twenty-four-hour immersion into the white-pillared past, there are accommodations available in private homes during the pilgrimage at reasonable rates, including a few houses on the tour. (For those arrangements contact The Room Committee, Natchez Pilgrimage, P.O. Box 347, Natchez, Mississippi 39120; telephone (601) 446-6631).

But there are other Natchez attractions, such as the seventy-eight-acre Grand Village with displays and diggings describing the history of the mound-building Natchez Indians. The first European settlers in the area were the French. They were followed by the British and then the Spanish, who laid out the town in a grid square of eight intersecting streets, an orderly arrangement for in-town strolling.

Three miles from Natchez is the town of Washington, the home of Jefferson College, where Aaron Burr's treason trial took place. Jefferson Davis attended the school for a time, and Andy Jackson used it as a campsite after the Battle of New Orleans. Old Hickory was marching his Tennessee militiamen along the old Natchez Trace, a five-hundred-mile, one-time Indian trail that ran all the way from Natchez to Nashville. It was the main overland route for tradesmen, settlers, ruffians, and the "Kaintucks" walking home from New Orleans after floating their goods down the Ohio and Mississippi rivers.

For brochures on these attractions and information on homes open to the public year round, stop at the Natchez-Adams County Chamber of Commerce at the corner of Jefferson and Commerce streets. An excellent walking-tour guide, a self-conducted stroll into the past, is available at the Chamber, itself a historic structure dating from 1826, on a lot granted by the Spanish in 1796.

Not far from the Chamber is the beautifully restored Natchez Eola Hotel, at 110 North Pearl Street. A multimillion-dollar project completed in mid-1982, it was originally built in 1927 but by the 1970s had fallen on hard times, its seven stories and 132 rooms deserted. It's now a crowning glory in the downtown renewal of Natchez: the tallest building in the city, and the ideal observation point for looking out, from the seventh-floor Moonflower lounge, across the town, the majestic Mississippi, and what, on a clear day, appears to be half the Old Confederacy. The food in the Eola's Cafe LaSalle is also worth noting, and the setting in the courtyard of the glass-enclosed Juleps restaurant is superb, the seafood salads a memorable explosion from the deep.

Other restaurants of note in Natchez also overlook the Mississippi: the Captain's Nest high on the bluffs with a sensational view of the river and live entertainment at night, the Natchez Landing for informal atmosphere and hickory-smoked ribs, and the Cock of the Walk close by. There the specialty is catfish, proudly praised by locals as the best in the South. The name commemorates the memory of one of Natchez's most notorious sons, Mike Fink, a flatboatman who prided himself on being the Cock of the Walk. The Walk was Natchez-Under-the-Hill, now known as Silver Street but once a spread of Sodom and sleaze, where murder and piracy were as common as gambling and prostitution. It was on Silver Street that the pirate Lafitte sold contraband slaves to the Spanish governor, and it's where the paddle-wheelers dock and discharge their passengers today for sightseeing in Natchez. Silver Street is also the site of the Silver Street Inn, one of five antebellum buildings that take overnight guests.

The Burn, Natchez, Mississippi

THE BURN
Natchez, Mississippi

The Burn was the first of the town's five historic buildings to take in overnight guests on a regular basis, and when it first blazed that trail back in 1978 it was the Harpers, Bobbie and Buzz, who were responsible. A dynamic, antique-loving couple who had previously restored a nearby home, the Wigwam, they took an 1832 Greek Revival mansion and worked their special brand of magic, stocking the several floors with furnishings from their superlative antique store in town. The Harpers were also instrumental in encouraging other owners of historic homes to do the same: restore their structures and then take in guests, feed them breakfast, and fill them with useful information about their lovely city. They even encouraged the Riches to get the Natchez fever and purchase Monmouth, then in dire need of someone with money who cared.

The Harpers, alas! have departed Natchez for different, possibly greener, pastures, and the present owner of the Burn, who happens to be the town mayor, is now overseeing the half dozen accommodations spread out in the former *garçonière,* the hideaway where the young man of the family was sent to be on his own and learn the ways of the world— but with home and hearth not too far distant in case he needed help or ran into some difficulty exercising his independence.

The rooms are at the rear of the Burn, which is graced by a three-acre profusion of azaleas and camellias highlighted by a century-old cascading Lady Banksia rose bush, and they contain furnishings from the late Federal, Empire, and Victorian periods, some featuring four-poster tester beds with an acanthus leaf and pineapple design—the symbol of hospitality—carved in the style of Prudent Mallard, the New Orleans cabinetmaker so popular in Natchez.

There's a splendid little courtyard, a well-tended garden, and even a swimming pool, unique among the antebellum inns of Natchez.

THE BURN, 712 North Union Street, Natchez, Mississippi 39120. Telephone: (601) 445-8566. Accommodations: six double rooms, each with a private bath; televisions but no telephones. Rates: expensive; full breakfast and tour of home included. No young children or pets. No credit cards, but personal checks are accepted. Open all year.
Getting there: The Burn is in the north end of town, three blocks from Pilgrimage headquarters in Stanton Hall.

LINDEN
Natchez, Mississippi

Jeanette Sanders Feltus, a quiet personification of the Old South charm that is encountered everywhere in Natchez, is the fifth generation of her family to live in this gem of Federal architecture, a majestically tranquil plantation home that was built about the time Jefferson was succeeding John Adams as President of the United States.

Shaded by towering cedars and gnarled oaks, Linden is one of the homes featured on the famous spring and fall pilgrimages, and it's on the National Register of Historic Places. Naturally.

The origins of the property go all the way back to a Spanish land grant in 1785. Jeanette's family took over in 1849, and the many rooms, filled with eighteenth- and nineteenth-century antiques, are strategically dotted with portraits of the Feltus family, including one of Jeanette's stunning daughter, who will be the sixth generation of continuous ownership and residency.

The porcelain is from China, the crystal from France, and there is an early painting by Audubon, but the hospitality, the graciousness, is strictly Southern, Natchez style. The rooms are immaculate, and they provide the overnight guest a great sense of place. And comfort. Also provided are breakfasts of ham and eggs, hand-beaten biscuits, grits (of course), orange juice, coffee or tea, and, if desired by the visitors, a good deal of personal advice about what to see and do in the area. Before breakfast, early-morning coffee is served on the back gallery, a shaded retreat with a grand view of the grounds of this historic home.

LINDEN, 1 Linden Place, Natchez, Mississippi 39120. Telephone: (601) 445-5472. Accommodations: five rooms, one with anteroom, each with a private bath. No televisions or telephones. Rates: expensive; includes full breakfast, early-morning coffee, and tour of the house. No children under ten; no pets. No charge cards, but personal checks are accepted. Open all year.
Getting there: Take State Street east from downtown and the Mississippi River directly to the John A. Quitman Parkway. At the intersection with Melrose Avenue, turn right. Linden Place is the first street on the left.

MONMOUTH
Natchez, Mississippi

The magnificent Monmouth was built in 1818 by a native of Monmouth, New Jersey, John Hankinson, but he lived in the mansion only a short time before contracting yellow fever and dying in his beloved home. His grave is tucked into a shaded corner of the carefully manicured twenty-six acres of the estate.

In 1826 John Anthony Quitman purchased Monmouth and, with his beautiful bride Eliza, moved in after altering the facade from classic Federal to early Greek Revival, adding stately pillars and a second-floor gallery porch. He also installed marble fireplaces and made Monmouth one of the grandest of all the grand homes in Natchez, while building an enviable reputation as soldier and statesman. Chancellor and governor of Mississippi, U.S. Congressman and a hero of the Mexican War, Quitman was one of the most popular men in America, and was generally considered to be a prime candidate for vice-president. But in 1856, while attending a banquet in Washington in honor of President Buchanan he was poisoned—or so most people thought at the time—and he died, after a lingering illness, two years later at Monmouth.

Guests today can sleep in General Quitman's magnificent massive four-poster bed. A high-ceilinged room in the main building filled with period antiques but blessed with a thoroughly modern bathroom, it's now known as the honeymoon suite, and guests staying there who are actually on their wedding trip or are celebrating an anniversary are greeted with a bottle of champagne on ice in a glistening silver bucket.

When not occupied, the Quitman bedroom is part of the tour of the manison, which has been painstakingly filled with an eye-popping array of antiques. Among the highlights are the cypress *faux bois* doors painted to resemble oak, the Aubusson carpets, the vases and sconces of Sèvres china, a pair of French bisque candleholders used in the movie *Gone With the Wind*, handsome Adams door frames, front-entry wallpaper of American scenes (including Natural Bridge, Niagara Falls, and the Boston waterfront) identical to that found in the White House. The dining room with its New York Empire table, its Federal sideboard, and a complete set of exquisitely hand-painted china is an absolute stunner, as is the gentlemen's parlor with the Mallard pieces—recently refinished and recovered in an almost incredible shade of blue—that were original to the Quitman home.

Other pieces dating from the General's era are his desk, the gold sword he received from the President in recognition of his courageous leadership in the Mexican War, and the red handkerchief he waved in September 1847, indicating the victory of his troops in capturing Mexico City.

There are other mementos, along with a small collection of Civil War weapons, maps, letters, shells, and swords. They have been collected and handsomely displayed by the present owners of Monmouth, who have poured loving care and concern—and money—into a full-scale, glorious restoration of the mansion and the adjoining slave quarters, the latter a total shambles when they bought the property in 1978. They now contain accommodations as well as a gathering place for all the guests to have their freshly made plantation breakfasts. Other accommodations are a few hundred feet away, in handsome little cottages that have been furnished with great style and flair.

The present owners are the Ronald Riches of Los Angeles and the Mason Gordons of Palos Verdes; their resident manager, an ebullient, enthusiastic woman of great charm and wit, is Marguerte Guercio. She's been on the scene ever since the restoration began in earnest and the first overnight guests started arriving. She is a very caring and competent innkeeper.

MONMOUTH, P.O. Box 1736, John A. Quitman Parkway and Melrose Avenue, Natchez, Mississippi 39120. Telephone: (601) 442-5852. Accommodations: honeymoon suite and ten other rooms, each with a private bath and all but the suite with a television and telephone. Rates: moderate to expensive; includes full breakfast and a tour of Monmouth. No pets. Cards: MC, V. Open all year.
Getting there: Take State Street east from downtown and the Mississippi River directly onto the John A. Quitman Parkway. Monmouth is on a prominence to the right of the intersection of the Parkway with Melrose Avenue.

RAVENNASIDE
Natchez, Mississippi

Historians, hikers, and drivers alike have reason to make a pilgrimage to Ravennaside, a carefully restored mansion now owned by Mr. and Mrs. John Van Hook. For years it was home to "Sweet Auntie" Roane Fleming Byrnes, president of the Natchez Trace Association from 1936 until her death in 1970. "Sweet Auntie" worked tirelessly for her beloved Trace, that 500-mile trail that ran from Natchez to Nashville, a historic route that she wanted to see preserved in more than memory. The map she used in planning her strategy now hangs in Ravennaside in

Ravennaside, Natchez, Mississippi

the warming kitchen, a place she used to call her "War Room," and in the mansion's Trace Room there's wallpaper with scenes of the famed overland route, which is now part of the national park system.

Ravennaside was built by the parents of Mrs. Byrnes expressly for the purpose of entertaining the rich, well-born, and able of city and state, and, thanks to the Van Hooks of McLoud, Oklahoma, the elegance of that entertainment can be appreciated today. Since purchasing Ravennaside in 1973 they have diligently restored the pillared assemblage of architectural styles—some Federal, a pushed-out facade of Greek Revival, a three-story Victorian turret of a tower with a wraparound gallery—to its present sparkling state.

It took some fifty-five gallons of stripper to take the layers of paint off the grand center-hall staircase, now as brilliantly restored as the fantastic parquet floor in the Gold Room. There's a stained-glass window believed to be an early Tiffany, a brass whaling ship lamp that's been in the house since the 1880s, and a variety of rooms for overnighters, including one with a massive mahogany bed and a great wall basin of marble; a room that's all blue, another that's decorated in reds; one room with a bed of brass, another with a bed sporting a half-tester.

RAVENNASIDE, 601 South Union Street, Natchez, Mississippi 39120. Telephone: (601) 442-8015. Accommodations: four rooms in main house, two in garden cottage; two rooms share a bath, others have a private bath; one room with Victorian claw-foot tub. Rates: moderate, including full breakfast and a tour of mansion. No pets. No cards, but personal checks are accepted. Open all year.
Getting there: Union Street is between Commerce and Rankin, and Ravennaside is a block south of Orleans, on the east side of the street.

SILVER STREET INN
Natchez, Mississippi

Natchez-Under-the-Hill, that notorious waterfront hangout of cutthroats and scum, pirates and gamblers, used to be called "hell on earth with bells attached," but it's now considered a model of urban renewal. Not Disney World cute or splashily modern, it is instead a successful capturing of the past—without all the shady characters that once disgraced the town. Today there's an ole-timey saloon (without the trapdoor through which customers regularly disappeared, only to reappear the following day floating in the Mississippi), some shops, the easy-to-recommend informal feederies Natchez Landing and Cock of the Walk, and a beautifully restored former house of ill repute.

It's now known as the Silver Street Inn, a second-floor intimate spread of just four rooms, reached via the "keeping room" with its fireplace and collection of rugged antiques, including a hard-to-find Mississippi huntboard, a dry sink made of cypress, and an early country cupboard. Two of the rooms open onto the gallery overlooking the mighty Mississippi and Silver Street; the other two face a small interior courtyard, a perfect staging area for a quiet Continental breakfast.

The structure dates from 1840, and restoration on it began in 1979—it was then a shell of its former self, but with the aid of the State Department of Archives and History, the construction of the galleries was accurately gauged, the proper colors determined, and the original walls saved. The rebirth of this bawdy house, this onetime "Cesspool of the South" commenced with a trio of midwives assisting: first-time innkeepers Lucille Barraza, Peggie Herrington, and Mary Lessley.

Those energetic ladies not only went into one of the most trying— and most rewarding—of trades, they also opened a women's clothing store on the ground floor of the inn, where shoppers can sip coffee or hot spiced tea while warming up by the fireplace.

SILVER STREET INN, 1 Silver Street; P.O. Box 1224, Natchez, Mississippi 39120. Telephone: (601) 442-4221. Accommodations: four rooms, each with a private bath; no televisions or telephones. Rates: moderate; includes Continental breakfast; kitchen facilities available. Pets permitted, but inquire. Cards: AE, MC, V. Open all year.
Getting there: Silver Street is at the western end of State Street, past the intersection with Broadway, leading down to the river from the Esplanade, the old Place d'Armes. The inn is on the left-hand side of the street, clearly marked.

LOUISIANA

GLENCOE PLANTATION
Wilson, Louisiana

It's not antebellum and it's not included in the usual rosters of Louisiana plantations, but it is a fantastic example of—take a deep breath—the Queen Anne style of Victorian Gothic. Built in 1870 but destroyed by fire twenty-eight years later, Glencoe was rebuilt on the same charred foundations. The present ramble of a structure with its towers, turrets, and dormers, its double-decker steamboat-gallery porches, and its gingerbread trim was completed in 1903.

Opened as an inn in 1981, Glencoe and its spacious grounds have a tennis court and swimming pool, fishing holes, and ample room for quiet strolls. There's a full bar, and dining arrangements are made for groups when reserved in advance. The high-ceilinged rooms are oversize, filled with period pieces. And, as are so many of the inns in Louisiana and elsewhere, it is on the National Register of Historic Places.

GLENCOE PLANTATION, Louisiana Highway 68, P.O. Box 178, Wilson, Louisiana 70789. Telephone: (504) 629-5387. Accommodations: four rooms, all with private baths; no televisions or telephones. Rates: moderate; includes full plantation breakfast. Inquire about small children and pets. Cards: MC, V. Open year round.
Getting there: Glencoe is on State Road 68, 4-1/2 miles north of Jackson.

ASPHODEL PLANTATION
Jackson, Louisiana

Webster tells us that the asphodel is any of various plants of the lily family. In *The Odyssey* Homer spoke of an asphodel meadow in the fields of Elysium. To the Greek poets the asphodel was a narcissus; to the English and French, it meant the daffodil.

Asphodel Plantation is in the heart of those parishes the French knowingly called the Felicianas. Here John James Audubon once wandered, painting and sketching, trapping and shooting. Here cotton fields once brought prosperity and position to their owners, financing magnificent mansions: Asphodel, Catalpa, the Cottage, the Myrtles, Oakley, Parlange, and Rosedown, all now open to the public. Dozens of other plantation houses were destroyed by Yankee troops or the ravages of time, including the forty-room Afton Villa, which burned in 1963. But its gardens, laid out by a French landscape designer, still exist behind an impressive wrought-iron barrier and Gothic gatehouse. The Yankees passed by these, according to local lore, because they thought the entrance, with its mile-long alley of oaks, led only to a cemetery.

East Feliciana Parish with its 1840 courthouse, now a national monument, boasts the largest concentration of Greek Revival buildings in the United States. And much of the surrounding countryside remains as Audubon found it in the 1820s: "Rich magnolias covered with fragrant blossoms, the holly, the beech, the tall yellow poplar, the hilly ground and even the red clay, all excited my imagination. Such an entire change in the face of nature in so short a time seems almost supernatural. . . ."

The modest central section of the mansion of Asphodel was built in 1820; later the owners added two wings and a sixty-five-foot open gallery overlooking their own fields of Elysium. This antebellum house is now the private home of Robert and Marcelle Reese Couhig, who have furnished it in a classic American style Marcelle calls "because we like it." This translates to a signed Chippendale chair, Dutch corner tables, a Mallard sideboard, an 1830 Steinway, a portrait of Queen Victoria's surgeon general, a Limoges tureen, an American-made Empire secretary, and modern live-in rooms designed by Marcelle for utility. These are cleverly tucked into the ground-level foundations without destroying the profile of this 160-year-old structure.

Asphodel Plantation was an ideal place to raise six children. When they started leaving home, Marcelle, or "Nootsie" as she tells you to call her a few cyclonic seconds after your first encounter with this dynamo of restless energy and creativity, started casting about for other careers. Now that she has nine grandchildren, she can look proudly at other offspring such as a quarterly newspaper and a cleverly assembled cookbook. "We have finally spawned in this delightful if somewhat earthy land a group of literate sophisticates who do not believe that dinner is a survival kit," she writes in her introduction.

She has also created a small village of originality in a grove of beech, dogwood, and pine at one end of the plantation's five hundred acres, reached from the Asphodel mansion either by highway or by a footpath running along a creek and past stocked ponds. The central building of the complex, called the Inn, was moved to the site from Jackson, nine miles away. This old town house, with a back wing built in the 1780s and the front in the 1830s, now houses the lounge, the fireside sitting room, and the dining room where Nootsie's culinary philosophy is put into practice. There are great breads, chicken curry, red beans with ham and rice, shrimp given the Creole and gumbo treatment, quiches, and English trifle.

Across the courtyard is the gift shop cum gourmet-kitchen store, where Nootsie holds court for as long as she can stand still. At one end is a breakfast room where grits and eggs, bacon, and biscuits pour forth. Overhead are some of the rental rooms; others are scattered in neighboring cottages that look as though they might have been shipped from New England, the North Woods, or the Carolina mountains. The furnishings are spartan, the decor reminiscent more of a summer camp than the antebellum South. But the appeal of Asphodel is not the room you sleep in. It's the setting in the woods, the proximity to all those plantations and sleepy little towns, and the personality of the lady in charge.

ASPHODEL PLANTATION, Jackson, Louisiana 70748. Telephone: (504) 654-6868. Accommodations: 20 rooms and suites; single and king-size beds; all rooms with private baths; televisions but no telephones. Rates: moderate. Meal service: breakfast, lunch, and dinner. Full bar service. Children welcome but pets discouraged. Cards: MC, V. Open all year except Christmas Day.
Getting there: Asphodel is between Baton Rouge and St. Francisville, eight miles from U.S. 61 on State Road 68.

WAKEFIELD PLANTATION
Wakefield, Louisiana

The Sinclairs are the current owners of this Creole raised cottage with its notable Federal door and its Greek Revival brick pillars fronting a broad gallery. Named for the *Vicar of Wakefield* and built by Lewis Stirling in the 1830s, the twelve-room home with its fourteen-foot ceilings is filled with eighteenth- and nineteenth-century antiques: a Babcock piano with brass candle holders, a marble-topped pier table with the obligatory petticoat mirror for the ladies to check their underpinnings, a pair of matching Empire sofas, a magnificent forty-foot mahogany dining table, rosewood chairs with needlepoint cushions, a Belgian marble mantel, and the original gold-leaf curtain rods. There are also mini-collections of firearms, buttons, dolls. Wakefield used to be a floor taller, but in 1877 the upper level was removed to another site. It was the only way an estate could be settled!

Upstairs are the rooms for overnight guests, four-poster retreats with still more antiques. They are perfect places to retire after a day of touring the many plantations in the area. In the immediate vicinity are Asphodel and the Myrtles, both described in this book; the Cottage Plantation with its hundred-foot gallery and ten original outbuildings from the early years of the nineteenth century; the late-Victorian Catalpa Plantation; and the Oakley House in Audubon State Park, the West Indies–style home where Audubon lived and taught.

Four miles south are the Afton Villa Gardens, a twisting avenue of live oak and azaleas, all that remains of a Gothic mansion that burned in 1963; and farther south is Rosedown Plantation, twenty-eight acres of meticulously manicured grounds with a breathtaking approach and furnishings that are the very definition of the word *opulent.*

The visitor to the Louisiana parishes known as the Felicianas—what a happy name for the area—is advised to allow several days for leisurely exploration and study. All the plantations and gardens described above are open to the public, and there are many more that can be viewed from the roads.

WAKEFIELD PLANTATION, Highway 61, P.O. Box 41, Wakefield, Louisiana 70784. Telephone: (504) 635-3988. Accommodations: three rooms, one with a private bath, two that share; no televisions or telephones. Rates: inexpensive to moderate; includes complimentary Continental breakfast. No pets. No cards. Open year round.
Getting there: Wakefield is 8 miles north of St. Francisville on the west side of Highway 61.

THE MYRTLES PLANTATION
St. Francisville, Louisiana

The name, romantically, is attributed to the fact that a young couple met and fell in love under the myrtle trees, but it's the dozens and dozens of giant twisted oaks, festooned with eerie Spanish moss, that distinguish this gabled plantation dating from 1796. That's when Gen. David Bradford, a wealthy judge from Pennsylvania, arrived on the scene—he was fleeing from the forces of President Washington. The leader of the Whiskey Rebellion was welcomed by the Spanish and given a land grant of 650 acres from Baron de Corondelet; it's on a portion of that original grant that the Myrtles stands.

Later owners improved the property considerably, adding a magnificent entry hall and grand staircase in the 1840s, filling it with superb examples of the fine art of plaster work and intricate *faux bois*—five different varieties of *faux bois* executed by imported European craftsmen. The chandelier is Baccarat; the bronze, brass, and pewter gasalier unique; and the pair of matched parlors with twin Carrara marble mantels and gilded French mirrors a joy to behold.

Upstairs the rooms have been converted to take overnight guests, and while they are not as stunning as those on the ground floor, they nonetheless give the visitor the warm sensation of living in an antebellum home in the heart of Louisiana's plantation country.

THE MYRTLES PLANTATION, Highway 61, P.O. Box 387, St. Francisville, Louisiana 70775. Telephone: (504) 635-6277. Accommodations: five rooms, all with private baths; no telephones or televisions. Rates: moderate. No pets. No credit cards. Open year round.
Getting there: St. Francisville is 25 miles north of Baton Rouge via U.S. 61, and the Myrtles is a couple of miles north of St. Francisville on 61, on the west side of the road.

PROPINQUITY
St. Francisville, Louisiana

Propinquity, we are advised in the charming, highly personal little brochure composed by owners Charles and Gladys Seif, means "close to history, kinfolk, friends, the street, the town, and the hearts of its owners."

Propinquity is indeed close to history: it's the oldest house in St. Francisville, with origins going back to 1809. That's when Scotsman John Mills, who had arrived earlier from Natchez to organize a trading post where Bayou Sara emptied into the Mississippi River, built his solid Creole Classic home, using nearly 200,000 bricks in the process.

Through the years it's served as a store, a bank, and an apartment building, but in 1966 the two-story structure with its second-floor gallery porch was completely restored. Eleven years later the Seifs took over, and they've filled their pride and joy with love. And antiques: matching crystal chandeliers dating from 1790; a trio of Audubon originals (he was a friend of Propinquity owners in the 1830s); American Victorian, French, and German pieces of furniture interspersed with more modern ones.

Upstairs, the bedroom suite has a Prudent Mallard four-poster with a tester, a trundle bed, and a sleigh bed; the other bedroom has a mahogany tester bed with a rare pair of roller rods: one at the foot to roll back the covers, one at the head to press out the lumps in the mattresses, which were made of feathers or Spanish moss. Between the rooms, each of which has a private bath, is a sitting room with a cypress mantel, an inlaid tilt-top Boulle table, and a Victorian swooning couch.

Propinquity is on the National Register of Historic Places and its owners are treasures: she lived in the house as a child; he's retired from the Defense Department. Together they personify that definition of "Propinquity."

PROPINQUITY, 523 Royal Street, Box 814, St. Francisville, Louisiana 70775. Telephone: (504) 635-6855. Accommodations: single suite with two bedrooms and private baths. Rates: moderate; includes complimentary breakfast of yellow grits, homemade fig preserves, and other Southern specialties. No children or pets. No cards, but personal checks are accepted. Open year round.

Getting there: Propinquity is in the center of town, on a prominence at the corner of Johnson and Royal streets.

ESTORGE HOUSE
Opelousas, Louisiana

The Acadian doctor who was the attending physician at the miraculous rebirth of both Mintmere Plantation and the Broussard House in New Iberia worked the same kind of reincarnation forty miles north.

Dr. Roy P. Boucvalt took a run-down, forgotten bit of Acadia's past and with time, talent, and a fair portion of treasure brought an 1827 gem back to its original sparkle. A neo-Classical three-story mansion that, like Shadows-on-the-Teche in New Iberia, combines Creole and Greek Revival elements, it is a town house built by Pierre La Beche with a metal roof, lead flashing, double-frame Norman truss joints, random-width cypress floorboards, Carrara marble mantels, panel shutters, and pivot-knob hardware.

The millwork in the house survived beautifully intact, and Boucvalt has left a section of the wall exposed to show the brick and post construction. In the 155-year-old home he built three suites, modern in terms of amenities but filled with the kind of period pieces that do not destroy the spirit of the place.

Opelousas, in the northern marches of Cajun Country, is a one-time trading post now known as the Sweet Potato Capital of Louisiana, a center of rice and sugar cane cultivation. It's within easy reach of Lafayette with its many Cajun restaurants and its fascinating Acadian Village on Mouton Road just south of State Road 342—a well-tended complex of homes, stores, and a church moved to the spot as living history exemplars of life in Cajun bayou country. Acadian handicrafts are for sale in the village shop.

In the other direction, across the Mississippi River, are the parishes of West and East Feliciana with all their plantations; only six miles to the north is an almost totally unspoiled town called Washington. In the decades following the War Between the States it was the largest steamboat port between New Orleans and St. Louis, but the arrival of the railroad and changes in the Atchafalaya Basin made navigation more difficult, and after the last steamboat transited the town in 1900, Washington steadily declined. But many of the architectural treasures of those glorious days survived, including a good many antebellum homes now being restored. Washington is a must tour for anyone fortunate enough to be staying at the Estorge House.

ESTORGE HOUSE, 427 North Market Street, Opelousas, Louisiana 70570. Telephone: (318) 948-4592. Accommodations: two suites on second floor, one on ground floor, each with a private bath; central telephone. Rates: expensive. Well-behaved children only; no pets. No cards, but personal checks are welcome. Open year round.

Getting there: Market Street runs from the center of town, and the Estorge House is four blocks north of the courthouse.

MINTMERE PLANTATION
New Iberia, Louisiana

Dr. Roy P. Boucvalt is a crusader. He not only gave new life to an antebellum mansion along Bayou Teche; he transported to the site a true early-Acadian *bousillage* house, meaning one constructed of cypress, mud, and moss. But when he finished the restoration on those two echoes of his Acadian heritage he was still not content. He went north to Opelousas, where he bought an 1827 early–Greek Revival derelict on two acres and worked another miracle of revitalization, opening another inn to the public. (See Estorge House, preceding.)

The *bousillage* home, now in the front of the doctor's New Iberia property, was built by Armand Broussard, son of Joseph "Beausoleil" Broussard, leader of the first Acadian exiles to settle in Teche country. The son participated in the Galvez Expedition during the American Revolution and was with Andy Jackson at the Battle of New Orleans. In 1790 he built his mud and moss home. Two centuries later, Dr. Boucvalt rescued it.

The good doctor, an anesthesiologist with a degree from the University of Pennsylvania Medical School, has an admirable goal: to preserve Acadian architecture as a descendant of those who built the homes and helped decorate them. Thus he was willing to move the Broussard House by barge on the Bayou Teche from Loreauville. He restored the original floors, doors, and hand-wrought iron hardware, and opened the house as a museum. He also moved a splendid example of a West Indian cottage to a far corner of his land, near the slight rise of Teche Ridge, the western end of the Mississippi alluvial flood plain.

In the same spirit he converted the Mintmere Plantation in half a dozen years from a derelict slated for destruction into a thing of beauty. A Greek Revival Louisiana raised cottage, Mintmere was built in 1857. During the War Between the States it became the headquarters of the occupying Yankees, the home of the famed Kansas-judge-turned-warrior, Gen. Alfred Lee.

Today Mintmere sparkles with the results of Boucvalt's dedication, and, if the guests arrive late, after the curator has departed for the day, he leads the tour himself, enthusiastically explaining that the Audubon

Mintmere Plantation, New Iberia, Louisiana

on the wall was the great painter's first sketch done in Louisiana—of the native iris—describing the fine little George Catlin portrait, and explaining his use of paint on the restored walls rather than a copy of the original hideous purple Victorian wallpaper, the kind of paper he dismisses as "malignant."

To the rear of the house—actually the front, for these mansions of the sugar barons were built facing the water—is the suite of rooms available for overnight guests: a pair of bedrooms with a bath and a large wicker-filled sitting room that sports a barber chair. It is rented to two couples or a family traveling together; if a single couple reserves it the other bedroom is not rented.

Included in the amenities is a Mintmere breakfast prepared and presented by the marvelous Hertis, who is straight out of central casting. His omelet with bacon and ham is glorious, his buttery biscuits unbelievable, and his coffee straight Creole.

New Iberia was settled by Spaniards and Canary Islanders dispatched here in the late 1700s to experiment with the raising of flax and hemp. A few yards down the street from Mintmere is another property that must be seen. Shadows-on-the-Teche, a beautifully preserved jewel built in the 1830s, was painstakingly restored and refurbished in the 1920s and again in the 1960s when it became a property of the National Trust for Historic Preservation.

MINTMERE PLANTATION, 1400 East Main, New Iberia, Louisiana 70560. Telephone: (318) 364-6210. Accommodations: a suite with two bedrooms, private or shared baths, telephones; no televisions. Rates: expensive; includes a full plantation breakfast and tours of both homes. Well-behaved children only; no pets. No cards, but personal checks are welcome. Open year round.
Getting there: Mintmere is a mile from the center of New Iberia and a long block from Shadows-on-the-Teche.

NOTTOWAY
White Castle, Louisiana

There are more than three hundred plantations still gracing the landscape in Louisiana, but Nottoway is the largest; in fact, it's the largest in the South, a three-story Goliath with sixty-four rooms, sixteen-foot ceilings, a couple of hundred windows, ring-around double gallery porches, and an astounding total of fifty-three-hundred square feet of space—a veritable antebellum Southern castle completed just in time to qualify as antebellum, in 1859.

It was designed by one of the greatest architects of the nineteenth century, Henry Howard of New Orleans. He was told by John Hamden Randolph, "Build me the finest home on the river."

It took four years to finish, using virgin cypress cut from plantation forests and thousands of bricks fired in plantation kilns, employing craftsmen to carve the imposing Corinthian columns that support the stunning plasterwork of the arches and cornices of the White Ballroom, and importing Dresden doorknobs, Italian marble mantels, and crystal chandeliers.

Eighty percent of the glass was made on the grounds, and the innovative engineers even designed a gas plant to burn rosin and pipe the gas to sconces to light the rooms. There was hot and cold running water, toilets that flushed, sixteen coal-burning fireplaces, a sewage treatment plant, and a bowling alley on the ground floor.

Spared during the War Between the States, Nottoway was named after a county in Randolph's native Virginia. The first Union forces on the scene came up the river by gunboat, but the commander had been a guest at Nottoway the previous year and after firing one round as a calling card, he rushed to the mansion to apologize to Mrs. Randolph and made certain that all the Yankees camped outside, not inside the magnificently furnished home.

When the last Randolph sold the house in 1889, most of the original furnishings were removed, but the morning room where the ladies gathered after breakfast is now filled with wicker that was left over in the attic, and the master bedroom has the original Brazilian rosewood furniture, including a half-tester bed. There are also Randolph chandeliers in two of the other bedrooms.

Randolph, the master of more than seventy-one hundred acres of sugar cane, fifty-seven house servants, and over a thousand slaves, could afford the best; and those in charge today, owner Arlin Dease and curator Steve Saunders, have worked diligently to return the Greek Revival–Italianate Nottoway to its days of glory. The silver doorknobs have been polished, the plaster medallions and friezes carefully restored, the twenty-two columns and acres of walls repaired and painted, the interior filled once again with furniture authentic to the 1850s. A prize piece is the seventeen-foot mahogany dining table made in Natchez, currently covered with gold service plates. The draperies are copies of those Scarlett tore down to make her dress in *Gone With the Wind.*

Six of the sixty-four rooms of Nottoway were opened to the inn-hopping public in July 1980: two on the third floor, the most elaborately furnished and the most expensive; two on the ground floor, a bit

Nottoway Plantation, White Castle, Louisiana

cramped; and two in the *garçonnière,* that detached building where bachelor sons could find a measure of privacy to sow their wild oats.

Guests are greeted on arrival with chilled champagne or a mint julep, and in the mornings wake-up coffee is delivered as prelude to the planter's breakfast with such specialties as eggs Benedict and sweet-potato biscuits. For those who like to remain near the premises, walking along the Mississippi, watching the river traffic, exploring the land where cane was once king, there's a ground-floor feedery that features for lunch such Louisiana fare as shrimp étouffée and chicken stew. Adjoining are gift stores that sell various guidebooks and local handicrafts.

NOTTOWAY, Highway 405, P.O. Box 160, White Castle, Louisiana 70788. Telephone: (504) 545-2730. Accommodations: six rooms, all with private baths and private entrances; no telephones or televisions. Rates: expensive; includes planter's breakfast, a drink on arrival, champagne in the room. No children under 12; no pets. Cards: AE, MC, V. Open year round.
Getting there: Nottoway is on the great River Road (State Road 405) with access from State Road 1, two miles north of White Castle and 18 south of Baton Rouge.

NEW ORLEANS

Atlanta is the South's most popular convention center, and Orlando, with its several worlds orbiting around Walt's wonderful world, is the number-one tourist destination, but New Orleans with all its happenings remains the country's most fascinating city. "The Big Easy," it calls itself, and "America's European Masterpiece." It is a Mecca for pleasure-seekers of all ages, a living work of art with 2-1/2 centuries of history vibrating with the clashes and cooperation of the French and Spanish, and with African, Irish, Italian, and German influences added to the melting pot.

You can ride one of the last remaining streetcars in the country, or cruise the Mississippi on a paddle-wheeler—more than five thousand ships transit the port of New Orleans each year. You can watch the Sugar Bowl in the Superdome, or make a pilgrimage to the Chalmette Battlefield, where, in 1815, Gen. Andy Jackson and his ragtail assemblage of back-country militia and pirates defeated superior British forces in the Battle of New Orleans.

New Orleans has it all: an opera, a symphony, Broadway shows, a fine zoo and a nature center, mansions in the Garden District to be toured, wonderful window shopping in the French Quarter, and, of course, all that jazz! And fine food, whether French or Italian, Creole and Cajun, or oysters shucked before your very eyes. It's a year-round festival, with a Spring Fiesta in April or May, the Food Festival in July or August, a Jazz and Heritage Festival in April or May, and, of course, Mardi Gras in February or March. Mardi Gras is organized madness, with parades by various societies called *krewes*, and a generally inebriated mass revelry that is surprisingly orderly—in its own way. Until the stroke of midnight ushers in Ash Wednesday, Bacchus serves as patron saint, and there's convincing evidence everywhere that, as some sage said long ago, to really enjoy Mardi Gras, you have to have the body of a seventeen-year-old and the mind of a twelve-year-old.

Whenever you visit this exciting city, there's something special going on, and the New Orleans Tourist and Convention Commission at 334 Royal Street (New Orleans, Louisiana 70116; telephone 504-566-5011) can provide schedules and additional information. And whenever you visit, there's no shortage of quiet little inns and hostelries to suit all tastes and all sizes of bank account.

THE COLUMNS
New Orleans, Louisiana

Brooke Shields fans take note! *Pretty Baby* was filmed in this magnificent mansion tucked into the trees in New Orleans's famed Garden District. Constructed in 1888 by a local tobacco merchant, and converted during World War I into an exclusive boardinghouse and during World War II into a small hotel of note, this handsome monument of the Victorian age is a treasure house of stained glass, richly carved mahogany, massive winding stairways, and high-ceilinged reception rooms. The former library is now a lounge with a beautiful bar; that's where stills of Shields and her co-stars of *Pretty Baby* are to be seen: all the interiors of that saga of Storyville were filmed at this aptly named hostelry, the Columns.

More Italianate than Southern in style, the Columns stands on St. Charles Avenue, route of New Orleans's last remaining streetcar, which glides the traveler past the many mansions of the Garden District, past Tulane and Loyola universities, ending directly downtown, near the French Quarter.

Claire and Jacques Creppel are the happy proprietors of the Columns and have been busily engaged in full-scale restoration, gradually expanding their intimate restaurant into something of value in this city of good eating. Stuffed eggplant appetizers and entrées of fresh rabbit, trout in a cream sauce sprinkled with green peppercorns, and, of course, gumbo are among the featured attractions in the dining room, which serves three meals a day as well as high tea.

The rooms are comfortable without being elaborate, and the Creppels are in the process of installing telephones and televisions, but one of the joys of staying in this century-old Victorian echo is the escape from such modern interruptions.

THE COLUMNS, 3811 St. Charles Avenue, New Orleans, Louisiana 70115. Telephone: (504) 899-9308. Accommodations: 22 rooms, half with private baths, one suite; some rooms with telephone and television. Rates: inexpensive to moderate, including full breakfast and morning paper (rates are double during Mardi Gras). No pets. Cards: AE, MC, V. Open year round.
Getting there: St. Charles Avenue is the main artery running through the Garden District; there's a streetcar stop in front of the Columns.

THE CORNSTALK HOTEL
New Orleans, Louisiana

The most famous fence in New Orleans dramatically graces the front of this boldly Victorian mansion. For more than a century and a half the cast-iron creation with golden ears of corn crowning its length has been a landmark, giving the name to this crisply white stone two-story inn, which in July 1982 was happily taken over by Debbie and David Spencer. He's a local attorney, she's a realtor; together they've worked a needed refurbishing, with new carpeting and paint, and the additions of thick, luxurious quilts and bedspreads and an overall dressing-up of the fourteen rooms. It's fully air conditioned, of course, and the Spencers are planning to install a small sidewalk cafe out front, between the inn and the famous fence.

THE CORNSTALK HOTEL, 915 Royal Street, New Orleans, Louisiana 70116. Telephone: (504) 523-1515. Accommodations: 14 rooms, all with private baths, color televisions, and telephones; some with double beds, some with twins. Rates: expensive, with special rates for the Sugar Bowl, Mardi Gras, and other New Orleans happenings; a deposit of one night's tariff is required to guarantee reservation. Continental breakfast is included. Children permitted but not pets. Cards: AE, MC, V. Open all year.
Getting there: Royal Street is in the French Quarter, and there's direct limousine service from the airport.

The Cornstalk Hotel, New Orleans, Louisiana

FRENCH QUARTER MAISONNETTES
New Orleans, Louisiana

Mrs. Junius Underwood is the charming woman in charge here, and though she's Boston and New England to the core, she's enough of a French Quarter convert to refer to herself as the chatelaine. And although she likes to tell her guests that "I'm the only one in this business who didn't plan to be ... I *backed into* this innkeeping business in 1962," she has displayed her caring professionalism as an innkeeper by preparing a compact little guide with information on museums and galleries, land and water tours, and structures and sites not to miss while walking the French Quarter. Want to know where to find the famous muffuletta, or the best pralines in town, or fried oysters on French bread, or the nearest pharmacy and grocery store? It's all in Mrs. Underwood's information-packed flyer, along with a reliable listing of restaurants, including such special spots as Tujague's on Decatur, four blocks away. Mrs. Underwood describes it as "something different. Not a tourist attraction. No menu," and she lists the hours and the telephone number to call to find out what they are serving that day. Bourbon Street's Famous Door is praised for its "outstanding orchestra," Pat O'Brien's as something considered a must stop by most tourists, and Lafitte's Blacksmith Shop as a place to have a nightcap when walking home. As for "Girlie Shows," this unique innkeeper advises that they are "all up and down Bourbon Street. Just peek in the door for 20 seconds and you've seen the show."

And if you peek through the iron gate of the old carriage house entrance that bars all but Maisonnettes guests, you'll want to pass through the interior gate with its fan-shaped spokes, walk into the flagstone courtyard with its feathery oak and cherry laurels, its three-tiered seventeenth-century French fountain, and its diminutive spiral staircase designed especially for the resident cats.

The seven suites—the maisonnettes—open into the courtyard. They are modernized quarters, transformed from a town house built by a prominent New Orleans family in the 1820s—their family plantation site is now uptown New Orleans.

There's more history closer to the Maisonnettes: next door is the Archbishop Antoine Blanc Memorial, identified as the city's "oldest and most historic building, erected 1745–1752." Close by is the 1734 Ursuline Convent, and across the street the Beauregard House. Mrs. Underwood will tell you about them, and much more: she's a gracious and valuable source of information on her adopted town.

FRENCH QUARTER MAISONNETTES, 1130 Chartres Street, New Orleans, Louisiana 70116. Telephone: (504) 524-9918. Accommodations: seven suites, all with private baths; no televisions or telephones. Rates: inexpensive to moderate, including morning newspaper. No children under 12; well-behaved pets permitted. No credit cards, but personal checks are accepted. Open from August 1 to June 30.
Getting there: Chartres Street is between Ursulines and Governor Nichols streets; the Maisonnettes are marked at the street entrance by a pair of iron horse heads that have been in place for more than a century and a half.

HOTEL MAISON DE VILLE
New Orleans, Louisiana

In this *maison* that was converted from a private home to a hotel in the 1920s, you will luxuriate in the lap of history—the slave quarters out back date from 1743. Rooms are beautifully furnished with period antiques: there's a front bedroom with an eighteenth-century four-poster, other rooms with fireplaces and oil portraits, and bathrooms of marble and brass. In three of the front bedrooms you can have morning coffee on your own balcony; in the back rooms the balconies look out on a quiet little brick courtyard, surrounded by wrought iron and lush greenery.

Your day at Maison de Ville starts with silver tray service: freshly squeezed orange juice, New Orleans coffee (spiked with chicory), croissants or brioches, a fresh flower, and the morning paper. In the afternoons, sherry, tea, and cookies or soft drinks are served in the handsomely appointed, intimate lobby. And when you return from dinner at one of the excellent area restaurants, many of which are within walking distance, there's a decanter of port.

It's all included in the tariff, along with garage parking and two leftovers from the grand old days of innkeeping: shoes are shined when left outside your door, and there's a concierge on duty around the clock to help with your travel requirements, make reservations, and organize touring.

This is all part of Maison's pampering, whether you stay in the main building or in one of the Audubon cottages a block away on Dauphine Street. The cottages are clustered around a swimming pool, but each has an individual courtyard. The name is no idle label: John James Audubon lived in cottage No. 1 from 1821 until 1822 with his wife and two sons, tutoring, sketching, and painting. Three of the cottages were constructed in a vintage New Orleans manner, the so-

Hotel Maison de Ville, New Orleans, Louisiana

called Creole brick and post style using bricks hand formed from Mississippi River clay. There are more bricks in the courtyards, in the entry walk, and along walls and dividers. And inside the cottages, the color tones and furnishings are the epitome of quiet, expensive taste. It's hard to believe that the hotel and cottages are just a block from that Bourbon Street of Sodom and sleaze, in the heart of this vital port city that bustles with so many things to do and see.

HOTEL MAISON DE VILLE, 727 Rue Toulouse, New Orleans, Louisiana 70130. Telephone: (504) 561-5858. Accommodations: 12 rooms and two suites in hotel; single, double, twin, and king-size beds; two rooms and five suites in Audubon Cottages; all with private baths, televisions, and telephones. Rates: expensive. Meal service: complimentary Continental breakfast. No bar service, but setups are provided and you can order from a nearby lounge. Children are welcome; pets preferred in cottages only. No credit cards. Open all year.
Getting there: The Maison de Ville is in the very heart of the French Quarter between Bourbon (a pedestrian street closed to traffic for most of its length) and Royal.

LAFITTE GUEST HOUSE
New Orleans, Louisiana

This grand three-story town house, built in 1849, was reborn in 1979. That's when the present owners completed their total restoration and refurbishing of this classic French Quarter structure, with its double front and side balconies enclosed with lacy wrought iron, its vine-covered wall, and its cozy little courtyard. The boldly Victorian lobby, brimming with superb antiques, includes a richly carved mahogany mantel, a wedding cake-stacked sideboard, and a Chinese writing desk that was given to a Hearst by the king of Italy.

The guest rooms sparkle with antiques, brightly patterned bedspreads and draperies, four-posters with full or half testers, glistening chandeliers, and black marble mantelpieces. The attic room, one of my favorites, is perfect for viewing the action on Bourbon Street; but the third-floor room with its balcony also provides a bit of panorama, and it's a happy retreat for a leisurely breakfast or a late afternoon drink while discussing which of the city's many attractions to take on at night.

LAFITTE GUEST HOUSE, 1003 Bourbon Street, New Orleans, Louisiana 70116. Telephone: (504) 581-2678. Accommodations: fourteen rooms, all with modern tiled baths; no televisions or telephones. Rates: moderate to expensive; includes complimentary Continental breakfast. No pets. Cards: AE, MC, V. Open year round.

Getting there: The inn is on the corner of Bourbon Street and St. Phillip.

LAMOTHE HOUSE
New Orleans, Louisiana

For a greater appreciation of this splendid little hostelry, buy, beg, or borrow the volumes of *New Orleans Architecture* that feature this landmark and the neighboring array of structural design and achievement along the Esplanade. You will read that the history of Lamothe House is "full of lawsuits, bankruptcies, auction sales, mortgages from banks long out of existence, partnerships, building and rebuilding, and surveys. The long list of French names associated with the property is rivaled only by that of the civil sheriffs in their suits of seizure."

Construction was begun around 1800 by brothers Jean and Pierre Lamothe, who had arrived in New Orleans from Santo Domingo, established a successful plantation in St. Charles parish, and, as was the custom in those days, decided to build a town house. They each had families, so had to have a double entrance, although the original structure had a porte cochere, a carriageway through the middle. In 1860, hand-carved Corinthian columns were added to the front doors.

The design was relatively simple: on the ground floor were double parlors on either side of a common, high-ceilinged hallway that now serves as a dramatic entryway with oversize gilt-framed mirrors. The parlors, with their handsomely embossed ceilings and medallions, now serve as suites, one named for Lafayette, with twin four-poster beds, and one named for the great nineteenth-century New Orleans furniture maker, Prudent Mallard—the bed and armoire came from his shop. There are two more suites on the third floor, as well as single rooms that formerly housed servants. On the second floor are the former party rooms, with their elaborate black marble mantels, double-leaded overdoors, crystal chandeliers, and, in the room now used as lobby-registration area, an overwhelming Victorian light fixture.

Past the lobby is the formal dining room, with its long banquet table where guests gather each morning for juice, coffee, and sweet rolls while they discuss their touring for the day. Giving aid and advice is the innkeeper, Mimi Munson Langguth (Mrs. Kenneth). She has taken over the responsibilities of hostessing from her mother, Mrs. Edward P. Munson, who for many years presided with great charm and grace at the day's *petit déjeuner,* while dispensing coffee from a two-hundred-

Lamothe House, New Orleans, Louisiana

year-old Sheffield silver urn and planning café brûlot parties under the magnolia and sweet olive trees in the garden. The narrow two-story wings that once housed the servants are now the second-floor gallery rooms flanking the patio, not as elaborate as the suites, but still something special.

LAMOTHE HOUSE, 621 Esplanade Avenue, New Orleans, Louisiana 70116. Telephone: (504) 947-1161. Accommodations: 10 rooms and four suites, all with private baths, televisions, and telephones. Rates: moderate. Meal service: complimentary breakfast. No bar service. Children welcome; pets not allowed. Cards: AE, MC, V. Open September 1 through mid-July.
Getting there: Take the Orleans Avenue exit of Interstate 10 to Claiborne Avenue, then go east seven blocks and turn right on Esplanade. Proceed ten blocks; the inn is on the flank of the French Quarter.

NOBLE ARMS INN
New Orleans, Louisiana

For the past two years the new owners of this French Quarter, Rue Royale hideaway have been working a miracle of revival and restoration. When I made my inspection tour, Nick Falcone, one of the owners, was wielding a paint brush out front and resident manager Ronda Jones was painting inside.

The results spell the rebirth of an 1820 town house that served for years as apartments for law students at Loyola. The old brick has all been scraped clean, the hardwood floors sanded down and refinished, and the rooms furnished comfortably, but not with period pieces or reproductions. The three-story interior courtyard is an intimate stone, brick, and wood retreat for enjoying the complimentary mint julep or sazerac that greets incoming guests, and the complimentary Continental breakfast consisting of juice, coffee, or tea, and whatever Ronda picks up at a nearby bakery on the way to the inn.

Nine of the inn's fifteen rooms are in the main building and are the larger of the accommodations, including the Beauregard and Bonaparte suites. A half dozen single rooms are in the second, adjoining building. Room No. 10 is a favorite of mine: it has a brass couch and a cushy queen bed; but No. 11 is also a winner, with its Williamsburg flower prints, its comfortable twin beds, and a balcony overlooking Rue Royale.

NOBLE ARMS INN, 1006 Royal Street, New Orleans, Louisiana 70116. Telephone: (504) 524-2222. Accommodations: 15 rooms, all with private baths, color televisions, and telephones; a pair of suites; queen- and twin-size beds; most rooms have kitchenettes. Rates: moderate, including Continental breakfast. No pets. Cards: AE, MC, V. Open all year.
Getting there: Royal Street is in the French Quarter.

PARK VIEW
New Orleans, Louisiana

The name is an apt one. This inn looks out on Audubon Park, an ample expanse of greenery, home of the recently revitalized zoo, and the site of the great Cotton Exposition of 1885. The Park View was built a year earlier as a hotel to house guests to that Exposition—the first such guest house to be built in the city.

It's now popular with parents of students at nearby Tulane and Loyola universities; overseas visitors, especially those who are looking to stretch travel budgets; and those who want to stay in the quiet Garden District, avoiding the bustle of the French Quarter and the downtown hotels. By famed St. Charles streetcar, that bustle is only minutes away, and the line operates around the clock, every fifteen minutes until midnight and then once an hour until 7:00 am.

Since 1981 the Park View has been on the National Register of Historic Places, and there is an air of historic Victorian elegance about the large ground-floor public rooms, the cut glass in the lobby doors, the glistening crystal of the chandelier. The somewhat spartan dining room, where a complimentary Continental breakfast is served, has a splendid view of the park. Rooms are more functional than fancy, but there is a scattering of antiques and period pieces, and some of the rooms have balconies overlooking St. Charles Avenue or the park.

PARK VIEW, 7004 St. Charles Avenue, New Orleans, Louisiana 70118. Telephone: (504) 861-7564. Accommodations: 25 rooms, half with private baths; no telephones or televisions, but there is a television room off the lobby and pay phones are located on each floor. Rates: inexpensive (moderate during Mardi Gras and other special events); includes complimentary Continental breakfast. Preferably no children; no pets. Cards: AE, MC, V. Open year round.
Getting there: From town take St. Charles Avenue past Audubon Park to Walnut Street; the Park View is on the corner and is distinguished by its wraparound porches and the flags hanging from its second floor.

Park View, New Orleans, Louisiana

PRINCE CONTI HOTEL
New Orleans, Louisiana

One of the Crescent City's premier properties, European Elegant style, the Prince Conti was named for the French nobleman who was an important backer of the Bienville expedition that founded New Orleans. And it's loyal enough to its namesake to have a French château of a lobby graced by an eighteenth-century Trumeau painting, a Louis XV marble mantel matched by Louis XV armchairs covered in their original Aubusson tapestry, and an authentic eighteenth-century Baccarat crystal and bronze dome chandelier.

Many of the rooms are furnished with period antiques. Among my favorites is No. 234 with its bed that's a woodcarver's dream, No. 232 looking out on the street and boasting a massive four-poster, No. 303 with its pair of Colonial twin tester beds, and No. 217, the Empress Eugenie Room, with its early Victorian bed and a marble-topped dresser of heavily carved redwood.

A Continental breakfast on a silver tray, accompanied with a fresh flower and a newspaper, is served in the room, and there's a quiet little "Petit Bar" in the adjoining La Galerie on the ground floor.

PRINCE CONTI HOTEL, 830 Rue Conti, New Orleans, Louisiana 70112. Telephone: (504) 529-4172 (toll free: 1-800-535-7908). Accommodations: 50 rooms and suites, all with private baths, color televisions, and telephones. Rates: expensive, including Continental breakfast. Inquire about pets. Cards: AC. Open all year.
Getting there: Conti Street is in the French Quarter.

PROVINCIAL
New Orleans, Louisiana

I know it used to have "Motel" and not "Inn" in its name, but this charming two-story hostelry in the French Quarter, close to all the wonders and delights of Jackson Square, is such a haven—despite its size—that I consider it more a sophisticated country inn than a city motel. The ancient brick buildings have been beautifully restored, as recognized by their receipt of the Vieux Carre Restoration Honor Award, and they wrap around five splendid little patios, one with a swimming pool.

Across one of the courtyards is the Honfleur Restaurant, an intimate, happily run retreat under the smiling management of Evelyn Revertiga, who is the very definition of New Orleans hospitality. Creole

Provincial, New Orleans, Louisiana

creations are the Honfleur specialty, but the menu is a simple one with gumbo, fried chicken, and a variety of sandwiches. In one corner is a small but fully stocked bar, in another a grand old hand-crafted bread cabinet from a Louisiana plantation.

After a restful evening in one of the individually furnished rooms—there's no motel-chain sameness at the Provincial—the Honfleur is the perfect gathering place for a plantation breakfast featuring creamy omelets, pancakes, French toast, and coffee as honest to its New Orleans origins as the room furnishings: French imports and local Creole creations.

PROVINCIAL, 1024 Rue Chartres, New Orleans, Louisiana 70116. Telephone: (504) 581-4995 (toll free: 1-800-535-7922). Accommodations: 96 rooms and suites, all with private baths, color televisions, and telephones; single, double, twin, and queen-size beds. Rates: moderate. No pets. Cards: AC. Open all year.
Getting there: Rue Chartres is in the French Quarter; the inn is between Ursulines and St. Philip streets, a block from the French Market.

THE SAINT ANN
New Orleans, Louisiana

Distinguishing a block of Conti Street is this delightful little retreat from all the bustle of the French Quarter. As soon as you enter the low-ceilinged lobby, you are greeted in the city's friendliest fashion by an accommodating concierge who will make your dining and entertainment arrangements.

Out front fly the colors of the country, the city, and also Napoleanic Colonial France, and inside there's the brick patio of a courtyard with flowing fountains, the fronds of palms, the fresh greenery of ferns, and a small pool—an ideal staging area for pre- and post-prandial sipping and a Continental breakfast. But at the Saint Ann I like to order from the menu labeled "Petit Déjeuner." It's not "petit" at all. Not with eggs Sardou, eggs Danton, eggs Benedict, and eggs Saint Ann—which translate to poached eggs on, respectively, creamed spinach and artichoke bottoms, chicken livers, smoked ham, or lump crab meat, all with hollandaise—or pan-browned corned beef hash or the Saint Ann version of *pain perdu.*

The courtyard with its gaslight is shaded by the five-storied structure. The bedrooms are small, but are expensively furnished, with bathrooms that define the word *luxury.* And I like the cypress bar, a blending of old and new nestled into a corner of the courtyard.

THE SAINT ANN, 717 Conti Street, New Orleans, Louisiana 70130. Telephone: (504) 581-1881 (toll free: 1-800-535-9730). Accommodations: 59 rooms, all with private baths and color televisions; some suites; king-, queen- and twin-size beds. Rates: expensive, including Continental breakfast. No pets. Cards: AC. Open all year.
Getting there: Conti Street is in the French Quarter.

ST. LOUIS HOTEL
New Orleans, Louisiana

Along with the Saint Ann and the Prince Conti, also in the French Quarter, this is a Mark Smith property—or, better said, a Mark Smith boutique hotel, one with enough caring concern by the concierge, enough fussy maintenance by the staff, and enough fine furnishings to mark it as an inn of great class. Created out of the old Regal Brewery warehouse and named for the French king who led the Seventh Crusade, the St. Louis is a brilliant example of adaptive restoration. No wonder it won the Vieux Carre Award of Excellence for building construction in 1973.

From the moment you enter the gentle arched doors, the St. Louis is a special experience, an escape to a more gracious age, French style. There are French antiques in the lobby, along with paintings, flowers and potted greenery, and richly patterned carpets over an imported French parquet floor that catches the light from the Italian chandeliers.

Across the lobby is the magnificent courtyard, bubbling with a fountain and lush with landscaping. High arches, fanned with delicately twisting wrought iron, rise four floors with interior gallery porches. All of it is spotless, looking as though it were painted yesterday. I could believe that Mark Smith has a shock crew of painters, something like a hospital trauma team—whenever a nick or scratch is spotted, they hurry to the scene with their brushes.

The rooms are handsomely appointed, with cushy side chairs, writing tables and desks, dream-inducing beds with thick, expensive spreads. That's the operative word at the St. Louis: "expensive." Their new restaurant, L'Escale, staffed by white-gloved waiters and a maître d' who for years had the same position at Doro's in San Francisco, is the latest entrant in the Eating City's *haute cuisine* sweepstakes. Chefs were imported from France and assistants were recruited from the ranks of recent graduates of Hyde Park's Culinary Institute, and when last I experienced L'Escale the fixed-price menu, a so-called *Soirée Parisienne,* was pegged at $95. The minimum charge when ordering à la carte was $55.

But for those guests who don't want to take that costly route, the immediate area offers many alternatives. Moran's Italian restaurant is next door, Begue's is across the street, and the Absinthe House is a few yards away. And there are dozens of other restaurants dotting the French Quarter.

ST. LOUIS HOTEL, 730 Rue Bienville, New Orleans, Louisiana 70130. Telephone: (504) 581-7300 (toll free: 1-800-535-9706). Accommodations: 66 rooms and suites, with twin, double, queen- and king-size beds; all rooms with private baths, televisions and telephones, shoeshine machines, terry-cloth bathrobes; some fireplaces. Rates: expensive. Well-behaved children and pets permitted. Cards: AC. Open year round.
Getting there: The St. Louis is in the French Quarter.

623 URSULINES
New Orleans, Louisiana

Jim Weirich and Don Heil, both enthusiastic émigrés from St. Louis, are the innkeepers of this small, seven-suite hideaway shoehorned into a vintage Vieux Carre structure dating from 1825. Graceful gateways and iron railings distinguish the facade, and there's a splendid flagstone walkway leading to the courtyard with its two-story gallery porch and its original brick patio dotted with plantings.

The innkeepers live on the premises, behind that brightly polished brass doorplate (at first I thought Swiss were living there, for it is sometimes said that for a good Swiss hausfrau the purpose of life is polishing the brass on her front door!). Jim explains that his definition of a true inn is one in which the owner-innkeeper lives. Apparently it's something he learned from Mrs. Junius Underwood, who's in charge of the nearby French Quarter Maisonnettes. He readily admits he learned a great deal about the inn-keeping business from that lovely lady.

Jim and Don have been in the business since 1980, and in that time they have learned much and are affable hosts to their guests, providing them with detailed advice about the restaurants, the nightlife, and the happenings in this city with so much to offer the visitor.

The accommodations are comfortable and simply furnished and all look out on the courtyard, the ideal haven for a sip or two before taking on New Orleans at night.

623 URSULINES, 623 Ursulines Street, New Orleans, Louisiana 70116. Telephone: (504) 529-5489. Accommodations: seven suites, all with private baths; black and white televisions but no telephones. Rates: inexpensive to moderate, including morning paper. Well-behaved children and pets permitted. No credit cards, but personal checks are accepted. Open year round.

Getting there: 623 is between Royal and Chartres; do not confuse it with the Ursuline Guest House a block away—that is an all-male hostelry.

ARKANSAS

EUREKA SPRINGS
Eureka Springs, Arkansas

Eureka Springs is a tale of two cities: there's the neon newness and bright lights of the highway-straddling motels and fried-food fast-feeders on the outskirts, and the time-stood-still inner core. Lovers of the Victorian era of architecture should put on blinders until they hit the high ground in the mountain-hugging town. Then they too can shout "Eureka!", not because they've found some miraculous cure in the healing waters, as that pioneer in the 1870s did when drinking and bathing in the springs, but because they have never seen such a stunning collection of pure Victoriana.

The gingerbread of Gothic Revival marches up and down the steeply pitched dormered roofs that shade rounded porches bright with the fresh paint of restoration. Preservation is not a fetish in Eureka Springs, it's a way of life all along the twists and turns of the arteries that wind through the heart of this delightful little town. There are 16 S-shaped streets, 50 U and 51 V curves, with only 6 of the more than 200 roads carrying the same name from the left side to the right of the intersections.

Many tourists find their way to this northwest corner of Arkansas to attend the annual Passion Play in summer and early fall. The amphitheater is on a mini-mountain named Oberammergau, close to the giant-sized Christ of the Ozarks statue, seven stories tall with an arm span of 65 feet. There's also a museum of the Holy Land, a Christ Only Art Gallery, and a museum boasting the largest collection of Bibles in the world.

On Spring Street in town is the Eureka Springs Historical Museum, with a wealth of furnishings, documents, photographs, and other memorabilia detailing the past, and not far distant is Hatchet

Hall, home of hatchet-wielding Carry Nation. The famous temperance crusader made her last public appearance in Eureka Springs, in Basin Park.

The in-town park is now used for summer concerts and down-home country-music shows. In May of each year the town organizes an antique show, and later in the month a sidewalk arts and crafts happening. In September the antique autos come to Eureka Springs, and the following month there's the Ozark Folk Festival, which marks the end of the high season in this section of the country.

From November through March the pace slows, and many of the stores shutter their doors while owners rest up for another invasion in the spring. Those stores exhibit a surprising level of taste. So do several memorable restaurants in town, as we discovered while working through veggie omelets, shrimp-stuffed avocado, and eggs Sausalito at the Crescent and New Orleans hotels; munching al fresco at the Pita Hut on tofu and tabouli, hummus and falafel; and dining on coquilles St. Jacques, vol-au-vent, and scampi in more formal surroundings at the excellent Plaza on Main Street.

And we were overjoyed to learn that Eureka Springs has its own puffing and chugging ride into the past: a train that is pulled by a 1906 Baldwin No. 1, considered to be the oldest woodburning "cabbage-head" in the country. Another engine used on the Eureka Springs and North Arkansas Railway started its locomotive life pulling construction material during the building of the Panama Canal. Trains depart from a depot dating from 1913, which is now on the National Register of Historic Places.

Two square miles of the town are also in the Register, and there's no end to the photographic possibilities or the feeling of being lost in time, especially when spending the night in one of the historic hostelries.

CRESCENT COTTAGE
Eureka Springs, Arkansas

This gingerbread-trimmed pink gem, so perfectly preserved and lovingly tended by owners Bernice and Erwin Pereboom (who also own the Queen Anne–Carpenter Gothic Rosalie House museum), was built in 1881 by Powell Clayton, the first governor of Arkansas after the War Between the States.

A two-story frame house with a Gothic-inspired turret out front and glorious views of the mountains from the back rooms and the garden, the Crescent Cottage is in the historic district, convenient to

269

the heart of town by foot or trolley. The trackless tram stops in front of the Cottage at thirty-minute intervals.

From two to six people can stay in the Crescent, making it a home away from home, utilizing the facilities of the fully equipped kitchen, relaxing on the porch and in the Victorian parlor, enjoying the art work of Bernice Pereboom. A late-blooming talent, she started painting a few years ago, and her primitives, proudly hanging throughout the Cottage, have a charming Grandma Moses quality.

CRESCENT COTTAGE, 211 Spring Street, Eureka Springs, Arkansas 72632. Telephone: (501) 253-7691. Accommodations: suite with four rooms, private bath, private entrance, fully equipped kitchen, television, and telephone. Rates: moderate. No pets. No cards, but personal checks are welcome. Open year round.

Getting there: Spring Street is one of the two main thoroughfares; it starts near the Basin Spring Park and winds up the mountain toward the Crescent Hotel. The Cottage is on the right side of the street, across from a small parklike lot.

CRESCENT HOTEL
Eureka Springs, Arkansas

The best view of the Ozarks is not from some scenic overlook or Forest Service fire tower. It's from the Top of the Crescent Lounge, a patio filled with wicker on the rooftop of a mountain-dominating castle. Built of stone from local quarries, the Crescent Hotel was completed in 1886 at a cost of $294,000 and dubbed the "Grand Lady of the Ozarks."

Her stables once housed a hundred horses, and an orchestra played for the wealthy who filled the four floors, lounging in the gargantuan lobby with its huge stone fireplace, resting in their elegantly appointed Victorian rooms.

The country's Gilded Age was the Grand Lady's Golden Age, but by 1908 the hotel was open only during summer months; the rest of the year it was a junior college for girls—an exclusive one, of course. The Great Depression brought a succession of owners struggling for survival, including an eccentric who painted all the walls lavender and drove an orchid-colored car. He ran the Crescent as a hospital for cancer patients, advertising his own miracle cure until the federal government put him behind bars for mail fraud.

After World War II the Crescent was reborn as a hotel, and in the 1970s new owners worked an extensive renovation and refurbishing, spending considerably more on the Victorian furnishings and the

Crescent Hotel, Eureka Springs, Arkansas

revitalized public rooms than the hotel cost to construct. Another new ownership team continued the process, and I'm sure the Crescent has not looked as good within most guests' memories. It sparkles with new life: outside along manicured paths past the swimming pool and into the woods, inside in the handsomely appointed Crystal Room with its walls of windows, its soft carpeting, and general air of elegance. The menu is basically Continental, with Crescent waffles and omelets among the specialties.

To work off the calories there's that new pool, tennis and shuffle-board, hiking trails, and, of course, all the strolling and shopping temptations in town.

CRESCENT HOTEL, Prospect Street, Eureka Springs, Arkansas 72632. Telephone: (501) 253-9766. Accommodations: 76 rooms and suites; double, twin, and king-size beds; all rooms with private baths, televisions, and telephones. Rates: moderate. Meal service: Breakfast, lunch, and dinner; full bar. Children and pets welcome, but inquire about pets. Cards: AE, MC, V. Open all year.
Getting there: Follow Route 62B from the center of Eureka Springs directly to the front door of the hotel.

DAIRY HOLLOW HOUSE
Eureka Springs, Arkansas

Anyone familiar with the writings of Crescent Dragonwagon should proceed at full speed to Eureka Springs and check in to this retreat off the beaten path—unique even in this town that time remembered. With husband Ned Shank and musician-friend Bill Haymes, Crescent revivified a simple frame farmhouse built by dairyman Daniel McIntyre in the 1880s. Two years were devoted to the reincarnation as floors were sanded and refinished, doors were stripped, modern bathrooms and a heating/cooling system installed, and antiques appropriate to the period carefully selected.

The Rose Room has a marble-topped, cherry wood Victorian-Eastlake gentleman's bureau that used to be in the Crescent Hotel, a marvelous old claw-footed tub big enough for two, a comfortable double bed covered with a handmade quilt in the Dutch Rose–Captive Beauty pattern.

The Iris room with its ornately swirled cast-iron twin beds, covered with quilts in two of America's earliest patterns, Bear's Paw and Goose Tracks, has an oak bureau with a hand-tatted lace scarf and is as softly blue in color as the Rose room is pink and raspberry and rose. Both rooms have antique hooked rugs and handwoven window shades.

A local artisan made the etched glass panels set into the doors, and there's a changing art gallery of works by local artists in rooms and parlor, a common room where the special "from-scratch" breakfast, as they call it, is prepared. This starts with herb tea or regular tea, coffee or café au lait—delivered to the room with the morning paper if desired—then fresh fruit or freshly squeezed orange juice, followed by a basket of fresh-baked whole-wheat butterhorns, a loaf of special bread, or a fantastic German baked pancake sprinkled with powdered sugar.

The parlor also has a writing table, various board games, and information on the sights and sites of Eureka Springs. Out the doors are wildflowers and woods that serve as a backdrop through the windows framed by ruffled calico curtains. The carefully tended gardens surrounding the hollow welcome the guest with their fragrance, informing the visitor at first sniff and sight that this is a very special place.

DAIRY HOLLOW HOUSE, P.O. Box 221, Eureka Springs, Arkansas 72632. Telephone: (501) 253-7444. Accommodations: two bedrooms, each with a private bath, private entrance, separate common room/parlor;

no telephones or televisions. Rates: moderate; includes breakfast. No small children or pets. Cards: AE, MC, V. Open year round.

Getting there: Follow Spring Street up the mountain toward the Crescent Hotel and watch for the little signs pointing the way to the house.

LAKE LUCERNE RESORT
Eureka Springs, Arkansas

Visitors to Eureka Springs who want to relax on a beach, do a bit of boating on a small lake and sunning on a small deck or, at a different time of the year, to sit before their own fireplace in their own cottage, should consider Lake Lucerne. On the outskirts of Eureka Springs, it's a 40-acre reincarnation of the 560-acre Lake Lucerne oasis, which was generally considered to be *the* place to go in the 1950s. Included in those 40 acres purchased by Mariellen and Leo Chandler is the lake, which was first developed in the 1880s for the Eureka Springs Sanitarium.

The Chandlers trucked in their very own beach, modernized the swimming pool, brought in rental rowboats, restored two of the units and added another three, installed the modern amenities, and created in the process an inn for all seasons—even winter when there's ice-skating on the lake.

There are lace curtains on the windows, attractive linens, and prints by Maxfield Parrish and other illustrators of children's books on the walls—all imparting a fairyland image to the cottages.

LAKE LUCERNE RESORT, P.O. Box 441, Eureka Springs, Arkansas 72632. Telephone: (501) 253-8085. Accommodations: five cottages with two and three bedrooms, fully equipped kitchens, fireplaces, color televisions, private sundecks; no telephones. Rates: moderate. Kennel for pets on premises. No cards, but personal checks are welcome. Open year round.

Getting there: The resort is two miles from downtown Eureka Springs off Highway 23S; turn left at the Ford dealership and follow the signs.

NEW ORLEANS HOTEL
Eureka Springs, Arkansas

For full-scale, total immersion into the Victorian past of this special corner of Arkansas, plan to check into a Spring Street hotel smack in the center of all the history: the New Orleans with its lacy French Quarter balconies. Built in 1892 and opened as the Wadsworth, the hotel is on the National Register of Historic Places and is steadily being brought back to its original glory and grandeur. Under the dedicated tutelage of owner-manager-front desk clerk-doorman-sometimes bellhop Phil Schloss, the modern additions, false ceilings, and shag carpeting have been removed and the original glitter brought back.

Manning the desk behind a vintage beauty of a cash register, grabbing a coffee from the French Market restaurant off the lobby, setting up the chairs for the weekly meeting of the Ukulele Club, which sings and strums its merry way each and every Saturday night, Phil is an escapee from the Chicago corporate world, a quietly enthusiastic jack-of-all-trades who has adopted his new home with sincerity and intelligence.

The Hiking Club of Eureka Springs also meets in the New Orleans lobby—on Sundays before striding out for their weekly explorations of town and country—and there's a steady procession of other regulars en route to the French Market for some uncommonly good hash browns, eggs Sausalito, or prime rib. On a lower level is the Quarter, a bistro of a bar reached by the side staircase leading to the parking lot out back—everything in this town seems to be built on a steep incline.

No two rooms are alike at the New Orleans (though all are simple, almost spartan), and, as Schloss writes in his brochure, "we are still working toward the goal of having each room a distinctive Victorian setting... not all the furniture and furnishings are antique (yet)... but that's the direction we are heading (Backward!)"

With the convenience of an in-town location and the trolley stopping out front, a guest sitting on the balcony of the New Orleans can contemplate the best of all possible worlds.

NEW ORLEANS HOTEL, 63 Spring Street, Eureka Springs, Arkansas 72632. Telephone: (501) 253-8630. Accommodations: 24 rooms; six share baths, eighteen have private baths, front rooms have a semi-sitting room; no telephones or televisions. Rates: inexpensive. No pets. No cards, but personal checks are welcome. Open year round.
Getting there: Spring Street is the extension of South Main that enters town as Route 62 B; the New Orleans is on the right side of the street, just before it takes a sharp turn to the left.

OZARK FOLK CENTER LODGE
Mountain View, Arkansas

In the geographic heart of the Ozarks, in the Stone County seat of the aptly named town of Mountain View, the Ozark Folk Center was opened in May 1973. Owned by the town, funded by a federal grant and under operating lease by the state Department of Parks and Tourism, the Center consists of some half a hundred cedar and native stone structures spread around eighty acres of the 915-acre wooded site.

It's a painless introduction to life in the Ozarks, vintage 1820–1920, with a large parking lot at the foot of the hill, an efficient Visitors' Center, a General Store for a bit of early-on stoking, and a tram to take the lazy to the entrance—those who want to stretch muscles and test hearts can climb the stairs.

Once inside, past the gift store with handicrafts made by the more than four hundred craftsmen who are members of the cooperative Ozark Foothills Craft Guild, the visitor to the center walks among craft demonstrations and daytime music presentations. Native artisans demonstrate and discuss the fine arts of basketry and broom-making, candle-dipping and woodcarving, printing and shingle splitting, spinning, dyeing, and doll-making with shriveled apple and corn shucks.

The locals doing the talking are articulate, and the subjects are interesting to those whose only knowledge of the area comes from the exaggerations of hillbilly shows. The 1060-seat auditorium with its tentlike cedar roof is the setting for regularly scheduled evening performances—such programs as dancers doing the square and round dances of the Ozarks as well as the jig, and musicians strumming on five-string banjos, mountain dulcimers and picking bows, mandolins and fiddles. There are also singers who perform ballads and gospel songs passed down from generation to generation. Close by is the education center with its library of resource material for those who want to research Ozark traditions and folklore.

The Folk Center's dining room is a real zinger—never have I tasted better coleslaw or fried chicken: fresh and perfectly prepared. The turnip greens and corn bread, the catfish and hush puppies, the carrot salad and apple pie with crust like a sugar cookie are all fantastically good. And where else can one find a pea salad made with egg and pimiento? A local woman is responsible for the salads; another bakes the pies.

Down the hill from the center, reached by a wilderness path from the restaurant, or by a paved road, are the overnight accommodations: modern octagon-shaped duplex cabins with all the modern conveniences

276

in a rustic setting. For those who want to attend several of the concerts, and to dig a little deeper into the history and culture of the people of the Ozarks, there's no better place to stay. The lodge provides a swimming pool and a game room for its guests.

OZARK FOLK CENTER LODGE, Mountain View, Arkansas 72560. Telephone: (501) 269-3871. Accommodations: 60 units, each with a private bath, two double beds, color television, telephone. Rates: inexpensive; lower during winter season when only part of the lodge cabins remain open. No pets. No cards, but personal checks are welcome. Open year round.
Getting there: The Center is on Spur 382 off State Road 9 a few minutes north of the center of Mountain View; the signs make it impossible to miss.

LAKEFRONT LODGE
Edgemont, Arkansas

The forty thousand-acre Greers Ferry Lake might just be the cleanest body of water in the country. Each September a couple thousand local residents and visitors walk the 276 miles of the waterfront picking up anything and everything that doesn't belong there—tons of trash.

At Fred and Patricia Janssen's Lakefront Lodge I have the feeling they do this kind of clean-up every day. The only hostelry on the lake with a lodge, restaurant, and boat dock is spotless. The small gardens are carefully manicured and the restaurant with its solid country fare looks scrubbed clean daily. And I like all the benches and the ole-timey swings once used for front-porch courting.

Sparkling across the horizon is the lake, a fisherman's dream with walleye, largemouth and striped bass, and a new hybrid bass—the fiercest of fighters—rainbow trout, crappies, channel catfish. There are more than a dozen areas for protected swimming, and rental equipment and instruction for scuba diving and water skiing. In August there's the annual Greers Ferry Lake and Little Red River Annual Water Festival with professional water-ski shows, a hot-air balloon race over the lake, a rodeo, dances, a hootenanny, and fish fries.

Close to the lodge is a trout hatchery, located below the dam and operated by the U.S. Fish and Wildlife Service. Three miles east of Heber Springs, on Highway 110, is a swinging bridge across the Little Red River, and south of Heber Springs is Bridal Veil Falls and Sugar Loaf Mountain with its sensational view of the lovely lake.

277

LAKEFRONT LODGE, P.O. Box 5, Edgemont, Arkansas 72044. Telephone: (501) 723-4243. Accommodations: 17 rooms directly overlooking the lake, all with private baths, televisions; no telephones; some kitchenettes. Rates: inexpensive. Inquire about pets. No cards, but personal checks are welcome. Open year round.

Getting there: The resort is on Devil's Fork and Middle Fork, the prime fishing area of the lake, a quarter mile east of Edgemont on Highway 16 and a mile west after crossing the Edgemont Bridge.

RED APPLE INN
Heber Springs

Sixty-five miles north of Little Rock, this happy retreat in the rolling hills surrounding the forty thousand-acre Greers Ferry Lake provides the ultimate opportunity for escape, for breathing clean mountain air, for being pampered by an ever-smiling staff in a setting that is as brightly polished as its name implies.

For the sportsman who wants more out of his holiday than just sitting on his porch or looking out the dining room windows at tree-top level, there's a nine-hole executive golf course, three lighted tennis courts, shuffleboard, rental bikes, and, at the Eden Isle Marina—the largest on the lake—sail and fishing boats, party barges, and numerous guides to help you land the big one. Immediately behind the hotel is a spectacular swimming pool set in the rocks, beautifully landscaped and boasting its own waterfall. Of course there is also a multitude of hiking trails for wandering among the wild flowers shaded by maples and oaks, dogwood, flowering crab, and wild cherry.

But don't expect to return to a rustically simple room after communing with nature. The designers of the Red Apple Inn had a love affair with Spain when they built this hideaway in the 1960s, and they furnished the rooms—each one differently—with heavy carved furniture, elaborate headboards, massive chairs and tables, and oversize lamps. Each room also has the most modern of bathrooms, with a dressing room adjoining.

There's more Spanish in the reds of the public rooms, including the After Five cocktail lounge off the lobby with its ornate gate made in 1505 for the Governor's Palace in Seville. The lounge is a private club in a dry country, open to all inn guests. There's a certain air of formality about the inn, as all guests are required to dress for dinner and for drinks in the After Five lounge. That means coats and ties for men, dresses or appropriate pants suits for women. It's one of "the niceties in life," declares the Red Apple Inn. We agree. Working through the

Sunday buffet with prime rib at center stage, diving into the made-out-back muffins or digging into the relish bowl and the excellent salad with a sour cream-peppercorn dressing, dining on brook trout or strip sirloin accompanied with corn pudding and one of the best stuffed tomatoes I've ever tasted, it's comforting to the spirit to look around the dining room and see people in more than sports clothes.

There's enough informality during the day, especially if one wanders around the woods or goes into the somnolent little settlement of Heber Springs. Chief among its attractions is the Seven Springs Craft Shop with its quilts, wood and pottery handicrafts, woven and leather goods. The shop is an outlet of the Ozark Foothills Handicraft Guild, founded in 1962 as a statewide cooperative to promote quality craftsmanship—there are now more than four hundred members.

Each year since 1966 the Guild has been the prime mover behind the annual October Ozark Frontier Trail Festival and Craft Show in Heber Springs. In addition to an antique show and sale, parades, and horseshoe pitching competitions, there are demonstrations of blacksmithing, basketry, spinning and weaving, vegetable dyeing, and the workings of a sorghum mill.

RED APPLE INN, Eden Isle, Heber Springs, Arkansas 72543. Telephone: (501) 362-3111. Accommodations: 58 rooms, all with private baths, telephones, televisions; some rooms with fireplaces, most with private balconies. Rates: moderate to expensive. Meal service: breakfast, lunch, and dinner. Full bar service. No pets. Cards: AE, DC, MC. V. Open year round.
Getting there: Follow U.S. 65 from Little Rock to State Road 25 two miles north of Greenbrier; take 25 to Heber Springs. The inn is on Eden Isle, four miles west of Heber Springs; there are numerous signs pointing the way.

MARLSGATE PLANTATION
Scott, Arkansas

William P. Dortch is the third William P. Dortch to live in Marlsgate, a Taralike echo of the Southern past named for an ancestor's home in Carlile, England. But it's not an antebellum home. When the Yankees swarmed through the lowlands of Arkansas, they burned the plantations and confiscated the crops.

Marlsgate was not built until this century, when it was completed in 1904 after four years of hand work. The brick was specially made, the pressed tin ceilings fourteen feet overhead were imported from St.

Marlsgate Plantation, Scott, Arkansas

Louis, and the beveled glass mirrors on many of the doors and the stained glass framing the imposing central staircase came from other cities. William and his wife Nancy, who wears vintage long gowns during the regularly conducted tours of the home, have filled their eleven thousand square feet of stage with family heirlooms and Arkansas antiques.

On the walls of the bedroom suite available for overnight guests are blueprints of the house as drawn up by its architect, Charles Thompson. There's also a fireplace with the original oak mantel, and an adjoining sitting room, the Blue Room, otherwise known as the library. The sun porch is a splendid place for the complimentary breakfast, while dinner, also included in the price of the room, is served in the strikingly appointed dining room with its walnut table that seats twenty.

During special occasions that table is filled. Marlsgate is available for catering and can accommodate groups of up to forty people for luncheon or dinner. Some two hundred guests can easily be handled for weddings and receptions.

That's how Nancy Dortch got into the inn-keeping business. After hosting so many groups she took a breather in Savannah and experienced first hand the pleasures of staying in a home converted in part to an inn. But she decided to add dinner to the usual breakfast, which gives the Dortchs an additional opportunity to get to know their guests. In turn the visitors learn about the energetic Dortchs, including their family history and how the family china and silver were buried in the Arkansas River during the War Between the State;. Bill can also discuss the farming of cotton and pecans on his extensive acreage.

MARLSGATE PLANTATION Box 26, Scott, Arkansas 72142. Telephone: (501) 961-1063. Accommodations: single suite with a private bath, sitting room, television; no telephone. Rates: expensive; includes complimentary breakfast and dinner. No pets. No cards, but personal checks are welcome. Open year round.

Getting there: Marlsgate is a 20-minutes' drive from downtown Little Rock. Drive east on East Broadway to Rose City and U.S. 165 toward England; go past Dixie Gin on right, and at Tull's Gulf Station bear left and proceed 2-1/2 miles to a four-way intersection. Drive through the intersection onto a gravel road for 2-1/2 more miles to Marlsgate's distinctive front-gate pillars, which match the Ionic columns of the two-story portico.

WILLIAMS HOUSE INN
Hot Springs, Arkansas

The glitter has gone from much of Bathhouse Row, that assemblage of buildings where tired tourists took the waters, sipping and soaking in the steaming outpourings of forty-seven springs. As early as 1832 the springs became a federal preserve, the first in the country and a forerunner of the National Park Service. In 1921 four square miles were established as the Hot Springs National Park, and those springs still give aching bones the full treatment in a series of baths. You start with a soaking, proceed to a sauna or a steambath, then to a packing room where an attendant applies hotpacks to your body. After showering you are ushered into the cooling room, then the dressing room.

The Park Service also supplies free water at a series of in-town faucets, and at the revitalized Arlington Hotel there are whirlpools and massages, a reflector sun deck, and a swimming pool complete with waterfalls and a water slide. The Arlington also provides the most sophisticated setting for dining in Hot Springs, but other high-flying hostelries, those which prospered during Prohibition and those which specialized in gambling right through the 1940s, are now only memories.

But there is still racetrack betting at nearby Oaklawn with its fifty-six-day season running from February to Easter, and the location of the town in the Ouachita range of mountains makes it a good base camp for exploring the park, the city, and the surrounding area.

And the Williams House Inn with its wraparound porches, its spacious sitting rooms, its tree-shaded setting on Quapaw Street—a name honoring the Indians who were using the springs long before DeSoto happened on the scene—is a happily-cared-for headquarters in Hot Springs.

Mary and Gary Riley are the innkeepers, émigrés from California who came to this area for the express purpose of finding just such an inn to buy and operate. They did not hesitate very long when they found this Victorian mansion, so solidly constructed with high ceilings, excellent workmanship, and even a carriage house, which will soon be made into an additional pair of accommodations.

Five rooms are already refurbished and filled with family heirlooms. On the ground floor is a reception room with a piano and a fireplace, a game room with cable television and comfortable chairs for reading and relaxing, and a large dining room with a family photo album of a wall detailing the genealogy—a most fitting bit of decor in this Victorian mansion.

The dining room is where guests are served the bountiful breakfasts: omelets on the weekends, and eggs Benedict, French toast, hash browns and grits, ham, bacon, or sausage and homemade biscuits during the week.

WILLIAMS HOUSE INN, 420 Quapaw Street, Hot Springs National Park, Arkansas 71901. Telephone: (501) 624-4275. Accommodations: five rooms, two with shared baths, three with private baths, one with a private sun porch, one with a sitting room; no telephones; television in common room. Rates: moderate; includes full breakfast. No children under five; no pets. No cards, but personal checks are welcome. Open year round.
Getting there: Drive south past the Bathhouse Row and Promenade on Central Avenue to the intersection with Prospect; proceed southwest on Prospect to where Quapaw enters. The inn is on the corner of Quapaw and Orange.

QUEEN WILHELMINA INN
Mena, Arkansas

The original Queen Wilhelmina Inn was built in the 1890s by the Kansas City Southern Railroad as a convenient stopover point for passengers traveling between Kansas City and Port Arthur. The inn, which sits twenty-seven hundred feet above sea level, was reached by donkey back in those days, since the rail line lay seven miles away at the foot of the mountain. The inn's breathtaking panoramic views span up to fifty miles on a clear day.

Why name a mountaintop inn for the ruling monarch of a pool-table-flat country with more than a thousand people per square mile, where the wide open spaces of these parts are nonexistent? The answer is simple. Dutch investors, both private and governmental, contributed three of the several millions needed to build the railroad.

The Queen never visited this elevated outpost just five miles from the Oklahoma border, but one of her ambassadors attended the dedication of the new Queen Wilhelmina Inn in 1975. Built on the site where the original building burned in 1973, the new inn is not an exact duplicate, but it comes close. At a cost of $1.3 million it is solidly constructed of stone and wood, with shapes and colors that do not insult the surrounding beauty. The inn's modern rooms have rugged, solid furnishings and are immaculately maintained. Two of the rooms have fireplaces.

The inn is part of the Queen Wilhelmina State Park, which offers active naturalist programs in the summer, including movie and slide presentations in the outdoor amphitheater near the inn. There are also many hiking trails, a nature center, a shop selling local handicrafts, a small zoo, a miniature golf course, and one of the largest miniature railroads in the country, chugging 1-1/2 miles around the crest of Rich Mountain.

This self-contained center of activity is spread along the only scenic highway in the Southwest, Talimena Skyline Drive. It begins at Mena and ends fifty-four miles away at Talihina, Oklahoma—thus its name. Running across the highest land between the Rockies and the Appalachians, the Skyline Drive winds through the 190,000 acres of the Ouachita National Forest (pronounce that Wash-a-tah if you want to sound like a Choctaw or Razorback) and along the summits of both Rich and Winding Stair mountains, one of the few ranges in the world that stretches east and west. The road was started in 1933 as a project of the Civilian Conservation Corps and was finally finished in 1970. Similar to its counterpart along the Blue Ridge, the Talimena Skyline Drive is extremely popular when the blooms of spring arrive and again when the frosts of fall change the colors.

The autumn spectacular is usually at its peak during the last few days in October and extends through the first week in November. During this period the inn's two dining rooms are filled to capacity with hungry hikers and drivers digging into generous buffet spreads or settling down to local specialties such as mountain-cured ham steak with red-eye gravy, ham hocks with beans and corn bread, and catfish with hush puppies.

QUEEN WILHELMINA INN, Rich Mountain, Mena, Arkansas 71953. Telephone: (501) 394-2863. Accommodations: 38 rooms with double and queen-size beds, all with private baths; televisions but no telephones. Rates: inexpensive. Meal service: breakfast, lunch, and dinner. No bar service. Children welcome; pets not allowed. Cards: MC, V. Open year round.
Getting there: Mena is on U.S. 71 eighty miles west of Hot Springs, 85 miles south of Fort Smith and 100 miles north of Texarkana. From Mena take State Highway 88 for 13 miles to the lodge. In winter months when ice and snow make summit-crossing 88 hazardous, take U.S. 270, six miles north of Mena at Acorn and then 272 the final two miles to the inn.

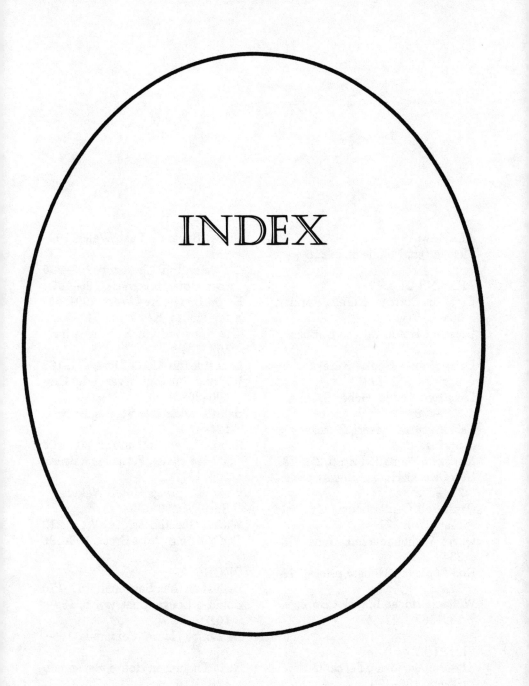

INDEX

286

VIRGINIA

WEST VIRGINIA

BIOGRAPHICAL NOTES

Robert W. Tolf has been a tireless traveler most of his life. In his teens he crisscrossed the United States several times with the aid of his thumb, and in college he hitchhiked across Europe and North Africa. After gaining a Harvard B.A. and a Rochester Ph.D., he joined the army, eager for more travel; then came the State Department and Foreign Service assignments in Scandinavia and Switzerland. In 1971 he settled in Florida, launching his writing career with the best-selling *How To Survive Your First Six Months In Florida*, now in its fifth revised edition. A former Senior Research Fellow of the Hoover Institution on War, Revolution and Peace, Tolf is Now the dean of Southern restaurant critics and Florida's premier travel writer. He is also an editor of *Florida Trend* magazine, and the author of numerous articles in a wide variety of national and international publications. His restaurant reviews, travel, and "Good Life" columns appear regularly in the *Fort Lauderdale News/Sun-Sentinel*. Since settling in Florida, Tolf has averaged almost two publications a year, including *Best Restaurants Florida*, *Best Restaurants Florida's Gold Coast* (both 101 Productions), and *The Russian Rockefellers: The Saga of the Nobel Family and the Russian Oil Industry*, which was awarded a Thomas Newcomen prize in 1980 as one of the best three books on business history published in this country during the preceding three years. His latest book is *Discover Florida: A Guide to the Unique Sites and Sights*, published by Manatee Books of Fort Lauderdale in 1982.